CHRISTIAN CLASSICS
DAY BY DAY

CHRISTIAN CLASSICS DAY BY DAY

Compiled by Robert Backhouse

Hodder & Stoughton
LONDON SYDNEY AUCKLAND

Copyright © 1995 by Robert Backhouse.

First published in Great Britain 1995.

The right of Robert Backhouse to be identified as the compiler
of the Work has been asserted by him in accordance with the
Copyright, Designs and Patents Act 1988.

10 9 8 7 6 5 4 3 2 1

British Library Cataloguing in Publication Data
A record for this book is available from the British Library

ISBN 0 340 63052 3

Designed and typeset by Watermark, Norfolk

Printed and bound in Great Britain by
Cox & Wyman Ltd, Reading, Berks.

Hodder and Stoughton Ltd
A Division of Hodder Headline PLC
338 Euston Road
London NW1 3BH

INTRODUCTION

C. S. Lewis once wrote an essay answering the question, 'Why should we read from books of the past?' ('On the Reading of Old Books', in *Undeceptions* (London, Geoffrey Bles, 1971), p. 162). He wrote, 'Every age has its own outlook. It is specially good at seeing certain truths and specially liable to make certain mistakes. We all, therefore, need the books that will correct the characteristic mistakes of our own period. And that means the old books. . . .'

The reader will be able to make up his or her mind about how the spiritual writings over the centuries provide a corrective to imbalances of our day. As James M. Houston has pointed out, 'contemporary literature is untried, lacks vintage, and often reflects the fads of the market-place. As C. S. Lewis has said: "A new book is still on trial, and the amateur is not in a position to judge it. . . . The only safety is to have a standard of plain, central Christianity ('mere Christianity' as Baxter called it), which puts the controversies of the moment in their proper perspective. Such a standard can only be acquired from old books. It is a good rule, after reading a new book, never to allow yourself another new one till you have read an old one in between. If that is too much for you, you should *read an old one to every three new ones.*"' ('A Guide to Devotional Reading', in *A Life of Prayer* by Teresa of Avila, ed. James M. Houston, Multnomah Press, 1983, p. 239, quoting C. S. Lewis, *God in the Dock*, Eerdmans, 1970.)

Certainly every follower of Christ and every Christian group would benefit from pondering more on the topics that these spiritual writers highlight: prayer, meditation, contemplation, and how to make progress in prayer; attending Holy Communion in a devotional way, concentrating on God's will in our times of devotion and not on any sensuous feelings we may be blessed with; not being overdepressed by our faults and sins; not giving undue place to our intellects, and focusing on the fruits of the Spirit, especially humility and patience. Perhaps one unifying theme in these authors' writings is their passionate desire for their readers to make progress in their spiritual walk with God. These authors did not avoid some of the very tough problems encountered in the spiritual life, such as spiritual dryness, apostasy, correcting a fellow Christian, hate in one's heart, and the danger of seeking revelations. In order to make progress in the inner spiritual life, they time and again point to our Lord's Sermon on the Mount, and to the Beatitudes in particular, and extracts from these are therefore included in this compilation. Pascal thought that everyone would benefit from spending time each morning being quiet in God's presence, and the readings in this book have been selected to this end.

Each page consists of the date, a heading, a verse of scripture and a reading. There is a page for every day of the year, including February 29th.

This book does not have a reading for a different saint through the year. However, the reader may care to note that certain dates have special readings for a number of saints' days, holy days and different seasons of the church's year: in January come 1 The circumcision of our Lord, 2 New Year, 24 Francis de Sales, 25 Conversion of St Paul, 27 St John Chrysostom, 28 St Thomas Aquinas; in February come 23 Polycarp's martyrdom (see also February 22 and 24), 24 Beginning of Lent; in March come 7 Perpetua's martyrdom (see also March 8), 31 Palm Sunday; in April come 5 Good Friday, 6 Easter Eve, 7 Easter Day; in May come 16 Ascension Day, 23 Pentecost, 24 John Wesley; in June comes 6 Corpus Christi; in August come 5 Transfiguration of our Lord, 11 St Clare of Assisi, 28 St Augustine, 31 John Bunyan; in September come 3 St Gregory the Great, 25 Lancelot Andrewes, 27 Harvest; in October come 4 St Francis of Assisi, 15 St Teresa of Avila, 17 St Ignatius, 31 Martyrs of the Reformation era; in November come 13 Charles Simeon, 30 Calling of the apostle Andrew; in December come 25 Christmas Day, 26 St Stephen's martyrdom, 27 St John the Evangelist.

Readings from February 24 to April 6 are in Lent, with many of them focusing on our Lord's passion and death. However, Lent, Easter and Christmas readings are not confined to any one time of the year in this book, as we are meant to be celebrating these events all through the year and not just on one particular day.

Most of the entries in this book do not follow on from the day before, but are complete in themselves. There is a deliberate randomness about the order of the entries, so that each day's meditation can stand on its own. However, occasionally there are a number of consecutive readings which are linked to a particular sequence of thought in the original author's writings. The following are examples of linked readings: January 16–23, readings from St John of the Cross; February 11–12, readings of St Francis of Assisi on the Lord's Prayer; February 14–16, readings on spiritual dryness by Madame Guyon; February 17–20, readings from St Augustine on the Lord's Prayer; March 11–12, The Dream of the Rood, from the 8th-century Anglo-Saxon; March 17–27, George Herbert's poem The Sacrifice; March 28–29, Robert Herrick's poem Rex Tragicus; September 21–22 My Dancing Day: meditations from the 15th century; November 6–12 St Teresa of Avila's seven mansions of the interior castle; December 8–11 Meditations from St Augustine.

At the beginning of each day there is a verse or two of scripture. The complete day's reading is often a meditation on this verse. Most of the verses were the choice of the original author. Sometimes it may be a help to look up the scripture verse in a Bible to see its context. Many Christian writers were in the habit of selecting a verse of scripture and then writing a short homily or meditation on it. This is how the word 'meditation' has often been thought of.

All the scripture references included in the readings from the classical writers themselves are those which were included by the original author. For many of us it shows how familiar they were with the scriptures, in comparison with our relative ignorance today. These scripture references have been retained so that further reading of the scripture verses and their contexts can be easily engaged in.

Sometimes seeing a scripture verse on its own strikes us in a different way from either hearing it read in church or reading it along with lots of other verses. It is also most instructive to see how spiritual writers of the past have found God speaking to them through particular verses of scripture.

Most of the readings are from very well known spiritual writers, nearly all drawn from the first nineteen centuries of the Christian era. There has been no conscious attempt to exclude any particular author, but rather a deliberate effort to include writers from differing Christian traditions. So Bernard of Clairvaux, Catherine of Siena, John of the Cross, Francis of Assisi are side by side with Madame Guyon, John Calvin, and John Bunyan.

It has been possible to include a number of most helpful writers whose work is not very accessible today. So some of the desert fathers are included here, such as Orsisius, Syncletica, and the man with the delightful name of John the Dwarf. Authors from the early Christian centuries are also featured, such as Synesius of Cyrene (375–430) and his meditation, 'Lord Jesus, think on me.' So as well as a good selection of well known, popular writers a number of lesser-known authors are also included.

It has been a conscious editorial policy to include a variety of styles of English in the contents. Sometimes the original has been only slightly updated, but at other times a more contemporary English style is employed. While this rules out uniformity of style throughout the book it allows us to read some authors, such as Wesley and George Herbert, in their original words.

No particular type of literature has been deliberately excluded. The most common form is a prose meditation or exposition of scripture, such as the extract from John Wesley's first sermon (January 1). A number of letters, such as Francis of Assisi's letter to Anthony (January 6) are included, as they often have specific spiritual directions in them. Poems and hymns are occasionally included as they have a very striking way of conveying a spiritual truth. Many of the writers in this book are sometimes called 'mystical' writers. However, the broader term 'spiritual writers' might be a more helpful term to use. For example, a reading from St Augustine's 'Confessions' might properly be thought of as 'mystical', but an extract from one of his sermons (such as that set for January 10) as 'spiritual'. Such divisions are rather artificial. Both, and many other types of spiritual writing, are included here.

Robert Backhouse
Norwich 1995

CIRCUMCISION OF OUR LORD

A man is a Jew if he is one inwardly; and circumcision is circumcision of the heart, by the Spirit, not by the written code (Romans 2:29).

Here is the sum of the perfect law, the circumcision of the heart. Let the spirit return to God that gave it, with the whole train of its affections.

Other sacrifices from us he would not accept, but the living sacrifice of the heart he has chosen. Let it be continually offered up to God through Christ, in flames of holy love. And let no creature be suffered to share with him, for he is a jealous God. He will not share his throne with another; he will reign without a rival. Let no design, no desire be admitted there, other than God for its ultimate object.

This is the way those children of God once walked, who though dead still speak to us: 'Desire not to live but to praise his name; let all your thoughts, words, and works tend to his glory.' 'Let your soul be filled with so entire a love for him, that you may love nothing but his sake.' 'Have a pure intention of heart, a steadfast regard to his glory in all your actions.' 'For then, and not till then, is that mind in us, which was in Christ Jesus, when in every prompting of our heart, in every word of our tongue, in every work of our hands, we pursue nothing that is not in relation to him, and in subordination to his pleasure'; when we also neither think, speak, nor act, to fulfil 'our own will, but the will of him who sent us' (see John 6:38); when, 'whether we eat or drink, or whatever we do,' we do it all 'to the glory of God' (see 1 Corinthians 10:31).

John Wesley, *A Plain Man's Guide to Holiness*

A NEW YEAR'S WISH

Love the LORD your God with all your heart and with all your soul and with all your strength. These commandments that I give you today are to be upon your hearts (Deuteronomy 6:5–6).

I wish you a happy new year with all my heart! May it be a year spent in complete simplicity and truth. We cannot control our feelings, only our wills. And we are not able to measure our wills. We cannot take it up, like a glove, and say, Here it is. You love your son without worrying all the time about how you feel about this love. In the same way, you should not worry about how you feel about your love for God. It is sufficient that we want to love and behave in the best way possible in the spirit of such love. God is not touchy and sensitive, as we are. Let us approach God directly, that is all we have to do.

Remember how Jesus Christ said, 'Whoever can be trusted with very little can also be trusted with very much, and whoever is dishonest with very little will also be dishonest with much' (Luke 16:10). I believe that a soul who sincerely longs after God does not worry about whether the activity he is engaged in is considered to be large or small. It is enough for him to know that he is doing it for God, who is infinitely great and who expects all his creatures to be completely devoted to bringing him glory and doing his will.

Archbishop Fénelon, *Christian Perfection*

A CLOUD OF UNKNOWING

Then you will understand the fear of the LORD and find the knowledge of God (Proverbs 2:5).

For at the first time when thou dost [this work] thou findest but a darkness, and as it were a cloud of unknowing, thou knowest not what, saying that thou feelest in thy will a naked intent unto God. This darkness and this cloud is, howsoever thou dost, between thee and thy God, and telleth thee that thou mayest not see him clearly by light of understanding in thy reason, nor feel him in sweetness of love in thine affection. And therefore shape thee to bide in this darkness as long as thou mayest, evermore crying after him that thou lovest. For if ever thou shalt feel him or see him, as it may be here, it behoveth always to be in this cloud in this darkness. And if thou wilt busily travail as I bid thee, I trust in his mercy that thou shalt not come thereto.

Then will he sometimes peradventure send out a beam of spiritual light, piercing this cloud of unknowing that is between thee and him; and show thee some of his secrets, about which man cannot speak. Then shalt thou feel thine affection inflamed with the fire of his love, far more than I can tell thee, or may or will at this time. For of that work that falleth only to God, dare I not take upon me to speak with my blabbering human tongue.

The Cloud of Unknowing

LIVING ALWAYS IN GOD'S PRESENCE

May the grace of the Lord Jesus Christ, and the love of God, and the fellowship of the Holy Spirit be with you all (2 Corinthians 13:14).

Having found in many books different methods of going to God, and diverse practices of the spiritual life, I thought this would serve rather to puzzle me, than facilitate what I sought after, which was nothing but how to become wholly God's. I renounced for the love of him everything that was not he; and I began to live as though there was none but he and I in the world. I worshipped him the oftenest that I could, keeping my mind in his holy presence, and recalling it as often as I found it wandered from him. I found no small pain in this exercise, and yet I continued it notwithstanding all the difficulties that occurred. I made this my business, as much all the day long as at the appointed times of prayer, and though I have done it very imperfectly, yet have I found great advantages by it. When we are faithful to keep ourselves in his holy presence, and set him always before us; this not only hinders our offending him but it also brings freedom, and if I may so speak, a familiarity with God wherewith we ask for the graces we stand in need of.

Brother Lawrence, *The Practice of the Presence of God*

EVERY MORNING

Because of the LORD's great love we are not consumed, for his compassions never fail. They are new every morning; great is your faithfulness (Lamentations 3:22–23).

Every morning compose your soul for a tranquil day, and all through it be careful often to recall your resolution, and bring yourself back to it, so to say. If something discomposes you, do not be upset, or troubled; but having discovered the fact, humble yourself gently before God, and try to bring your mind into a quiet attitude. Say to yourself, 'Well, I have made a false step; now I must go more carefully and watchfully.' Do this each time, however frequently you fall. When you are at peace use it profitably, making constant acts of meekness, and seeking to be calm even in the most trifling things. Above all, do not be discouraged; be patient; wait; strive to attain a calm, gentle spirit.

Francis de Sales, *Treatise on the Love of God*

LETTER TO ST ANTONY

'I am sending you out like sheep among wolves. Therefore be as shrewd as snakes and as innocent as doves' (Matthew 10:16).

To my well-beloved Brother Antony. Brother Francis sends you greetings in the Lord.

It will please me if you instruct the brothers the teachings of holy theology. But do this in such a way that you do not damage in yourself or others the spirit of holy prayer which we engage in according to the Rule. Adieu.

St Francis was asked if he would like learned brothers who had already been received into the Order to diligently study the holy scriptures. St Francis replied, 'I approve of this provided that they follow Christ's example in this. We are told that Christ preferred prayer to reading. So these brothers must not neglect the spirit of prayer. They must not study in order to become learned orators; rather, they should study so that they can put into practice in their own lives what they learn. Then, when they have done this themselves, they can suggest other people do the same. I want my friars to be true disciples of the gospel and to advance so much in the knowledge of the truth that they may grow in purity and innocence. They are not to separate the innocence of the dove from the wisdom of the serpent since these virtues were united in our good Master's teaching.'

St Francis of Assisi, *Letters*

NO BIGGER THAN A HAZELNUT

In the beginning was the Word, and the Word was with God, and the Word was God (John 1:1).

In this revelation the Lord showed me a tiny thing, no bigger than a hazelnut, lying in the palm of the hand, and as round as a ball. I looked at it, puzzled, and thought, 'What is it?'

The answer came: 'It is everything that is made.'

I wondered how it could survive. It was so small that I expected it to shrivel up and disappear.

Then I was answered, 'It exists now and always because God loves it.' Thus I understood that everything exists through the love of God.

In this small thing I saw three things: first God made it, second God loves it, and third God looks after it. But what he really means to me as Maker, Keeper and Lover, I cannot tell; I shall never know complete rest and true happiness until all that I am is united with him; until I am so joined to him that nothing on earth can come between my God and me. We need to understand the insignificance of creation, and to see every created thing as mere nothing, if we are to love and possess God who is uncreated. This is why we are restless in heart and soul: we seek our rest in things that are so trivial, in which there is no rest, instead of seeking to know God who is allpowerful, totally wise and good. God alone is true rest. He wants to be known and it makes him happy when we rest in him. Nothing less than God himself can satisfy us. This is why no one can find rest until he has let go of all created things. When of his own free will he has seen the world as nothing for love of him who is everything, then he can receive spiritual rest.

Lady Julian of Norwich, *Revelations of Divine Love*

CHRISTIAN MEETS THE INTERPRETER

'My grace is sufficient for you, for my power is made perfect in weakness' (2 Corinthians 12:9).

Then in my dream I saw the Interpreter take Christian by the hand and lead him into a place where there was a fire burning against the wall, and someone standing by, throwing a great deal of water on it to put it out. But the fire kept burning higher and hotter.

Then Christian said, 'What's the meaning of this?'

The Interpreter answered, 'This fire is the work of grace in the heart. The one who throws water on it to extinguish it is the devil. But, as you can see, in spite of that the fire burns higher and hotter. I'll show you the reason for that.'

He took him behind the wall where he saw a man holding a container of oil, out of which he continually and secretly threw oil into the fire.

Then Christian said, 'What does this mean?'

The Interpreter answered, 'This is Christ. With the oil of his grace he continually maintains the work already begun in the heart. In this way, no matter what the devil can do, the souls of Christ's people remain full of grace (2 Corinthians 12:9). And you saw the man standing behind the wall to keep the fire going to teach you that it's hard for people being tempted to see how this work of grace is maintained in the soul.'

John Bunyan, *The Pilgrim's Progress*

GOD'S LIGHT

The city does not need the sun or the moon to shine on it, for the glory of God gives it light, and the Lamb is its lamp (Revelation 21:23).

Holiness appeared to me to be of a sweet, pleasant, charming, serene, calm nature. It seemed to me, it brought an inexpressible purity, brightness, peacefulness, and ravishment to the soul; and that it made the soul like a field or garden of God, with all manner of pleasant flowers, that is all pleasant, delightful, and undisturbed; enjoying a sweet calm, and gently vivifying beams of the sun.

The soul of a true Christian appeared like a little white flower, as we see in the spring of the year, low and humble on the ground, opening its heart to receive the pleasant beams of the sun's glory; rejoicing, as it were, in a calm rapture; diffusing around a sweet fragrancy; standing peacefully and lovingly in the midst of other flowers round about, all in like manner opening their hearts to drink in the light of the sun.

Jonathan Edwards, *Diaries*

A WORD TO THE RICH

Command those who are rich in this present world not to be arrogant nor to put their hope in wealth, which is so uncertain, but to put their hope in God, who richly provides us with everything for our enjoyment (1 Timothy 6:17).

Nothing generates pride so easily as riches. The person who is rich and is not proud has trampled on riches and become dependent solely on God. If you are rich and proud it means you are not possessing but being possessed. Being rich and proud means being like the devil; what have you got when you are rich and proud, when you do not have God?

Possessing riches should mean that you know that what you have can be lost; so aim to possess what cannot be lost. Riches can indeed be lost; and I just hope that they become lost without making you lost at the same time.

The Psalmist mockingly addresses the rich who set their hopes on riches: 'Man is a mere phantom as he goes to and fro: He bustles about, but only in vain; he heaps up wealth, not knowing who will get it' (Psalm 39:6). The living can observe how true this is about the dead; they can own the property of many dead people without it being owned by their children. Those who are supposed to inherit it either squander it by riotous living or get cheated of it through some sharp practice. While great effort is put into gaining its possession, the one who gains possession also loses possession of himself.

Many people are killed on account of their wealth. They all leave behind them here what they used to own. Since they never did with their wealth what Christ told them to do with it, how are they going to face him when they meet him? So take great care that your riches are real riches. God himself 'richly provides us with everything for our enjoyment.'

St Augustine, *Sermons*

O FOR A CLOSER WALK WITH GOD

'Remain in me, and I will remain in you' (John 15:4).

O for a closer walk with God,
  A calm and heavenly frame;
A light to shine upon the road
  That leads me to the Lamb!

Return, O holy Dove, return,
  Sweet messenger of rest;
I hate the sins that made thee mourn,
  And drove thee from my breast.

The dearest idol I have known,
  Whate'er that idol be,
Help me to tear it from thy throne,
  And worship only thee.

So shall my walk be close with God,
  Calm and serene my frame;
So purer light shall mark the road
  That leads me to the Lamb.

William Cowper

THE BEATITUDES

'It is more blessed to give than to receive' (Acts 20:35).

Now when [Jesus] saw the crowds, he went up on a mountainside
and sat down. His disciples came to him, and he began to teach
them, saying:
  'Blessed are the poor in spirit,
    for theirs is the kingdom of heaven.
  Blessed are those who mourn,
    for they will be comforted.
  Blessed are the meek,
    for they will inherit the earth.
  Blessed are those who hunger and thirst for righteousness,
    for they will be filled.
  Blessed are the merciful,
    for they will be shown mercy.
  Blessed are the pure in heart,
    for they will see God.
  Blessed are the peacemakers,
    for they will be called sons of God.
  Blessed are those who are persecuted because of righteousness,
    for theirs is the kingdom of heaven.
  Blessed are you when people insult you, persecute you and
falsely say all kinds of evil against you because of me. Rejoice and
be glad, because great is your reward in heaven, for in the same
way they persecuted the prophets who were before you.'
Matthew 5:1–12

COMING TO THE TRUE LIGHT

'Whoever wants to save his life will lose it, but whoever loses his life for me will find it' (Matthew 16:25).

Let no one suppose that we may come to the true Light and perfect understanding and to the Christ-like life through asking many questions, or through hearsay, or through reading and study and great learning. Indeed, nobody can come to the true Light so long as he at all values anything, or remains pursuing his own pleasures and desires. Christ himself has declared, 'If anyone comes to me and does not hate his father and mother, his wife and children, his brothers and sisters – yes, even his own life – he cannot be my disciple' (Luke 14:26).

By this Christ means: 'He who does not forsake and lose everything, can never know me, the eternal truth, nor receive my life.' Though this had never been stated before by any human voice, yet now the Truth himself declares it, for it is indeed true.

But so long as a person loves anything, and especially himself, above God, he is deceived and grows blind and so is incapable of receiving anything that is good. For what is most pleasant and profitable for himself and what is his, these he maintains are the best, and he loves them above everything else. Thus he never comes to the Truth.

Theologia Germanica

GOD'S WILL

Going a little farther, he fell with his face to the ground and prayed, 'My Father, if it is possible, may this cup be taken from me. Yet not as I will, but as you will.' . . . He went away a second time and prayed, 'My Father, if it is not possible for this cup to be taken away unless I drink it, may your will be done.' (Matthew 26:39, 42).

Resignation to the will of God is the whole of piety.

It includes in it all that is good, and it is a source of the most settled quiet and composure of mind. Our resignation to the will of God may be said to be perfect, when our will is lost and resolved up into God's; when we rest in his will as our end, as being itself most just, and right, and good. And where is the impossibility of such an affection to what is just and right and good, such a loyalty of heart to the Governor of the universe, as shall prevail over all sinister indirect desires of our own?

Joseph Butler, *Sermons*

ALL IS FROM GOD

For those God foreknew he also predestined to be conformed to the likeness of his Son, that he might be the firstborn among many brothers. And those he predestined, he also called; those he called, he also justified; those he justified, he also glorified (Romans 8:29–30).

I believe that I cannot by my own reason or strength believe in Jesus Christ my Lord, or come to him;
but the Holy Spirit has called me through the gospel,
enlightened me by his gifts,
and sanctified
and preserved me in the true faith.
In like manner as he
calls,
gathers,
enlightens,
and sanctifies the whole Christian Church on earth,
and preserves it in union with Jesus Christ in the true faith;
in which Christian Church he daily forgives abundantly all my sins,
and the sins of all believers,
and will raise me up
and all the dead at the last day,
and will grant everlasting life to me
and to all who believe in Christ.
This is most certainly true.
Amen.

Martin Luther, *Table-Talk*

BY A SECRET LADDER

Your thunder was heard in the whirlwind, your lightning lit up the world; the earth trembled and quaked. Your path led through the sea, your way through the mighty waters, though your footprints were not seen (Psalm 77:18–19).

The darkness experienced in contemplation has often been described as a 'secret'. Mystical theology has been called secret wisdom by theologians. St Thomas says that this comes into the soul by means of love. The soul's understanding and other faculties are unaware of this because it happens secretly and in darkness. The soul receives it by means of the Holy Spirit and the soul's faculties do not acquire it. The Bride in the Song of Songs correctly says that this happens without the soul's knowledge or understanding and that is why it is called a secret. In addition to the soul's not understanding it nobody else understands it, not even the devil himself, for the master who teaches it to the soul lives within it.

This isn't the only reason it is called secret. It is also called secret because of what it does in the soul. It is secret in the darknesses and the distressful time of purification when the soul is purified by this wisdom of life. While this is happening, the soul cannot talk about it and in the same way after the soul has been illumined the soul still remains silent. Apart from not wanting to talk about it, the soul cannot find the words to express such an exquisite spiritual experience. So it would still remain secret and hidden, even if the soul did want to talk about it and find the correct words for this. This inner wisdom is so singleminded and so all-embracing and so spiritual that it doesn't enter the soul's mind in disguise. Therefore the soul's sense and imagination know that it is experiencing something most unusual and delightful but does not know what.

St John of the Cross, *The Dark Night of the Soul*

PURE SPIRIT

Moses trembled with fear and did not dare to look (Acts 7:32).

One of the characteristics of God's way of communicating is that it is very intimate and spiritual in its relationship to the soul. It goes beyond all the senses which immediately stand before it in silence.

The Bible has a number of examples of this. Jeremiah was a man who was unable to describe this experience, '"Ah, Sovereign Lord," I said, "I do not know how to speak; I am only a child"' (Jeremiah 1:6). Moses was another person who couldn't speak about this inner experience. 'Moses said to the Lord, "O Lord, I have never been eloquent, neither in the past nor since you have spoken to your servant. I am slow of speech and tongue"' (Exodus 4:10). Moses says to God that after he has spoken to him he does not know how to speak and Luke adds in the Acts of the Apostles, 'Moses trembled with fear and did not dare to look' (Acts 7:32). The inner mind did not dare to meditate on this and it could not speak about the parts that it did understand. The wisdom of this contemplation is the way that God speaks to the soul in pure spirit and as the senses are not purely spiritual they cannot understand it and so it is hidden from them and they are powerless to understand or talk about it.

St John of the Cross, *The Dark Night of the Soul*

SECRET WISDOM IS LIKE A LADDER

He had a dream in which he saw a stairway [ladder AV] resting on the earth, with its top reaching to heaven, and the angels of God were ascending and descending on it (Genesis 28:12).

The nature of the state of perfection is made up of the perfect love of God and total contempt for oneself. The state of perfection cannot exist unless the soul has both knowledge of God and knowledge of self. The soul has to acquire first one and then the other, and it finds itself exalted by the knowledge of God and humbled through knowledge of itself. This climbing up and down the ladder comes to an end when the soul reaches God which is where the top of the ladder leads it. This ladder of contemplation which comes down from God was experienced by Jacob (see Genesis 28:12).

The Bible says that all this happened at night while Jacob was asleep, to show how the road to God is a secret one and how much it differs from man's knowledge. For example, what men regard as most valuable – pleasing and consoling experiences of God – are actually of little value for the soul; whereas what men consider the worst possible experience – to lose oneself and become nothing – is of the greatest value.

We come now to the most important reason for this secret contemplation being likened to a ladder. God's loving knowledge which fires the soul brings it alight with love, lifts it up rung by rung until it arrives in the presence of its creator God. Only love unites and cements the soul with God.

St John of the Cross, *The Dark Night of the Soul*

THE MYSTICAL LADDER OF DIVINE LOVE: STEPS 1 AND 2

Look to the LORD and his strength; seek his face always (Psalm 105:4).

Step 1

There are ten steps on this ladder of love which the soul finds before arriving in God's presence. St Bernard and St Thomas interpreted them as follows. The first step of love makes the soul quite ill, but this turns out to be to the soul's advantage. This illness is not terminal for it ends in the glory of God. During this illness the soul loses its taste for sin and everything else that does not come from God, for God's own sake. In this step of love the soul loses its taste for the incidentals of this life just as a sick person loses his appetite for food. The soul would not be so ill if it had not experienced the heat of God. As the soul climbs on to the first rung of this ladder of purifying contemplation it finds that it ceases to take pleasure in things of the world.

Step 2

The second step makes the soul continually seek after God. As David advises, the soul does continually 'look to the Lord and his strength' and 'seek his face always' (Psalm 105:4). Magdalene was so caught up in her search for Jesus that she did not even notice the angels in the tomb. When the soul is on this rung of the ladder it is so anxious to find God that it looks everywhere for him. Whatever it may be thinking about, its thoughts always return to God. Whatever the soul is talking about its conversation always gravitates towards God. As the soul eats and sleeps it can think of nothing other than its longing for God. During this step the soul begins to recover from its illness and discover new strength in God's love. Through this new strength it then moves on to the third rung of the ladder in this night of purification.

St John of the Cross, *The Dark Night of the Soul*

THE MYSTICAL LADDER OF DIVINE LOVE: STEPS 3 AND 4

So Jacob served seven years to get Rachel, but they seemed like only a few days to him because of his love for her (Genesis 29:20).

Step 3

The third step of this ladder of love gives the soul strength for action and so inspires it that it does not stop. About this David says, 'Blessed is the man who fears the Lord, who finds great delight in his commands' (Psalm 112:1). If reverence, which is a child of love, causes the soul to be so keen to work, you can imagine what happens when the soul receives God's perfect love. On this step of the ladder the soul reckons that great works carried out for God are nothing. It regards numerous things it does for God as being only a few things and feels that when it has served God for a long time, it is but a short time because of the fires of love which are now burning in it.

Another wonderful experience on this third step of the ladder is that it thinks of itself as being much worse than all the other souls. The soul is like this because God's love is teaching us all the time how much reverence God deserves. Also the soul now realises that all it does for God is flawed and nothing it does is worthy of Almighty God. On this third rung of the ladder the soul never condemns anybody else and it is free of presumption itself.

Step 4

The fourth step of this ladder of love enables the soul to go on suffering for God tirelessly. St Augustine has said, 'Love can make light of everything, even the things that weigh you down most of all.' This fourth step of love is a very high one because the soul's love for God is so true. The soul longs to suffer for Almighty God who is all the time giving it joy and other delightful spiritual experiences.

St John of the Cross, *The Dark Night of the Soul*

THE MYSTICAL LADDER OF DIVINE LOVE: STEPS 5 AND 6

I run in the path of your commands, for you have set my heart free (Psalm 119:32).

Step 5

On the fifth step of the ladder the soul longs for God with complete abandon. The soul is now like the lover who finds the shortest separation from her loved one to be completely intolerable. When the soul can't be with its lover it pines and faints as the Psalmist says, 'My soul yearns, even faints, for the courts of the Lord . . .' (Psalm 84:2). On this fifth step the soul is so much in love with God that it feels as if it will die if it is deprived of this. Hungry men become like scavenging dogs who prowl around the city in search of food. This deep hunger in the soul is totally satisfied when it meets divine love.

Step 6

The sixth step of the ladder makes the soul run towards God very fast. The soul is full of hope and it can run without tiring; its love is so strong that it can run quickly. Isaiah the prophet spoke about this when he said, '. . . but those who hope in the Lord will renew their strength. They will soar on wings like eagles; they will run and not grow weary, they will walk and not be faint' (Isaiah 40:31). On the sixth rung of the ladder the souls no longer collapse as they did on the fifth rung. The Psalmist also makes reference to the sixth step when he says, 'As the deer pants for streams of water, so my soul pants for you, O God' (Psalm 42:1). The soul has now been made nearly completely pure and its love knows no bounds.

St John of the Cross, *The Dark Night of the Soul*

THE MYSTICAL LADDER OF DIVINE LOVE: STEPS 7 AND 8

Delight yourself in the LORD and he will give you the desires of your heart (Psalm 37:4).

Step 7

On the seventh rung of the ladder the soul becomes passionate in its boldness. Now the soul throws caution to the winds because of the blessings that God showers on it. As the apostle Paul wrote, so the soul 'always protects, always trusts, always hopes, always perseveres' (1 Corinthians 13:7). Moses spoke about this seventh step on the ladder when he said, 'Oh, what a great sin these people have committed! They have made themselves gods of gold. But now, please forgive their sin – but if not, then blot me out of the book you have written' (Exodus 32:31–32). When people pray like this God answers their prayers. So David can say, 'Delight yourself in the Lord and he will give you the desires of your heart' (Psalm 37:4). On this seventh rung of the ladder the Bride boldly said, 'Let him kiss me with the kisses of his mouth . . .' (Song of Songs 1:2). It is most important to note here that the soul should never presume to be as bold as this unless it experiences strong spiritual blessings from God. For if the soul does not remain humble it will fall back to lower rungs on the ladder. On this seventh step God fills the soul with power and courage to be bold in the ecstasy of its love; and then it moves on to the eighth step.

Step 8

On the eighth step of the ladder of love the soul is enabled to embrace God so strongly that it never lets him go. This is similar to what the Bride says, 'I held him and would not let him go . . .' (Song of Songs 3:4). The soul is not totally satisfied with staying on this step of the ladder and is impatient to move on.

St John of the Cross, *The Dark Night of the Soul*

THE MYSTICAL LADDER OF DIVINE LOVE:
STEPS 9 AND 10

Dear friends, now we are children of God, and what we will be has not yet been made known. But we know that when he appears, we shall be like him, for we shall see him as he is (1 John 3:2).

Step 9

On the ninth step of love the soul is aflame with passion for God. The soul has now arrived and is perfect in its passion for God. This comes about through the Holy Spirit as a result of the soul being united to God. This is why St Gregory said about the apostles that when the Holy Spirit could be seen descending on them they had an inner burning sensation of God's passionate love.

Step 10

The tenth and final step of this secret ladder of love enables the soul to be completely assimilated by God. This happens through a completely clear and very close vision of God. Once the soul leaves the ninth step of the ladder it ceases to be a human being. There are only very few of these souls. St Matthew says of them, 'Blessed are the pure in heart, for they will see God' (Matthew 5:8). Through this vision they become exactly like God, as St John says, 'But we know that when he appears, we shall be like him, for we shall see him as he is' (1 John 3:2). This is not because the soul is able to contain God – that is impossible. It is because the soul becomes like God and God has called it to be one with him. The soul is assimilated by God on the final step because it has this completely clear vision of God; everything is now open to it. So our Saviour says, 'In that day you will no longer ask me anything' (John 16:23). But until that day arrives the soul will not be complete because it has not been fully assimilated by God. Through this love and mystical knowledge of God the soul travels upwards above everything and above itself towards God. The soul is like flames of fire which are always burning and leaping upwards.

St John of the Cross, *The Dark Night of the Soul*

NEVER RUSH

This is what the Sovereign LORD, the Holy One of Israel says: 'In repentance and rest is your salvation, in quietness and trust is your strength' (Isaiah 30:15).

Never be in a hurry; do everything quietly and in a calm spirit. Do not lose your inward peace for anything whatsoever, even if your whole world seems upset.

Commend all to God, and then lie still and be at rest in his arms. Whatever happens, abide steadfast in a determination to cling simply to God, trusting to his eternal love for you; and if you find that you have wandered forth from this shelter, recall your heart quietly and simply. Maintain a holy simplicity of mind, and do not smother yourself with a host of cares, wishes, or longings, under any pretext.

Be patient with everyone, but above all with yourself. I mean, do not be disturbed because of your imperfections, and always rise up bravely from a fall. I am glad that you make a daily new beginning; there is no better means of progress in the spiritual life than to be continually beginning afresh, and never to think that we have done enough.

Francis de Sales, *Introduction to a Devout Life*

CONVERSION OF ST PAUL

As he neared Damascus (Acts 9:3).

Meanwhile, Saul was still breathing out murderous threats against the Lord's disciples. He went to the high priest and asked him for letters to the synagogues in Damascus, so that if he found any there who belonged to the Way, whether men or women, he might take them as prisoners to Jerusalem. As he neared Damascus on his journey, suddenly a light from heaven flashed around him. He fell to the ground and heard a voice say to him, 'Saul, Saul, why do you persecute me?'

'Who are you, Lord?' Saul asked.

'I am Jesus, whom you are persecuting,' he replied. 'Now get up and go into the city, and you will be told what you must do.'

The men travelling with Saul stood there speechless; they heard the sound but did not see anyone. Saul got up from the ground, but when he opened his eyes he could see nothing. So they led him by the hand into Damascus. For three days he was blind, and did not eat or drink anything.

In Damascus there was a disciple named Ananias. The Lord called to him in a vision, 'Ananias!'

'Yes, Lord,' he answered.

The Lord told him, 'Go to the house of Judas on Straight Street and ask him for a man from Tarsus named Saul, for he is praying. In a vision he has seen a man named Ananias come and place his hands on him to restore his sight.'

'Lord,' Ananias answered, 'I have heard many reports about this man and all the harm he has done to your saints in Jerusalem. And he has come here with authority from the chief priests to arrest all who call on your name.'

But the Lord said to Ananias, 'Go! This man is my chosen instrument to carry my name before the Gentiles and their kings and before the people of Israel. I will show him how much he must suffer for my name.'

St Luke, The Acts of the Apostles 9:1–16

TRULY TURN TO GOD

Therefore, if anyone is in Christ, he is a new creation; the old has gone, the new has come! (2 Corinthians 5:17)

Everyone alive on this wretched earth, exiled as we are, knows that one cannot be filled with eternal love or anointed with heavenly perfume unless one is truly turned to God. A person must be truly turned to God. In one's innermost thoughts all earthly things must be turned away from, before one can experience even just a little of God's love. This conversion happens even in ordinary love; a person loves and is ardent only for what is fitting and worthy of love, and this is less so in a person who is less worthy of love.

God is worthy to be loved; heavenly things are worthy of great love; all earthly things deserve little or no love unless out of necessity. Undoubtedly, then, a person is turned to Christ as long as he desires nothing but Christ. To be free from fleshly desire, and to hate every kind of evil, is the context of a true turning to God. It is a leaving of those things which beguile and render one defenceless, so that a person finds earthly things tasteless and, except for the barest necessities, seeking worldly possessions pointless.

Richard Rolle, *The Fire of Love*

LONG-SUFFERING

The fruit of the Spirit is . . . long-suffering (Galatians 5:22, AV).

A certain wise man said: 'A man who is long-suffering is abundant in understanding.' When compared with a strong city, he said it was stronger than that, for it is both an invincible weapon and a sort of impregnable tower, easily beating off all attackers. Just as a spark which falls into the keep does not harm, as it is quickly extinguished, so whatever unexpected thing falls on a long-suffering soul speedily vanishes, but the soul it does not disturb. It is true that there is nothing so impenetrable as long-suffering.

You may talk about armies, money, horses, walls, arms, or anything else, but you will name nothing like long-suffering. For he who is surrounded by these, being overcome by anger, is upset, like a worthless child, and fills all with confusion and tempest. But the long-suffering person, settled as it were in a harbour, enjoys a profound calm. Even though he may be surrounded with loss, the rock is not moved: even though you bruise him with stripes, you have not wounded his soul. The possessor of this passive virtue has a kind of long and noble soul, whose great strength is love.

St John Chrysostom, *Sermons*

ADVICE FOR STUDENTS

Whatever your hand finds to do, do it with all your might, for in the grave, where you are going, there is neither working nor planning nor knowledge nor wisdom (Ecclesiastes 9:10).

To a disciple (1270)
You have asked me, John, most dear to me in Christ, how you should set about studying in order to build up a rich store of knowledge. This is the advice I give you on the subject.
1. Do not plunge straight into the sea, but rather enter it by way of little streams, because it is wise to work upward from the easier to the more difficult.
2. I would have you slow to speak, and slow to go to the parlour.
3. Cherish purity of conscience.
4. Never forget your times of prayer.
5. Love to stay in your own cell if you want to gain access to God's wine cellar.
6. Show a cheerful face to everyone.
7. Never pry into other people's business.
8. Do not become over familiar with anyone, because familiarity breeds contempt and gives a pretext for neglecting serious work.
9. Take care not to interfere in the words and actions of outsiders.
10. Do not waste time in useless talking.
11. Be sure to follow in the footsteps of good and holy men.
12. Do not concentrate on the personality of the speaker, but treasure up in your mind anything profitable he may happen to say.
13. See that you thoroughly grasp whatever you read and hear.
14. Check up on doubtful points.
15. Do your best to hoard up whatever you can in that little bookcase of your mind; you want to fill it as full as possible.
16. Do not concern yourself with things beyond your competence.

By following this path, you will throw out leaves and bear serviceable fruit in the vineyard of the Lord of Hosts all the days of your life. If you stick to this advice you will reach the goal of your desires. Farewell.

Thomas Aquinas, *Letters*

CONTEMPT FOR WORLDLY VANITIES

'Whoever follows me will never walk in darkness, but will have the light of life' (John 8:12).

These are the words of Christ; by which we are taught that it is only by a conformity to his life and Spirit, that we can be truly enlightened, and delivered from all blindness of heart. Therefore, let it be the principal employment of our minds to meditate on the life of Christ.

The teaching of Christ infinitely transcends all the teachings of the holiest men, and those who have the Spirit of Christ, may find in it 'hidden manna' (see Revelation 2:17). But it happens that many, though they frequently hear this teaching, take no pleasure in it. He can only happily receive and truly delight in Christ's teaching, who continually endeavours to acquire the Spirit and imitate the life of Christ.

Of what benefit are your most subtle enquiries into the mystery of the blessed Trinity, if you are devoid of humility, and, therefore, profane the Trinity? It is not profound speculations, but a holy life, that makes a man righteous and good, and dear to God. I had rather feel compunction, than be able to give the most accurate definition of it. If you could memorise the whole Bible, along with all the precepts of the philosophers, how would that benefit you without the love and grace of God. Everything is vanity with the one exception of the love of God and being entirely devoted to his service.

The Imitation of Christ, ascribed to Thomas à Kempis

THE SONG OF ANGELS

Then the devil left him [Jesus], and angels came and attended him (Matthew 4:11).

When a soul is purified by the love of God, illumined by wisdom, stabled by the might of God, then is the eye of the soul opened to view spiritual things, such as angels and heavenly beings. Then the purified soul is able to feel the touch and hear the voice of good angels. This feeling and hearing is not bodily but spiritual. For when the soul is lifted up and ravished out of sensuality, and away from all earthly things, then in great fervour and light (if our Lord wills) the soul may hear and feel heavenly sound, made by the presence of angels as they love God. This is the song of the angels.

For the sovereign and essential joy is in the love of God by himself and for himself. Following this, and secondly, comes the communing and viewing angels and heavenly beings. So whoever wishes to hear the angel's song must take care not to delude himself, to give himself over to his own imagination or to be deceived by the devil. It is necessary for him to have perfect love. This occurs when all vain love, fear, joy and sorrow is thrown out of the heart, so that it only loves God, only fears God, and only derives joy and sorrow from God.

Walter Hilton, *The Scale of Perfection*

THE TWO RAPTURES

I know a man in Christ who fourteen years ago was caught up to the third heaven. Whether it was in the body or out of the body I do not know – God knows (2 Corinthians 12:2).

The closer and more present God is to a soul, the purer is his love. This is how one rejoices more purely in God. He feels more strongly God's goodness and loving-kindness which is bound to be poured out in those who love him. With incomparable joy it fills to overflowing the hearts of the just.

With great purity the spirit is totally established in a single desire for eternity, and looks up continually, with freedom, towards heavenly things. It is so caught up that it is ravished from every other thing to which it does not turn and cannot love.

But this ravishing, however, is clearly to be understood in two ways. In one way, he is so ravished out of bodily feeling that at the time of rapture he cannot feel whatever is done in or from the flesh. He is not, however, dead, but alive, because the soul yet quickens the body. In this way the saints and the elect are sometimes enraptured for the benefit and instruction of others, as Paul was ravished in the third heaven. In this way too sinners are sometimes ravished so that they may see the joy of the blessed or the punishments of the damned, in order that they themselves or others may be corrected. And we read of many such examples.

In the other way, it is called the rapture of the raising of the mind to God by contemplation. This is found in all the perfect lovers of God, and in no one unless they love God. It is correctly called rapture or ravishing, like the other, because it does a certain violence, as it were, against nature. Moreover, it is truly supernatural, since it may change a man from a vile sinner to a son of God, who is carried up into God, full of spiritual joy.

Richard Rolle, *The Fire of Love*

PROGRESS IN THE DIVINE LIFE

He is a double-minded man, unstable in all he does (James 1:8).

I cannot tell you how much I love you. But that which of all things I have most at heart, with regard to you, is the real progress of your soul in the divine life. Heaven seems to be awakened in you. It is a tender plant. It requires stillness, meekness, and the unity of the heart, totally given up to the unknown workings of the Spirit of God, which will do all its work in the calm soul, that has no hunger or desire but to escape out of the mire of its earthly life into its lost union and life in God.

I mention this, out of a fear of your giving in to an eagerness about many things, which, though seemingly innocent, yet divide and weaken the workings of the divine life within you. The only foundation for taking comfort in the enjoyments of this life is in the assurance that a wise and good God governs the world. The more we discover God in everything, the more we seek him in every place, the more we look up to him in all our actions, the more we conform to his will, the more we act according to his wisdom and imitate his goodness, so much the more we enjoy God. Then we share in the divine nature and heighten and increase all that is happy and comfortable in human life.

William Law, *A Serious Call to a Devout and Holy Life*

FORGIVE IMMEDIATELY

'Forgive, and you will be forgiven' (Luke 6:37).

I know how to give comfort not to a small number but to the vast mass of Christians, and I know that you long to hear about this. 'Forgive, and you will be forgiven' (Luke 6:37), said Christ. That is what you have to do, and if you don't do it, you will perish.

When you are told, 'Your enemy is asking your pardon,' you must forgive at once. Is that also asking too much of you? It seemed too much to ask you to love your enemy while he is speaking against you; is it too much to ask you to forgive a man on his knees before you? What do you say to that? He was raging against you, and you hated him. I'd rather you didn't hate him even then; I'd rather you remembered, even then as you endured his ravings, the Lord saying, 'Father, forgive them, for they do not know what they are doing' (Luke 23:34). Even at the moment when your enemy is raging against you, you should turn your eyes to the Lord your God and utter those words.

If you think it is too much for you to set your sights on your Lord, turn your thoughts to your fellow servant. St Stephen, as he was being stoned, knelt down under the hail of stones, and started praying for his enemies and said, 'Lord, do not hold this sin against them' (Acts 7:60). They were hurling stones, not asking for his forgiveness, and Stephen was praying for them. That's what I want you to be like. Exert yourself, stretch yourself a little. Why always drag your heart along the ground? Listen; lift up your heart, stretch it; love your enemies. If you can't love him while he is raging, love him at least while he is begging. Love the person who says to you, 'Brother, I have done you wrong; forgive me.' If you don't forgive him then, I don't say, 'You are cutting out the Lord's Prayer from your heart,' but, 'You are blotting yourself out of God's book.'

St Augustine, *Sermons*

EVERYONE IS CAPABLE OF PRAYER

'Watch and pray so that you will not fall into temptation. The spirit is willing, but the body is weak' (Matthew 26:41).

What a dreadful delusion has overshadowed most of mankind, as they suppose that they are not called to a state of prayer! The truth of the matter is that everyone who is called and who is capable of salvation is also called to and is capable of prayer.

Prayer is the application of the heart to God, and the internal exercise of love. St Paul has told us to 'pray continually' (1 Thessalonians 5:17); and our Lord said 'Watch and pray' (Matthew 26:41): and so everyone may, and indeed ought to practise prayer. I grant that meditation can only be attained by a few, for few are capable of it; and therefore, my beloved brethren, who are thirsty for salvation, meditative prayer is not the prayer which God requires of you, nor the one we would recommend for you.

Let everyone pray. We should live by prayer, as we should live by love. 'I counsel you to buy from me gold refined in the fire, so that you can become rich' (Revelation 3:18). This is easier to receive than we can imagine. Jesus himself said, 'If anyone is thirsty, let him come to me and drink' (John 7:37). So do not waste any precious moments in imitating some of the people in Jeremiah's day, of whom the prophet wrote: 'My people have committed two sins: they have forsaken me, the spring of living water, and have dug their own cisterns, broken cisterns that cannot hold water' (Jeremiah 2:13).

Madame Guyon, *A Short and Easy Method of Prayer*

GOD'S WILL

'. . . your will be done on earth as it is in heaven . . .' (Matthew 6:10).

True handing of oneself over to God's will consists in a thorough conformity to the whole will of God, who wills and does all (excepting sin) which comes to pass in the world. In order to do this we have only to embrace all events, good and bad, as he will.

In the greatest afflictions which can happen to the just, either from heaven or earth, they remain immovable in peace, and perfectly submissive to God, by an inward, loving regard to him, uniting in one all the powers of their souls.

We ought quietly to suffer whatever happens to us, to bear the defects of others and our own, to confess them to God in secret prayer, or with groans that words cannot express; but never to speak a sharp or peevish word, nor to murmur or complain; but thoroughly willing that God should treat you in the manner that pleases him. We are his lambs, and therefore ought to be ready to suffer, even to death, without complaining.

We are to bear with those we cannot amend, and to be content with offering them to God. This is true handing ourselves over to God's will. And since God has borne our infirmities, we may well bear those of each other for his sake.

To abandon all, to strip one's self of all, in order to seek and to follow Jesus Christ naked to Bethlehem, where he was born; naked, to the hall where he was scourged, and naked to Calvary, where he died on the cross, is so great a mercy, that neither the thing, nor the knowledge of it, is given to any, but through faith in the Son of God.

John Wesley, *A Plain Man's Guide to Holiness*

LOSS OF PEACE

'Peace I leave with you; my peace I give you. I do not give to you as the world gives. Do not let your hearts be troubled and do not be afraid' (John 14:27).

God is a tranquil being, and abides in a tranquil eternity. So must your spirit become a tranquil and clear little pool, wherein the serene light of God can be mirrored. Therefore shun all that is disquieting and distracting, both within and without.

Nothing in the whole world is worth the loss of your peace; even the faults which you have committed should only humble, but not disturb you.

God is full of joy, peace and happiness. Endeavour then to obtain a continually joyful and peaceful spirit. Avoid all anxious care, murmuring, and melancholy, which darkens your soul, and makes you unfit for friendship with God. If you perceive such feelings arising, turn gently away from them.

Gerhard Tersteegen, *Meditations*

HOW TO PRAY

One day Jesus was praying in a certain place. When he finished, one of his disciples said to him, 'Lord, teach us to pray' (Luke 11:1).

As you start to pray, no matter how long or short your prayers will be, make sure that your heart is totally convinced, without a shadow of doubt, that when you stop praying you will die. If you do this, you will see an overall view of your wretchedness and a particular view of the little time there is left for amendment of life. This will make your heart very fearful.

While you may in reality live longer, it is wrong to presume that this will happen and to assure your heart that this will be the case. This matter is totally in God's hands, and you must follow his will, now knowing whether you will live for many years or just for one more moment. So, if you want to pray wisely, you will follow the Psalmist in your heart. 'For God is the King of all the earth; sing to him a psalm of praise' (Psalm 47:7). Ensure, from the very start, that you say this reverently. For the Psalmist also says, 'The fear of the Lord is the beginning of wisdom' (Psalm 111:10).

Epistle of Prayer (14th century)

THE DUTY OF PRAISING GOD FOR HIS GOOD GIFTS

Pray continually (1 Thessalonians 5:17).

As the sea is the source of fountains and rivers so the Lord Jesus Christ is the source of every kind of virtue and knowledge. For who but the King of Glory is the Lord of every virtue? According to the song of Hannah he is the Lord God of knowledge (see 1 Samuel 2:3).

Self-control of the body, diligence in the heart and correct judgment form the will flow from a divine source. And that is not all. For anyone who has a keen intellect, or who is a powerful orator or has a saintly character also has his ability given to him by God. Every wise conversation that is full of knowledge has its origin in God, 'in whom are hidden all the treasures of wisdom and knowledge' (Colossians 2:3).

Do not pure intentions, just judgments, holy aspirations all stream from the same source? All waters constantly seek to return to the sea. They sometimes make their way there through hidden and underground tunnels so that they can continue their journey and they become visible again and useful to man. So why are those spiritual streams not constantly and wholeheartedly attributed to their legitimate source and allowed to continue to flow in the fields of our hearts?

Let the rivers of varying graces return to their source so that they may flow again. Let the heavenly rains rise again to their heavenly source so that they may be poured out again and even more abundantly on the earth. Do you ask, How does this happen? In the way that is laid down by the apostle Paul, 'give thanks in all circumstances' (1 Thessalonians 5:18). Whatever you may think that you have by way of wisdom and virtue, attribute it to the One who is the Power of God and the Wisdom of God, that is, to Christ.

Bernard of Clairvaux, *The Song of Songs*

STILL DEWS OF QUIETNESS

After the wind there was an earthquake, but the LORD was not in the earthquake. After the earthquake came a fire, but the LORD was not in the fire. And after the fire came a gentle whisper (1 Kings 19:11–12).

Dear Lord and Father of mankind,
    Forgive our foolish ways!
Reclothe us in our rightful mind,
In purer lives thy service find,
    In deeper reverence praise.

In simple trust like theirs who heard,
    Beside the Syrian sea,
The gracious calling of the Lord,
Let us, like them, without a word
    Rise up and follow thee.

O Sabbath rest by Galilee!
    O calm of hills above,
Where Jesus knelt to share with thee
The silence of eternity,
    Interpreted by love!

Drop thy still dews of quietness,
    Till all our strivings cease;
Take from our souls the strain and stress,
And let our ordered lives confess
    The beauty of thy peace.

Breathe through the heats of our desire
    Thy coolness and thy balm;
Let sense be dumb, let flesh retire;
Speak through the earthquake, wind, and fire,
    O still small voice of calm!

John Greenleaf Whittier

IN HOLINESS AND RIGHTEOUSNESS

'In holiness and righteousness before him all our days' (Luke 1:75).

We should serve our Lord in holiness. A person is holy who loves God above everything else. A person is righteous who loves other Christians as himself.

'In holiness' also means loving God deeply and having our emotions on fire for him, as happens to people who are very active. These deeds are profitable if they are done in God's sight and for God's sake and the sake of fellow Christians, and not for selfish motives and worldly rewards.

Hypocrites do many good deeds, but they do not do them to honour God, but to gain glory from the world. We must not do this. In all our service, both inner and outer, seek to experience and find joy in God. Do this, not just for one hour or one day, but for all your life. That is, for all the time you spend on earth, so that you may live with God in the everlasting bliss of heaven.

Walter Hilton, *The Scale of Perfection*

ENTERING THE HEAVENLY CITY

**'Blessed are those who are invited to the supper of the Lamb!'
(Revelation 19:9).**

Christian and Hopeful were drawing close to the gate, a company of the heavenly host came out to meet them. The two Shining Ones said: 'These are the men who loved our Lord when they were in the world, and have left everything for his holy name. He has sent us to fetch them and we have brought them up to here on their longed-for journey so that they may go in and look at their Redeemer with joy.'

'Open the gates,' commanded the King, 'that the righteous nation may enter, the nation that keeps faith' (Isaiah 26:2).

Now in my dream I saw that these two men went in at the gate. And behold, as they entered, they were transfigured, and garments were put on them that shone like gold. Others met them with harps and crowns, which they gave to them. The harps were for praise, the crowns were in token of honour. Then I heard in my dream that all the bells in the city rang out again for joy, and the pilgrims were told, 'Come and share your master's happiness!' (Matthew 25:21).

I also heard Christian and Hopeful singing aloud and saying, 'To him who sits on the throne and to the Lamb be praise and honour and glory and power, for ever and ever!' (Revelation 5:13).

John Bunyan, *The Pilgrim's Progress*

THE LORD'S PRAYER EXPLAINED (I)

'When you pray, say: "Father, hallowed be your name, your kingdom come. Give us each day our daily bread"' (Luke 11:2–3).

'Our Father'

'Our Father' most holy, our Creator, Redeemer, Saviour and Comforter.

'Who art in heaven'

May thy kingdom shine in us so that we may know the greatness of thy benefits, the breadth of thy promises, the height of thy majesty and the depth of thy judgments (see Ephesians 3:18).

'Thy kingdom come'

So that thou mayest reign in us by thy grace and mayest make us enter into thy kingdom, where thou art clearly seen, where there is the perfect love of thee, the blessed company of thee, the eternal enjoyment of thee.

'Thy will be done in earth as it is in heaven'

How we love thee with all our heart, thinking always about thee; with our whole soul, desiring thee always; with our whole mind, directing all our thoughts towards thee. We seek your honour in everything. With all our strength we submit our faculties to thee. All our spirits and bodies we submit to only obeying your love. We will love our neighbours as ourselves. We will do our utmost to encourage the whole world to love thee. We rejoice with those who rejoice as if the good fortune had been our own. We sympathise with the sad and never offend anyone.

St Francis of Assisi, *Rule*

THE LORD'S PRAYER EXPLAINED (II)

He [Jesus] said to them, 'When you pray, say: ". . . Give us each day our daily bread. Forgive us our sins, for we also forgive everyone who sins against us. And lead us not into temptation"' (Luke 11:2–4).

'Give us this day our daily bread'
Our Lord Jesus Christ, thy dear Son, reminds us of and makes us understand the love he has for us. He makes us venerate all that he has said, done and suffered for us.

'And forgive us our trespasses'
We are forgiven through thine ineffable mercy and by virtue of the passion of thy dear Son our Lord Jesus Christ.

'As we forgive them that trespass against us'
Grant, O Lord, that even though we do not completely forgive we may nevertheless be completely forgiven. May we truly love our enemies for thy sake; may we pray to thee devoutly for them and may we repay no one evil for evil. May we strive to be useful to everyone for thy sake.

'And lead us not into temptation'
Lead us not into hidden or open temptations, or sudden or persistent temptations.

'But deliver us from evil'
Deliver us from past evil, present evil and future evil. Amen.

St Francis of Assisi, *Rule*

CHRISTIAN DEVOTION

The sinful nature desires what is contrary to the Spirit, and the Spirit what is contrary to the sinful nature (Galatians 5:17).

Devotion refers neither to private nor public prayer. But prayers, whether private or public, are simply expressions of devotion. Devotion means a life given, or devoted, to God.

The devout man is, then, one who no longer obeys his own will, nor conforms to the way and spirit of the world, but obeys only the will of God. Such a man considers God in everything, serves God in everything, and makes every aspect of his life a part of devotion. He does everything in the name of God; in everything he conforms to God's rule, and brings glory to God.

We willingly accept that our prayers should be ruled and measured by God alone. We agree that in prayer we are to look to him and act wholly for him, and that we are only to pray in ways and for things that will bring him glory. Now if anyone wants to know why he is to be so absolutely God-centred in his prayers, he will discover that it is for the same reason that he should be as absolutely God-centred in all the other areas of his life. There is not one rule for prayer and a different rule for the rest of life. It is absurd and a mark of failure to pray prayers that are not in harmony with the will of God. It is equally absurd to follow any pattern of life and use any of our talents, abilities, time, or money, in ways that are not in accordance with the will of God and do not bring glory to his name.

William Law, *A Serious Call to a Devout and Holy Life*

SPIRITUAL DRYNESS

My soul is weary (Psalm 119:28).

There are some people who have become very tired with spiritual exercises, have become lukewarm and feel faint in their spirits as they walk in sadness along the ways of the Lord. What once filled them with joy now fills them with dryness and makes them tired, and they frequently grumble about their condition. They complain that their days and nights are long, and they say with Job, 'When I lie down I think, "How long before I get up?" The night drags on, and I toss till dawn' (Job 7:4).

When a soul is in this kind of state the Lord may, out of his compassion, come close to it as it travels and the One from heaven may speak heavenly things to the soul, or sing to us some delightful song from the Songs of Sion, or tell us something about the city of God, the peace of that city, the eternity of that peace or the certainty of that eternity. If the Lord does choose to do this I am certain that the wonder of this conversation will be like a soft couch to that tired, sleeping soul.

This heavenly talk will drive away all negative thinking from the mind and all weariness from the body. Do you not think that he who wrote, 'My soul is weary with sorrow; strengthen me according to your word' (Psalm 119:28), must have experienced this trial and prayed for this same heavenly assistance? And when you have received this heavenly blessing will you not also cry out, 'Oh, how I love your law! I meditate on it all day long' (Psalm 119:97)?

Bernard of Clairvaux, *The Song of Songs*

DRYNESS AND DESOLATION

My soul thirsts for you (Psalm 63:1).

I will now show you how the night of the senses is most helpful
in your spiritual life, with its dryness and desolation, as it floods
the soul with divine light. I shall do this by quoting from David,
where he describes with great clarity the mighty power which this
night has to enable the soul to reach this superior knowledge of
God. He says: 'O God, you are my God, earnestly I seek you; my
soul thirsts for you, my body longs for you, in a dry and weary
land where there is no water. I have seen you in the sanctuary and
beheld your power and your glory' (Psalm 63:1–2).

It is a wonderful thing that David says here. He tells us that his
preparation for the knowledge of the glory of God did not lie in
any of the spiritual delights and pleasures which he had experienced. Rather, his knowledge of the glory of God came as a result
of his times of dryness when he was divorced from his physical
nature. That is how we are to understand '. . . in a dry and weary
land where there is no water.'

David's description of the road he travelled along so that he
could meet God is no less wonderful. It did not come about
through his many divine meditations, but happened when he was
unable to think about God or to meditate on God; that is how we
are to understand the words of 'weary land'. So the way to find
out about God and about oneself is by means of this dark night
with all its dryness and emptiness. However, this night does not
give us such ample knowledge about God as the night of the spirit,
since this is only, as it were, the beginning of that night.

St John of the Cross, *The Dark Night of the Soul*

ARIDITY

Better is one day in your courts than a thousand elsewhere (Psalm 84:10).

As soon as the soul places herself by faith in the presence of God and maintains an attitude of prayer before him, let her remain like this for a little time in a profound and respectful silence.

But if, at the beginning, in making her act of faith she feels some small pleasant sensation of the divine presence; let her remain there without being concerned about the subject of her meditation, and proceed no further, but carefully cherish this feeling as long as it continues: as soon as it fades, she may bring the will to life with a thought about God's love. If this does not succeed in bringing her back her rich experience of God's presence, let her stay there for as long as this continues. The smouldering fire must be gently fanned, but as soon as it is burning brightly again we must stop blowing it in case we put it out completely through our own efforts.

I would warmly recommend that no one should finish praying without remaining for a further short time in God's presence in respectful silence. It is also very important for the soul to start praying in the correct frame of mind and spirit. The soul should have a pure and disinterested love, as it seeks nothing from God, but only to please him, and to do his will. Any servant who only works with an eye on his reward makes himself unworthy of any reward at all. Do not turn to prayer hoping to enjoy spiritual delights; rather come to prayer totally content to receive nothing or to receive great blessing from God's hand, which ever should be your heavenly Father's will at that time. This will enable you to live close to God in times of sadness as well as in times when you are being comforted by God. It will also prevent you from being surprised when you go through times of spiritual aridity or when you feel as if you are rejected by God.

Madame Guyon, *A Short and Easy Method of Prayer*

OUR FATHER

'Our Father in heaven, hallowed be your name, your kingdom come' (Matthew 6:9–10).

We have a Father in heaven, so we must pay attention to how we live on earth. People who have found such a Father should live in such a way that they deserve to come into the inheritance he has in store for them.

We say 'Our Father' all together, and is this not all-embracing generosity? The emperor says it, the beggar says it, the slave says it, and the master says it. Together, they all say, 'Our Father who art in heaven'. So they must realise that they are brothers, since they all have one Father. The master must not scorn to have as a brother the slave of his whom the Lord Christ was willing to have as a brother.

Then we say, 'Hallowed be thy name, thy kingdom come.' The hallowing of God's name is anything that makes us holy. His name, after all, is always holy. We also desire his kingdom to come. It will come, even if we do not wish it to come. The people it is going to come for are those who are told, 'Come, you who are blessed by my Father; take your inheritance, the kingdom prepared for you since the creation of the world' (Matthew 25:34). The people the kingdom is not coming for are those who will be told, 'Depart from me, you who are cursed, into the eternal fire' (Matthew 25:41). So when we say 'Thy kingdom come', we are praying that it may come for us. What does it mean for us? That it may find us good people. This is what we are praying for, that Christ may make us good, because then his kingdom will come for us.

St Augustine, *Sermons*

GOD'S WILL

'Your will be done on earth as it is in heaven' (Matthew 6:10).

Angels serve our Father in heaven, may we serve him on earth. The angels do not offend our Father in heaven, may we not offend him on earth. Just as the angels do our Father's will, so may we do his will. We are again praying that we may be good. When we carry out God's will, we are obviously doing our Father's will in us.

There is a second helpful way of understanding 'Thy will be done, as in heaven, so also on earth.' Here we are given God's commandment and we approve it and our minds approve it. 'For in my inner being I delight in God's law' (Romans 7:22). This is when God's will is done in heaven, because our spirit can be compared to heaven, and our flesh to earth. So, just as our mind approves of God's command, so does our flesh.

Here is a third way of understanding 'Your will be done on earth as it is in heaven.' We can take the church as heaven, because it is the bearer of God. Unbelievers are like the earth and they are told, 'for dust you are and to dust you will return' (Genesis 3:19). So when we pray for our enemies, the enemies of the church, those who are against the name of Christ, this is what we are praying for, that his will may be done, as in heaven, so also on earth. So, as in those who believe in our Father, so also those who take his name in vain, may they all come to heaven.

St Augustine, *Sermons*

DAILY BREAD

'Give us today our daily bread' (Matthew 6:11).

It can be taken quite simply that we pour out this prayer for our daily assistance, that we may have plenty of it; and if we don't have plenty, that we may not lack it entirely. He called it 'daily', 'as long as it is called Today' (Hebrews 3:13). Daily we live, daily we get up, daily we take our fill, daily we get hungry. May he give us our daily bread. Why didn't he also mention shelter? Our sustenance consists of food and drink, our shelter of clothing and a roof over our heads. People should desire nothing else, seeing that the apostle says, 'For we brought nothing into the world, and we can take nothing out of it. But if we have food and clothing, we will be content with that' (1 Timothy 6:7–8). Once greed is eliminated nature is seen to be what it is, rich.

There is also another reasonable way of understanding 'Give us today our daily bread.' Your daily food is your eucharist. The faithful know what they are receiving, and it is good for them to receive the daily bread that is so necessary for their pilgrimage on earth. They are begging for themselves, that they may become good, that they may persevere in goodness and in faith and in a good life. This is what they desire, this is what they are praying for, because if they do not persevere in a good life, they will be cut off from the bread. So, 'Give us today our daily bread' means may we live in such a way that we are not cut off from the altar.

And the word of God, which is opened up for you every day, and as it were is broken for you, is daily bread. Just as our stomachs are hungry for bread so our minds are hungry for spiritual bread. So, in simplicity, we ask for whatever is necessary for our soul and for our bodies in this life. All this is included in the words 'daily bread'.

St Augustine, *Sermons*

FORGIVE US OUR SINS

**'Forgive us our debts, as we also have forgiven our debtors'
(Matthew 6:12).**

When we pray, 'forgive us our debts', we are praying a true prayer. Is anybody alive who does not have debts? Is there anybody alive for whom this prayer is unnecessary? Of course, you can preen yourself, but you are unable to justify yourself. It's good to imitate the tax collector, and not to be self-satisfied like the Pharisee. For the Pharisee went up to the temple, boasted about his merits and kept his evil wounds covered up. But the tax collector knew very well why he went into the temple, as he said, 'God, have mercy on me, a sinner' (Luke 18:13).

My dear brothers, think about this prayer that the Lord Jesus prayed – just think about it. He taught his disciples to pray this prayer, those first great disciples, our rams and leaders in the Lord's flock. So if the rams pray for their sins to be forgiven, what should the lambs be doing?

There is one forgiveness of sins which is given only once. But there is another forgiveness of sins which is given to us every day. There is one forgiveness of sins that is given only once in holy baptism; but there is another forgiveness of sins which, as long as we are alive on earth, is given in the Lord's Prayer. That is why we pray on a daily basis, 'Forgive us our debts.'

St Augustine, *Sermons*

CHRIST'S BIRTH AND SUFFERINGS

'Glory to God in the highest and on earth peace to men of good will' (Luke 2:14).

He chose to be born away from a home in a stable, to be wrapped in swaddling clothes, to be nourished by virginal milk and to lie in a manger between an ox and an ass.

Now, then, my soul, embrace that divine manger; press your lips upon and kiss the boy's feet.

Then in your mind keep the shepherd's watch, marvel at the assembling host of angels, join in the heavenly melody, singing with your voice and heart: 'Glory to God in the highest and on earth peace to men of good will' (Luke 2:14).

. . . This blessed and most holy flesh – which you so chastely conceived, so sweetly nourished and fed with your milk, which you so often held on your lap, and kissed with your lips – you actually gazed upon with your bodily eyes now torn by the blows of the scourges, now pierced by the points of the thorns, now struck by the reed, now beaten by hands and fists, now pierced by nails and fixed to the wood of the cross, and torn by its own weight as it hung there.

Bonaventure, *Meditations*

POLYCARP'S MARTYRDOM

'Be faithful, even to the point of death, and I will give you the crown of life' (Revelation 2:10).

Late in the day Polycarp's pursuers came up together and found him hiding in a cottage, lying in an upper room. It was within Polycarp's power to flee from there to another place, but he refused to do so, saying, 'God's will be done.'

So when Polycarp heard them arrive he came down and talked with them. The soldiers were amazed at his age and his courage and that so much trouble had been taken to arrest such an elderly man.

The soldiers brought Polycarp back into the city, riding on a donkey. The head of the police, Herod, met him. Herod's father, Nicetes, transferred Polycarp into a carriage, sat next to him, and tried to make him change his mind. Nicetes urged Polycarp, 'Tell me, what harm is done if one says that Caesar is Lord. Go on, make a sacrifice to Caesar, and then you will save your skin.'

To start with Polycarp made no reply, but as they pressed him, he said, 'I do not intend to do what you advise me.'

Once they had failed to persuade Polycarp they dragged him from the carriage into the stadium where there was such a tremendous noise that it was impossible for anyone to be heard.

Church at Smyrna for the Church at Philomelium

FAITHFUL UNTO DEATH

I saw under the altar the souls of those who had been slain because of the word of God and the testimony they had maintained (Revelation 6:9).

Polycarp was brought before the Proconsul who also tried to persuade him to change his mind: 'Think of your old age. Just do as everybody else does and "Swear by the genius of Caesar; repent; say, 'Away with the Atheists.'" ['Atheists' here does not refer to people who do not believe in God, but to people, like Polycarp, who refused to acknowledge that Caesar was a divine god who should be worshipped and receive sacrifices.]

Polycarp then studied the crowd of lawless heathen in the stadium, waved his hand in their direction, looked up to heaven with a groan, and said, 'Away with the Atheists.'

The Proconsul was insistent and repeated, 'Swear, and we will release you; deny Christ.'

Polycarp replied:

> 'Eighty and six years have I served him,
>   and he has done me no wrong;
>   how then can I blaspheme my King who saved me?'

Still the Proconsul urged Polycarp: 'Swear by the genius of Caesar.'

'If you really think that I would, "Swear by the genius of Caesar" then you forget who I am. Take note, I am a Christian. If you want to learn the Christian faith, appoint a day, and grant me a hearing.'

The Proconsul replied, 'I have wild beasts and if you do not change your mind I will throw you to them.'

Polycarp said, 'Order them to be brought. We are not allowed to change our minds from what is good to what is evil, only to change from what is evil to what is good.'

The Proconsul said, 'As you despise the wild beasts, you will be destroyed by fire, if you do not change your mind.'

Church at Smyrna for the Church at Philomelium

MARTYRS IN HEAVEN

They were told to wait a little longer, until the number of their fellow-servants and brothers who were to be killed as they had been was completed (Revelation 6:10–11).

Polycarp said, 'The fire you threaten me with only burns for a short time and then it goes out. You are ignorant of the future fire of judgment which is never put out and which is reserved for the ungodly. So what are you waiting for? Do what you want to do. I have to be burnt alive.'

In a moment the mob collected logs and faggots from the workshops and the baths. . . . When the pyre had been completed they were about to nail Polycarp to the stake, but he said, 'Let me be as I am: he that gave me power to abide the fire will grant me too, without your making me fast with nails, to abide untroubled on the pyre.' So they did not nail him to the stake but just bound him to it. Polycarp put his hands behind him and was bound, like a godly ram out of a great flock for an offering, a whole burnt offering made ready and acceptable to God. Then he looked up to heaven and prayed: 'O Lord God Almighty, you are the Father of your much loved and blessed Son Jesus Christ, through whom we have received our knowledge of you. You are the God of the angels and the powers and the God of the whole creation and of everyone who worships you. I praise you that you have counted me worthy of this day and hour so that I can be counted as one of the martyrs in the suffering of Christ and then to the resurrection to eternal life of both the body and the soul with the Holy Spirit. May I be welcomed with them today into your presence as an acceptable sacrifice. As you planned that this should happen, may it now be fulfilled. . . . I praise you, bless you, and glorify you through the everlasting and heavenly high priest Jesus Christ, your much loved Son. It is through him we come to you in the company of the Holy Spirit, to whom we give glory now and for ever. Amen.'

As soon as Polycarp had completed his prayer and offered up his Amen the fire was kindled.

Church at Smyrna for the Church at Philomelium

REFRESHED BY THE CROSS

We know that just as you share in our sufferings, so also you share in our comfort (2 Corinthians 1:7).

'Daughter, if you seek virtue and spiritual strength you must follow Me. Because of my divine virtue I could have overcome all the power of the devil, but because of my manhood I overcame him through my death on the cross. From this example you see how you are to defeat your spiritual enemies; you are to take the cross, just as I did. You will discover the cross a source of great refreshment in your temptations, if you focus on the pains that I suffered during my crucifixion. Without doubt, the pains of the cross can be called refreshment in temptations. The more you suffer on account of my love, the more you will become like me. If you become like me in my passion, you will become like me in my joy.

'Therefore, my daughter, for the sake of my love suffer patiently every bitter experience and do not seek pleasurable experiences. Have no doubt that you will be strong enough to endure everything patiently.'

Catherine of Siena, *Treatise on Divine Providence*

CRUCIFIED WITH CHRIST

I have been crucified with Christ and I no longer live, but Christ lives in me. The life I live in the body, I live by faith in the Son of God, who loved me and gave himself for me (Galatians 2:20).

Let Christ crucified alone be enough for you. Suffer with him and take your rest with him, never rest or suffer without him. Strive with all your might to rid yourself of all selfish affections and inclinations and annihilate the self.

He who makes any account of himself, neither denies himself nor follows Christ.

Love hardships more than all pleasant things, and do not think that you are doing anything when you endure them. In this way you will please him who did not hesitate to die for you.

If you wish to attain the height of possessing Christ you must never seek him without his cross. Anybody who does not seek the cross of Christ is not seeking Christ's glory.

Desire to make yourself in suffering like our great God, who was humiliated and crucified; for life, if it is not imitating Christ, is worth nothing.

What does he know who does not know how to suffer for Christ? The greater and heavier the sufferings, the better is his lot who suffers.

All men desire to enter into the treasures and consolations of God; but few desire to enter into tribulations and sorrows for the Son of God.

St John of the Cross, *The Dark Night of the Soul*

PEACE WITH GOD

Therefore, since we have been justified through faith, we have peace with God through our Lord Jesus Christ, through whom we have gained access by faith into this grace in which we now stand (Romans 5:1–2).

Sweet Peace, where dost thou dwell? I humbly crave,
Let me once know.
I sought thee in a secret cave,
And ask'd if Peace were there.
A hollow wind did seem to answer, 'No;
Go seek elsewhere.'

I did; and going did a rainbow note:
Surely, thought I,
This is the lace of Peace's coat:
I will search out the matter.
But while I look'd, the clouds immediately
Did break and scatter.

Then went I to a garden, and did spy
A gallant flower,
The Crown Imperial. Sure, said I,
Peace at the root must dwell.
But when I digg'd, I saw a worm devour
What show'd so well . . .

George Herbert

THE GOD OF PEACE

The God of peace be with you all (Romans 15:33).

> Whom, when for Peace
> I did demand, he thus began:
> 'There was a Prince of old
> At Salem dwelt, who liv'd with good increase
> Of flock and fold.
>
> 'He sweetly liv'd: yet sweetness did not save
> His life from foes.
> But after death out of His grave
> There sprang twelve stalks of wheat;
> Which many wond'ring at, got some of those
> To plant and set.
>
> 'It prospered strangely, and did soon disperse
> Through all the earth;
> For they that taste it do rehearse
> That virtue lies therein;
> A secret virtue, bringing peace and mirth
> By flight of sin.
>
> 'Take of this grain, which in my garden grows,
> And grows for you;
> Make bread of it; and that repose
> And peace, which ev'ry where
> With so much earnestness you do pursue,
> Is only there.'
>
> George Herbert

READING HOLY SCRIPTURE

I delight in your commands because I love them (Psalm 119:47).

Not eloquence, but truth, is to be sought after in the holy Scriptures; every part of which ought to be read with the same spirit as that in which it was written. In these, as in all other books, it is improvement of holiness, not pleasure in the subtlety of the thought or sublimity of language, that must be principally regarded. We ought indeed to read those books that are simple and devout, with the same affection and delight as those of high speculation or profound erudition.

Whatever book you read, do not allow your mind to be influenced by the character of the writer, whether his literary attainments are great or small; but let your only motive to read, be, the pure love of truth. Do not ask who said this or that, but note carefully what is said. Men pass away like the shadows of the morning, but the word of the Lord endures for ever. And that Word, without respect of persons, in infinitely various ways speaks to everyone.

The profitable reading of the holy Scripture is often interrupted by the vain curiosity of our own minds, which prompts us to examine and discuss, and labour to comprehend, those parts, that should be meekly and submissively passed over. To derive spiritual improvement from reading, we must read with humility, simplicity, and faith; and not affect the character of profound learning.

Ask freely, and receive silently and respectfully, the instructions of holy men; and let not the parables and allegories of ancient times upset you, for they were not written without meaning, and without design.

The Imitation of Christ, ascribed to Thomas à Kempis

TO KEEP A TRUE LENT

At once the Spirit sent him out into the desert, and he was in the desert for forty days, being tempted by Satan. He was with the wild animals, and angels attended him (Mark 1:12–13).

Is this a Fast, to keep
  The larder lean?
    And clean
From fat of veals and sheep?

Is it to quit the dish
  Of flesh, yet still
    To fill
The platter high with fish?

Is it a fast an hour,
  Or ragg'd to go,
    Or show
A down-cast look and sour?

No: 'tis a Fast to dole
  Thy sheaf of wheat
    And meat
Unto the hungry soul.

It is to fast from strife
  And old debate,
    And hate;
To circumcise thy life.

To show a heart grief-rent;
  To starve thy sin,
    Not bin;
And that's to keep thy Lent.

Robert Herrick

SEEKING VISIONS

Dear friends, do not believe every spirit, but test the spirits to see whether they are from God, because many false prophets have gone out into the world (1 John 4:1).

There is one thing in our day that ought to make us afraid: people who have hardly begun to make their meditations, if they seem to hear anything in a brief recollection, pronounce it to have come from God; and so imagine, saying, God has spoken or I have had an answer from God, and it is not so: these people have been speaking to themselves, out of a longing for such communications.

He who should now enquire of God by vision or by revelation would offend him, because he does not fix his eyes on Christ alone. To such a person God's answer is: This is my beloved Son, in whom I am well pleased, hear him, and do not seek for new instructions for in him I have spoken and revealed all that may be desired and asked for; I have given him to be your brother, master, companion, ransom and reward.

We must be guided in all things by the teaching of Christ and his church. You are not to believe what you hear in a supernatural way, but only what you learn from the teaching of Christ and his ministers.

The soul that desires revelations undermines the perfect guidance of the faith, and opens a door for Satan to deceive by false revelations; for he knows well how to disguise them so that they appear to be good.

St John of the Cross, *The Dark Night of the Soul*

SILENCE OR SPEECH?

Now the Lord is the Spirit, and where the Spirit of the Lord is, there is freedom (2 Corinthians 3:17).

It is God whom you should be still for, if you are going to be still. It is God whom you should speak for, if you are going to speak. It is God whom you should fast for, if you are going to fast. It is God whom you should eat for, if you are going to eat. It is God whom you should be alone for, if you are going to be alone. It is God whom you should be in company for, if you are going to be in company. This principle should apply to every aspect of your life.

For silence is not God, neither is speaking God; fasting is not God, neither is eating God; being on one's own is not God, neither is being in company God. God is hidden between them. God is not to be found in any deed your soul may accomplish, but only through the love of your heart. God cannot be known through your powers of reason and he cannot be understood by thinking hard, but God may be loved with the genuine will of your heart. So choose God, and you will be speaking silently, and silently speaking; choose God, and you will be fasting as you eat, and eating when you fast. You choose God when you seek him with a pure heart.

Epistle of Discretion (14th century)

PREPARATIONS

Jesus sent Peter and John, saying, 'Go and make preparations for us to eat the Passover' (Luke 22:8).

Contemplation
At midnight; it is how Christ our Lord went from Bethany to Jerusalem up to and including the Last Supper.

Six Points
1. The first point meditates on the people at the Supper, in such a way that some benefit is derived from this.

2. The second point listens to what they say, and also derives some profit from this.

3. The third point derives some benefit from looking at what they are doing.

4. The fourth point considers what Christ our Lord suffers in his humanity, or wills to suffer, as recorded in the passage we are contemplating. I enter into this with all my being as I grieve, cry and am overcome by sorrow. In the same way I go through the other points which follow.

5. In the fifth point I consider how the divine one hides himself. Even though he was able to destroy his enemies, he chooses not to do so as he allows his most holy humanity to suffer so cruelly.

6. The sixth point considers how Christ our Lord suffers all these things for my sins, and how I should respond in suffering for him.

Ignatius of Loyola, *Spiritual Exercises*

IMAGINE CHRIST ON THE CROSS

**'You will find a colt tied there. . . . Untie it and bring it here'
(Mark 11:2).**

1. The first prelude calls to mind the history of how Christ our
Lord sent two disciples from Bethany to Jerusalem to prepare for
the Supper; and then himself came there with the other disciples;
and how, after having eaten the paschal lamb, and eaten supper, he
washed their feet and gave his most holy body and precious blood
to his disciples and spoke to them, before Judas went out to sell his
Lord.

2. The second prelude is imagining the place about which we
are to meditate. In this case it will be a consideration of the road
from Bethany to Jerusalem, whether it was wide or narrow, or
level or uneven. In a similar way meditate on the place of the
Supper, considering the type and size of room it was held in.

3. In the third prelude I ask for what I desire. I shall have heartfelt sorrow because my sins caused our Lord to go to his passion.

Imagining Christ our Lord present before me on the cross, to
make a colloquy with him, asking him how even though he is the
Creator, he has come to make himself man, and from eternal life
has come to temporal death, and in this way to die for my sins.
Again, reflecting on myself, to ask what have I done for Christ,
what am I doing for Christ, what ought I to do for Christ? Then
meditating on him in such a state, hanging upon the cross, to make
the reflections which may come to mind.

The colloquy is made, when it is made properly, as when a
friend speaks to a friend, or a servant to his master, asking sometimes for some grace, and at other times accusing oneself about
one's own evil deeds. End with an Our Father.

Ignatius of Loyola, *Spiritual Exercises*

THE USE OF MONEY

If anyone has material possessions and sees his brother in need but has not pity on him, how can the love of God be in him? (1 John 3:17).

If a man had eyes, hands and feet that he could remove to give to those who wanted them, and if he should then either lock them up in a chest, or please himself with some needless or ridiculous use of them, instead of giving them to brothers in need, wouldn't we have every justification in calling him an inhuman beast? If he chose rather to amuse himself with furnishing his house than to entitle himself to an eternal reward by giving those in need the eyes and hands they require, would we not justly class him mad?

Now money is very much in the same category as eyes and feet. If we lock it up in chests or waste it in needless and ridiculous expenses on ourselves while the poor and the distressed are in great need of it, or if we consume it on ridiculous ornaments or clothes while others are starving in nakedness, we are not far from the cruelty of the man who chooses wastefully to dispose of his hands and eyes rather than give them to those who need them. If we choose to indulge ourselves in the kind of expensive enjoyments which have no real value, things which aren't really necessary, rather than to gain for ourselves an eternal reward by disposing of our money well, we are guilty of the same madness.

Once we have satisfied our own reasonable needs, all the rest of our money is like spare eyes or spare hands. It is something that we cannot keep to ourselves, foolishly wasting it, but is something that can only be used well by giving it to those who need it.

William Law, *A Serious Call to a Devout and Holy Life*

PERPETUA'S MARTYRDOM

'Do not be afraid of those who kill the body but cannot kill the soul' (Matthew 10:28).

Certain young catechumens were arrested, among them Vibia Perpetua, well-born, liberally educated, honourably married, and having an infant son at her breast. She was about twenty-two.

'When I was still with my companions, and my father in his affection for me was endeavouring to overthrow my resolution, I said, "Father, do you see this waterpot lying here? Can it be called by any other name than what it is?"

'And he answered, "No."

'"So also I cannot call myself anything else than what I am, a Christian."

'Then my father, furious at the word "Christian", threw himself upon me as though to pluck out my eyes; but he was satisfied with annoying me; he was in fact vanquished, he and his devil's arguments. Then I thanked the Lord for being parted for a few days from my father, and was refreshed by his absence. During those few days we were baptised, and the Holy Spirit bade me make no other petition after the holy water save for bodily endurance. A few days later we were put in prison; and I was in great fear, because I had never known such darkness. What a day of horror! Terrible heat, thanks to the crowds! Rough handling by the soldiers! To crown all I was tormented there by anxiety for my baby. Then my baby was brought to me and I suckled him, for he was already faint for lack of food. I obtained leave for my baby to remain in prison with me and my prison suddenly became a palace to me, and I would rather have been there than anywhere else.

'The procurator Hilarian said to me: "Spare your father's white hairs; spare the tender years of your child. Offer a sacrifice for the safety of the Emperors."

'And I answered, "No."

'"Are you a Christian?" said Hilarian.

'And I answered: "I am."

'Then he sentenced all of us to the beasts.'

Adapted from John Foxe, *Acts and Monuments* [Perpetua was martyred 7th March, 203, in the amphitheatre at Carthage.]

A DAY OF VICTORY

'These are they who have come out of the great tribulation; they have washed their robes and made them white in the blood of the Lamb' (Revelation 7:14).

'I sent the deacon Pomponius to my father at once to ask for my baby. But my father refused to give him. And as God willed, neither had he any further wish for my breasts, nor did they become inflamed; that I might not be tortured by anxiety for the baby and pain in my breasts.'

The day of their victory dawned, and they proceeded from the prison to the amphitheatre, as if they were on their way to heaven, with happy and gracious looks; trembling, if at all, not with fear but joy. Perpetua followed with shining steps, as the true wife of Christ, as the darling of God, abashing with the high spirit in her eyes the gaze of all.

. . . For the young women the Devil made ready a mad heifer, an unusual animal selected for this reason, that he wished to match their sex with that of the beast. And so after being stripped and enclosed in nets they were brought into the arena. The people were horrified, beholding in the one a tender girl, in the other a woman fresh from child-birth, with milk dripping from her breasts.

They were brought into the open, that, when the sword pierced their bodies, these might lend their eyes for partners in the murder. When Perpetua's turn came to receive the sword, she was struck on the bone and cried out, and herself guided to her throat the wavering hand of the young untried gladiator. Perhaps so great a woman, who was feared by the unclean spirit, could not otherwise be slain except she willed.

Adapted from John Foxe, *Acts and Monuments*

SILENCE AND SOLITUDE

One of those days Jesus went out to a mountainside to pray, and spent the night praying to God (Luke 6:12).

Seek and set apart convenient times for retirement and self-examination, and frequently meditate on the benefits received from almighty God. Reject all studies that are merely curious; and read only what will rather produce compunction, than speculation. If you can refrain from unnecessary conversation and idle visits, and from hearing and telling something new, you will find both sufficient leisure for excellent meditation. The most eminent saints, where they were able, have shunned social meetings, and chosen to live to God in retirement and solitude.

Seneca said, as often as he mingled in people's company, he came out of it less humanised than he went in. Our own experience agrees with this.

It is much easier to be wholly silent, than not to exceed in talk: and it is much easier to keep concealed at home, than to preserve ourselves from sin abroad. He, therefore, who presses on to the perfection of the internal and spiritual life, must, with Jesus, withdraw from the multitude. No one can safely go abroad, who does not love to stay at home; no man can safely speak, who does not willingly hold his tongue; no one can safely govern, who will not be willingly governed; no one can safely command, who has not learned to obey; and no one can safely rejoice, unless he has the testimony of a good conscience.

The Imitation of Christ, ascribed to Thomas à Kempis

VICTORY OVER TRIALS

I beat my body and make it my slave so that after I have preached to others, I myself will not be disqualified for the prize (1 Corinthians 9:27).

'I'm truly glad,' said Evangelist to Christian, 'not that you've met with trials, but that you've come out on top, and despite many weaknesses you've continued on the way to this very day. I'm truly glad for my own sake as well as yours. I've sowed and you've reaped, and the day is coming, when "the sower and the reaper may be glad together" (John 4:36): that is, if you hold out; "for at the proper time we will reap a harvest if we do not give up" (Galatians 6:9). The crown is before you and it's incorruptible, so "Run in such a way as to get the prize" (1 Corinthians 9:24).

'There are some who set out for this crown, and after going a long way for it, someone else comes in and takes it from them!: "Hold on to what you have, so that no-one will take your crown" (Revelation 3:11). You are not out of the devil's firing line; "you have not yet resisted to the point of shedding your blood" (Hebrews 12:4): let the kingdom always be before you, and resolutely believe in the things that are invisible. Don't let anything on this side of the other world get within you, and, above all, watch your own hearts carefully and the evil desires within them, for they are "deceitful above all things and beyond cure" (Jeremiah 17:9). Set your faces like flint; you have all power in heaven and earth on your side.'

John Bunyan, *The Pilgrim's Progress*

THE DREAM OF THE ROOD (I)

He himself bore our sins in his body on the tree, so that we might die to sins and live for righteousness (1 Peter 2:24).

Hear while I tell about the best of dreams
Which came to me the middle of one night
While humankind were sleeping in their beds.
It was as though I saw a wondrous tree
Towering in the sky suffused with light. . .
                                 . . . the best
Of woods began to speak these words to me:
'It was long past – I still remember it –
That I was cut down at the copse's end,
Moved from my roots. Strong enemies there took me,
Told me to hold aloft their criminals,
Made me a spectacle. Men carried me
Upon their shoulders, set me on a hill,
A host of enemies there fastened me.
And then I saw the Lord of all mankind
Hasten with eager zeal that He might mount
Upon me. I durst not against God's word
Bend down or break, when I saw tremble all
The surface of the earth. Although I might
Have struck down all the foes, yet stood I fast.

The Dream of the Rood [This 8th-century poem and meditation
on the death of Christ is most unusually presented from the point
of view of the rood (or cross) on which Christ was crucified.]

THE DREAM OF THE ROOD (II)

The next day John saw Jesus coming towards him and said, 'Look, the Lamb of God, who takes away the sin of the world!' (John 1:29).

Then the young hero (who was God almighty)
Got ready, resolute and strong in heart.
He climbed onto the lofty gallows-tree,
Bold in the sight of many watching men,
When he intended to redeem mankind.
I trembled as the warrior embraced me.
But still I dared not bend down to the earth,
Fall to the ground. Upright I had to stand.
A rood I was raised up; and I held high
The noble King, the Lord of heaven above.
I dared not stoop. They pierced me with dark nails;
The scars can still be clearly seen on me,
The open wounds of malice. Yet might I
Not harm them. They reviled us both together.
I was made wet all over with the blood
Which poured out from His side, after He had
Sent forth His spirit. And I underwent
Full many a dire experience on that hill.
I saw the God of hosts stretched grimly out.
Darkness covered the Ruler's corpse with clouds,
His shining beauty; the shadows passed across,
Black in the darkness. All creation wept,
Bewailed the King's death; Christ was on the cross.
And yet I saw men coming from afar,
Hastening to the Prince. I watched it all.'

The Dream of the Rood

MEDITATIONS ON THE GOSPEL

'Eloi, Eloi, lama sabachthani?' (Mark 15:34)

These words teach us two things. First, that we must speak to God with perfect simplicity, telling him all our thoughts, even our complaints. We should express our joy, in gratitude give him thanks, in penitence ask his pardon, in our desires ask for fulfilment, in sorrow show him our grief. Since our sufferings are allowed by him we may make our complaint to God as our Lord did, but we should complain with all reverence, love, submission, unbounded and loving conformity to his will. Such his only Son showed for him, and we his children owe the same to him, so loaded with his graces as we are by this infinitely good and lovable Father.

Second, our Lord uses two words of Holy Scriptures in speaking to his Father. We should use words of Scripture too since they come from the Holy Spirit, use them in our longer prayers, as the ancient Jews used to do and as the Church does, the spouse of Christ. We can use them too as ejaculatory prayers as our Lord does here. He gives us this example in several places to show us that it was a habit with him, and that we should make it our habit. He uses words of Scripture to express the cry of his soul at those most solemn moments, in the temptation in the wilderness and on the cross. Two words of the Psalms are his last before his death. It is very clear we should follow this example of his. For the words of Scripture inspired by God are surely worth more than any words of ours. What better offering can we make to God, next to the Body of his Son, than the words his Sacred Heart has poured from heaven on to earth, his own holy words fallen from his own lips.

Charles de Foucauld, *Meditations*

LEARNING IN THE DESERT

When God, who set me apart from birth and called me by his grace, was pleased to reveal his Son in me so that I might preach him among the Gentiles, I did not consult any man, nor did I go up to Jerusalem to see those who were apostles before I was, but I went immediately into Arabia (Galatians 1:15–17).

The present moment is, as it were, a desert in which the simple soul sees nothing but God only, whom she enjoys, being solely occupied with his will for her; all else is left aside, forgotten, abandoned to providence. The soul like an instrument in God's hand only receives impressions and works so far as she is passively occupied with God or applied by him to some external purpose.

The will of God is in all things the rule, the method, the law, the simple and certain way of the soul. The invariable law, belonging to all times, all places, all states. It is a straight line which the soul follows with courage and fidelity, straying neither to the right nor to the left and unconcerned with what exceeds its grasp. All that is beyond it is received and performed in self-abandonment.

In one word, the soul is active as far as it is concerned with her present duty, but passive and abandoned as regards all the rest, where her only action is to await in peace the divine movement.

Jean-Pierre de Caussade, *The Sacrament of the Present Moment*

O SACRED HEAD

[They] twisted together a crown of thorns and set it on his head (Matthew 27:29).

O sacred head, sore wounded,
　　Defiled and put to scorn;
O kingly head, surrounded
　　With mocking crown of thorn:
What sorrow mars thy grandeur?
　　Can death thy bloom deflower?
O countenance whose splendour
　　The hosts of heaven adore.

Thy beauty, long-desired,
　　Hath vanished from our sight;
Thy power is all expired,
　　And quenched the light of light.
Ah me! for whom thou diest,
　　Hide not so far thy grace:
Show me, O Love most highest,
　　The brightness of thy face.

In thy most bitter passion
　　My heart to share doth cry,
With thee for my salvation
　　Upon the Cross to die.
Ah, keep my heart thus moved
　　To stand thy Cross beneath,
To mourn thee, well-beloved,
　　Yet thank thee for thy death.

My days are few, O fail not,
　　With thine immortal power,
To hold me that I quail not
　　In death's most fearful hour:
That I may fight befriended,
　　And see in my last strife
To me thine arms extended
　　Upon the Cross of life.

14th-century Latin hymn, trans. Robert Bridges

IGNORANCE AND KNOWLEDGE

For since in the wisdom of God the world through its wisdom did not know him, God was pleased through the foolishness of what was preached to save those who believe (1 Corinthians 1:21).

A distinction needs to be made between two kinds of ignorance: ignorance about ourselves and ignorance about God. Both kinds of ignorance must be avoided because they both lead us to be condemned by God. First of all we must ask whether every kind of ignorance leads to condemnation. It seems to me that this is not the case. There are many things we can be ignorant of which do not put our salvation at risk. For example you may be ignorant about some complicated piece of machinery without affecting your salvation.

Many people have been saved and please God in both their actions and character who are not at all familiar with the liberal arts, even though they do have their uses. How many people are mentioned in the Letter to the Hebrews as being dear to God and who know nothing about refined literature but who have a pure conscience and sincere love? (See Hebrews 11.)

Many other people pleased God, not on account of the literature they knew, but by the lives they lived. Peter and Andrew, the sons of Zebedee, and all their fellow disciples, were not drawn from the school of rhetoric or philosophy and yet the Saviour used them to spread the knowledge of salvation throughout the world. They did not possess greater wisdom than other men but God saved them because of their faith and gentleness. They told the world about the way of life, not through magnificent preaching, or from clever human learning, because the world can never know God from its own wisdom.

Bernard of Clairvaux, *The Song of Songs*

ALL YE, WHO PASS BY

'Is it nothing to you, all you who pass by? Look around and see. Is any suffering like my suffering that was inflicted on me?' (Lamentations 1:12).

O all ye, who pass by, whose eyes and mind
To worldly things are sharp, but to be blind;
To me, who took eyes that I might find you:
Was ever grief like mine?

Mine own Apostle, who the bag did bear,
Though he had all I had, did not forbear
To sell me also, and to put me there:
Was ever grief like mine?

For thirty pence he did my death devise,
Who at three hundred did the ointment prize,
Not half so sweet as my sweet sacrifice:
Was ever grief like mine?

Therefore my soul melts, and my heart's dear treasure
Drops blood (the only beads) my words to measure:
O let this cup pass, if it be thy pleasure:
Was ever grief like mine?

These drops being temper'd with a sinner's tears,
A balsam are for both the Hemispheres,
Curing all wounds, but mine; all, but my fears:
Was ever grief like mine?

George Herbert, 'The Sacrifice'

CLUBS AND STAVES

**Then the men stepped forward, seized Jesus and arrested him
(Matthew 26:50).**

Arise, arise, they come! Look how they run!
Alas! what haste they make to be undone!
How with their lanterns do they seek the sun:
Was ever grief like mine?

With clubs and staves they seek me, as a thief,
Who am the way of truth, the true relief,
Most true to those who are my greatest grief:
Was ever grief like mine?

Judas, dost thou betray me with a kiss?
Canst thou find hell about my lips? and miss
Of life, just at the gates of life and bliss?
Was ever grief like mine?

See, they lay hold on me, not with the hands
Of faith, but fury; yet at their commands
I suffer binding, who have loosed their bands:
Was ever grief like mine?

All my disciples fly, fear puts a bar
Betwixt my friends and me. They leave the star,
That brought the wise men of the East from far:
Was ever grief like mine?

George Herbert, 'The Sacrifice'

BEFORE HEROD

When he [Pilate] learned that Jesus was under Herod's jurisdiction, he sent him to Herod, who was also in Jerusalem at that time (Luke 23:7).

They bind, and lead me unto Herod: he
Sends me to Pilate. This makes them agree;
But yet friendship is my enmity:
Was ever grief like mine?

Herod and all his bands do set me light,
Who teach all hands to war, fingers to fight,
And only am the Lord of hosts and might:
Was ever grief like mine?

Herod in judgment sits, while I do stand;
Examines me with a censorious hand:
I him obey, who all things else command:
Was ever grief like mine?

The Jews accuse me with despitefulness;
And vying malice with my gentleness,
Pick quarrels with their only happiness:
Was ever grief like mine?

I answer nothing, but with patience prove
If stony hearts will melt with gentle love.
But who does hawk at eagles with a dove?
Was ever grief like mine?

George Herbert, 'The Sacrifice'

'CRUCIFY'

But they kept shouting, 'Crucify him! Crucify him!' (Luke 23:21).

> Hark how they cry aloud still, 'Crucify:
> It is not fit he live a day', they cry,
> Who cannot live less than eternally:
> Was ever grief like mine?
>
> Pilate a stranger holdeth off; but they,
> Mine own dear people, cry, 'Away, away,'
> With noises confused frighting the day:
> Was ever grief like mine?
>
> Yet still they shout, and cry, and stop their ears,
> Putting my life among their sins and fears,
> And therefore with my blood on them and theirs:
> Was ever grief like mine?
>
> They chose a murderer, and all agree
> In him to do themselves a courtesy;
> For it was their own cause who killed me:
> Was ever grief like mine?
>
> And a seditious murderer he was:
> But I the Prince of Peace; peace that doth pass
> All understanding, more than heaven doth glass:
> Was ever grief like mine?
>
> George Herbert, 'The Sacrifice'

HOW THEY SCOURGE ME!

He [Pilate] had Jesus flogged (Matthew 27:26).

Ah, how they scourge me! yet my tenderness
Doubles each lash: and yet their bitterness
Winds up my grief to a mysteriousness:
Was ever grief like mine?

They buffet me, and box me as they list,
Who grasp the earth and heaven with my fist,
And never yet, whom I would punish, miss'd:
Was ever grief like mine?

Behold, they spit on me in scornful wise;
Who with my spittle gave the blind man eyes,
Leaving his blindness to mine enemies:
Was ever grief like mine?

My face they cover, though it be divine.
As Moses' face was veiled, so is mine,
Lest on their double-dark souls either shine:
Was ever grief like mine?

Servants and abjects flout me; they are witty:
'Now prophesy who strikes thee,' is their ditty.
So they in me deny themselves all pity:
Was ever grief like mine?

George Herbert, 'The Sacrifice'

DELIVER'D UNTO DEATH

Then the governor's soldiers took Jesus into the Praetorium and gathered the whole company of soldiers round him (Matthew 27:27).

And now I am deliver'd unto death,
Which each one calls for so with utmost breath,
That he before me well-nigh suffereth:
Was ever grief like mine?

Weep not, dear friends, since I for both have wept,
When all my tears were blood, the while you slept:
Your tears your own fortunes should be kept:
Was ever grief like mine?

The soldiers lead me to the common hall;
There they deride me, they abuse me all:
Yet for twelve heavenly legions I could call:
Was ever grief like mine?

Then the scarlet robe they me array;
Which shows my blood to be the only way,
And cordial left to repair man's decay:
Was ever grief like mine?

Then on my head a crown of thorns I wear;
For these are all the grapes Sion doth bear,
Though I my vine planted and water'd there:
Was ever grief like mine?

So sits the earth's great curse in Adam's fall
Upon my head; so I remove it all
From th' earth unto my brows, and bear the thrall:
Was ever grief like mine?

George Herbert, 'The Sacrifice'

THEY STRIKE MY HEAD

They . . . took the staff and struck him on the head again and again (Matthew 27:30).

Then with the reed they gave to me before,
They strike my head, the rock from whence all store
Of heavenly blessings issue evermore:
Was ever grief like mine?

They bow their knees to me, and cry, 'Hail, King':
Whatever scoffs or scornfulness can bring,
I am the floor, the sink, where they it fling:
Was ever grief like mine?

Yet since man's sceptres are as frail as reeds,
And thorny all their crowns, bloody their weeds;
I, who am Truth, turn into truth their deeds:
Was ever grief like mine?

The soldiers also spit upon that face
Which angels did desire to have the grace,
And Prophets once to see, but found no place:
Was ever grief like mine?

Thus trimmed, forth they bring me to the rout,
Who 'Crucify him,' cry with one strong shout.
God holds his peace at man, and man cries out:
Was ever grief like mine?

They lead me in once more, and putting then
Mine own clothes on, they lead me out again.
Whom devils fly, thus is he toss'd of men:
Was ever grief like mine?

George Herbert, 'The Sacrifice'

SIMON BEARS IT

As they were going out, they met a man from Cyrene, named Simon, and they forced him to carry the cross (Matthew 27:32).

> And now weary of sport, glad to engross
> All spite in one, counting my life their loss,
> They carried me to my most bitter cross:
> Was ever grief like mine?
>
> My cross I bear myself, until I faint:
> Then Simon bears it for me by constraint,
> The decreed burden of each mortal Saint:
> Was ever grief like mine?
>
> 'O all ye who pass by, behold and see:'
> Man stole the fruit, but I must climb the tree;
> The tree of life to all, but only me:
> Was ever grief like mine?
>
> Lo, here I hang, charged with a world of sin,
> The greater world o' the two; for that came in
> By words, but this by sorrow I must win:
> Was ever grief like mine?
>
> Such sorrow, as if sinful man could feel,
> Or feel his part, he would not cease to kneel,
> Till all were melted, though he were all steel:
> Was ever grief like mine?
>
> George Herbert, 'The Sacrifice'

'O MY GOD, MY GOD!'

About the ninth hour Jesus cried out in a loud voice, 'Eloi, Eloi, lama sabachthani?' – which means, 'My God, my God, why have you forsaken me?' (Matthew 27:46).

But, 'O my God, my God!' why leav'st thou me,
The Son, in whom thou dost delight to be?
'My God, my God' –
Was ever grief like mine?

Shame tears my soul, my body many a wound;
Sharp nails pierce this, but sharper that confound;
Reproaches, which are free, while I am bound:
Was ever grief like mine?

Now heal thyself, Physician; now come down.
Alas! I did so, when I left my crown
And Father's smile for you, to feel his frown:
Was ever grief like mine?

In healing not myself, there doth consist
All that salvation, which ye now resist;
Your safety in my sickness doth subsist:
Was ever grief like mine?

Betwixt two thieves I spend my utmost breath,
As he that for some robbery suffereth.
Alas! what have I stolen from you? death:
Was ever grief like mine?

George Herbert, 'The Sacrifice'

NOW ALL IS FINISHED

Jesus said, 'It is finished.' With that, he bowed his head and gave up his spirit (John 19:30).

A king my title is, prefix'd on high;
Yet by my subjects I'm condemn'd to die
A servile death in servile company:
Was ever grief like mine?

They gave me vinegar mingled with gall,
But more with malice: yet, when they did call,
With Manna, Angels' food, I fed them all:
Was ever grief like mine?

They part my garments, and by lot dispose
My coat, the type of love, which once cured those
Who sought for help, never malicious foes:
Was ever grief like mine?

Nay, after death their spite shall farther go;
For they will pierce my side, I full well know;
That as sin came, so Sacraments might flow:
Was ever grief like mine?

But now I die; now all is finished.
My woe, man's weal: and now I bow my head:
Only let others say, when I am dead,
Never was grief like mine.

George Herbert, 'The Sacrifice'

THE WONDROUS CROSS

'They will look on the one they have pierced' (John 19:37).

When I survey the wondrous Cross,
  On which the Prince of glory died,
My richest gain I count but loss,
  And pour contempt on all my pride.

Forbid it, Lord, that I should boast
  Save in the death of Christ my God;
All the vain things that charm me most,
  I sacrifice them to his blood.

See from his head, his hands, his feet,
  Sorrow and love flow mingled down;
Did e'er such love and sorrow meet,
  Or thorns compose so rich a crown?

His dying crimson like a robe,
  Spreads o'er his body on the Tree;
Then am I dead to all the globe,
  And all the globe is dead to me.

Were the whole realm of nature mine,
  That were a present far too small;
Love so amazing, so divine,
  Demands my soul, my life, my all.

Isaac Watts

REX TRAGICUS (I),
OR CHRIST GOING TO HIS CROSS

Then they led him away to crucify him (Matthew 27:31).

Put off thy robe of purple, then go on
To the sad place of execution:
Thine hour is come; and the tormentor stands
Ready, to pierce thy tender feet, and hands.
Long before this, the base, the dull, the rude,
Th' inconstant and unpurged multitude
Yawn for thy coming; some ere this time cry,
How he defers, how loath he is to die!
Amongst this scum, the soldier with his spear,
And that sour fellow, with his vinegar,
His sponge, and stick, do ask why thou dost stay?
So do the scurf and bran too: Go thy way,
Thy way, thou guiltless Man, and satisfy
By thine approach, each their beholding eye.
Not as a thief, shalt thou ascend the mount,
But like a person of some high account:
The cross shall be thy stage; and thou shalt there
The spacious field have for thy theatre. . . .

Robert Herrick

REX TRAGICUS (II)

When they came to the place called the Skull, there they crucified him, along with the criminals – one on his right, the other on his left (Luke 23:33).

Thou art that Roscius, and that marked-out man,
That must this day act the tragedian,
To wonder and affrightment: Thou art He,
Whom all the flux of nations comes to see;
Not those poor thieves that act their parts with Thee:
Those act without regard, when once a King,
And God, as thou art, comes to suffering.
No, no, this scene from thee takes life and sense,
And soul and spirit, plot and excellence.
Then begin, great King! ascend thy throne,
And thence proceed to act thy passion
To such a height, to such a period raised,
As hell, and earth, and heaven may stand amazed.
God, and good angels guide thee; and so bless
Thee in thy several parts of bitterness;
That those, who see thee nailed unto the tree,
May (though they scorn Thee) praise and pity Thee.
And we (Thy lovers) while we see Thee keep
The laws of action, will both sigh and weep;
And bring our spices, and embalm Thee dead;
That done, we'll see Thee sweetly buried.

Robert Herrick

GETHSEMANE

Then Jesus went with his disciples to a place called Gethsemane, and he said to them, 'Sit here while I go over there and pray' (Matthew 26:36).

Jesus suffers the torments which men inflict upon him; but in his agony he suffers the torments which he inflicts on himself. This is a suffering from an almighty hand, for he must be almighty to bear it.

Jesus seeks some comfort at least in his three dearest friends, and they are asleep. He prays them to bear with him for a little, and they leave him with entire indifference, having so little compassion that it could not prevent their sleeping, even for a moment. And thus Jesus was left alone to the wrath of God.

Jesus is alone on the earth, with no one to feel and share his suffering, or even to know of it; he and heaven were alone.

Jesus is in a garden, not of delight as the first Adam, where he lost himself and the whole human race, but in one of agony, where he saved himself and the whole human race.

He suffers this affliction and desertion in the horror of the night.

I believe that Jesus never complained but on this single occasion; but then he complained as if he could no longer bear his extreme suffering. 'My soul is sorrowful, even unto death.'

Jesus seeks companionship and comfort from men. This is the sole occasion in all his life, as it seems to me. But he receives it not, for his disciples are asleep.

Jesus will be in agony even to the end of the world. We must not sleep during that time.

. . . Finding his chosen friends asleep, Jesus is vexed because of the danger to which they expose, not him, but themselves; he cautions them for their own good, with a sincere tenderness for them during their ingratitude, and warns them that the spirit is willing and the flesh is weak.

Jesus, finding them still asleep, without being restrained by any consideration for themselves or for him, has the kindness not to waken them, and leaves them to sleep.

Jesus prays, uncertain of the will of his Father, and fears death; but when he knows it, he goes forward to offer himself to death.

Blaise Pascal, *Pensées*

PALM SUNDAY

A very large crowd spread their cloaks on the road, while others cut branches from the trees and spread them on the road (Matthew 21:8).

> Come, drop your branches, strew the way
>   Plants of the day!
> Whom sufferings make most green and gay.
> The King of grief, the man of sorrow,
> Weeping still like the wet morrow,
> Your shades and freshness comes to borrow.
>
> Put on, put on your best array;
> Let the joy'd road make holy-day
> And flowers, that into fields do stray
> Or secret groves, keep the high-way.
>
> Hark! how the children shrill and high
>   Hosanna cry;
> Their joys provoke the distant sky,
> Where thrones and seraphins reply;
> And their own angels shine and sing
>   In a bright ring:
>   Such young, sweet mirth
>   Makes heaven and earth
>   Join in a joyful Symphony.
>
> The harmless young and the happy Ass
> Is in these joys an high partaker,
> Ordain'd and made to bear his Maker.
> Dear feast of Palms, of Flowers and Dew!
> Whose fruitful dawn sheds hopes and light;
> Thy bright solemnities did show,
> The third glad day through two sad nights.
>
> I'll get me up before the Sun,
> I'll cut me boughs off many a tree
> And all atone full early run
> To gather flowers to welcome thee.

Henry Vaughan

RIDE ON! RIDE ON IN MAJESTY!

Jesus found a young donkey and sat upon it (John 12:14).

Ride on! ride on in majesty!
Hark! all the tribes 'Hosanna' cry:
O Saviour meek, pursue Thy road
With palms and scattered garments strowed.

Ride on! ride on in majesty!
In lowly pomp ride on to die:
O Christ, Thy triumphs now begin
O'er captive death and conquered sin.

Ride on! ride on in majesty!
The winged squadrons of the sky
Look down with sad and wondering eyes
To see the approaching sacrifice.

Ride on! ride on in majesty!
Thy last and fiercest strife is nigh;
The Father on His sapphire throne
Awaits His own anointed Son.

Ride on! ride on in majesty!
In lowly pomp ride on to die;
Bow thy meek head to mortal pain,
Then take, O God, Thy power and reign.

Henry Hart Milman

FEW BEARERS OF THE CROSS

Then Jesus said to his disciples, 'If anyone would come after me, he must . . . take up his cross' (Matthew 16:24).

Jesus has many lovers of his heavenly kingdom, but few bearers of his cross.

He has many who desire to partake in his comforts, but few to share in his distress. He finds many companions to eat with, but few to fast with. Everyone is disposed to rejoice with Jesus, but few to suffer sorrow for his sake. Many follow him even to the breaking of the bread, but few to the drinking of the bitter cup. Many reverence his miracles, but few follow the ignominy of the cross. Many love Jesus, while they are free from adversity; many praise and bless him, while they receive his consolations: but if Jesus hide his face, and leave them just for a short time, their confidence is shaken, and they sink into grumbling and despair.

But those who love Jesus for Jesus' sake, and not for their own personal comfort, bless him in the depths of tribulation and distress, as well as in the highest state of consolation. Indeed, should he be willing to withhold his consolations from them, they would still continue to be willing to praise him, and to give him thanks.

The Imitation of Christ, ascribed to Thomas à Kempis

WITH YOUR WHOLE MIND

When they had crucified him (Matthew 27:35).

With your whole mind, you must imagine yourself present and consider diligently everything done against your Lord and all that is said and done by him and regarding him.

With your mind's eye, see some thrusting the cross into the earth, others equipped with nails and hammers, others with the ladder and other instruments, others giving orders about what should be done, and others stripping him.

Now for the first time the Mother beholds her Son thus taken and prepared for the anguish of death. She is saddened and shamed beyond measure when she sees him entirely nude: they did not leave him even his loincloth. Therefore she hurries and approaches the Son, embraces him, and girds him with the veil from her head. Oh, what bitterness her soul is in now! I do not believe that she could say a word to him: if she could have done more, she would have, but she could not help him further. The Son was torn furiously from her hands to the foot of the cross.

Meditations on the Life of Christ (14th century)

TAKE UP THY CROSS

'Anyone who does not take his cross and follow me is not worthy of me' (Matthew 10:38).

Take up thy cross, the Saviour said,
　　If thou wouldst my disciple be;
Deny thyself, the world forsake,
　　And humbly follow after me.

Take up thy cross; let not its weight
　　Fill thy weak spirit with alarm;
His strength shall bear thy spirit up,
　　And brace thy heart, and nerve thine arm.

Take up thy cross, nor heed the shame,
　　Nor let the foolish pride rebel;
The Lord for thee the Cross endured,
　　To save thy soul from death and hell.

Take up thy cross then in his strength,
　　And calmly every danger brave;
'Twill guide thee to a better home,
　　And lead to victory o'er the grave.

Take up thy cross, and follow Christ,
　　Nor think till death to lay it down;
For only he who bears the cross
　　May hope to wear the glorious crown.

To thee, great Lord, the One in Three,
　　All praise for evermore ascend;
O grant us in our home to see
　　The heavenly life that knows no end.

Charles Everest

GOOD FRIDAY

We all, like sheep, have gone astray, each of us has turned to his own way; and the LORD has laid on him the iniquity of us all (Isaiah 53:6).

He ran thus till he came to a place somewhat ascending; and upon that place stood a cross, and a little below in the bottom, a sepulchre. So I saw in my dream, that just as Christian came up to the cross, his burden loosed from off his shoulders, and fell from off his back; and began to tumble; and so continued to do, till it came to the mouth of the sepulchre, where it fell in, and I saw it no more.

Then was Christian glad and lightsome, and said with a merry heart, 'He hath given me rest, by his sorrow; and life, by his death.' Then he stood awhile to look and wonder; for it was very surprising to him, that the sight of the cross should thus ease him of his burden. He looked therefore, and looked again, even till the springs that were in his head sent the waters down his cheeks. Now as he stood looking and weeping, behold three shining ones came to him, and saluted him, with 'Peace be to thee.' The first said to him, 'Thy sins be forgiven.' The second stripped him of his rags, and clothed him with a change of raiment. The third put a mark on his forehead, gave him a roll with a seal on it which he bid him look on as he ran, and that he should give it in at the Celestial Gate. So the three went their way. Then Christian gave three leaps for joy, and went on singing.

> Thus far did I come laden with my sin,
> Nor could ought ease the grief that I was in,
> Till I came hither: What a place this is!
> Must here be the beginning of my bliss?
> Must here the burden fall from off my back?
> Must here the strings that bound it to me, crack?
> Blest cross! Blest sepulchre! Blest rather be
> The Man that there was put to shame for me.

John Bunyan, *The Pilgrim's Progress*

SEPULCHRE

Joseph took the body, wrapped it in a clean linen cloth, and placed it in his own new tomb that he had cut out of the rock (Matthew 27:59).

O blessed body! whither art thou thrown?
No lodging for thee, but a cold hard stone?
So many hearts on earth, and yet not one
    Receive thee?

Sure there is room without our hearts' good store;
For they can lodge transgressions by the score:
Thousands of toys dwell there, yet out of door
    They leave thee.

But that which shows them large, shows them unfit.
Whatever sin did this pure rock commit,
Which holds thee now? Who hath indited it
    Of murder?

Where our hard hearts took up of stones to brain thee,
And missing this, most falsely did arraign thee;
Only these stones in quiet entertain thee,
    And order.

And as of old, the Law by heavenly art
Was writ in stone: so thou, which also art
The letter of the word, find'st no fit heart
    To hold thee.

Yet do we still persist as we began,
And so should perish, but that nothing can,
Though it be cold, hard, from loving man
    Withhold thee.

George Herbert

EASTER DAY

The angel said to the women, 'Do not be afraid, for I know that you are looking for Jesus, who was crucified. He is not here; he has risen, just as he said. Come see the place where he lay' (Matthew 28:5–6).

Jesus Christ is risen to-day, Alleluia!
Our triumphant holy day, Alleluia!
Who did once, upon the Cross, Alleluia!
Suffer to redeem our loss. Alleluia!

Hymns of praise then let us sing, Alleluia!
Unto Christ, our heavenly King, Alleluia!
Who endured the Cross and grave, Alleluia!
Sinners to redeem and save. Alleluia!

But the pains that he endured, Alleluia!
Our salvation have procured; Alleluia!
Now above the sky he's King, Alleluia!
Where the angels ever sing. Alleluia!

Lyra Davidica

WERE YOU THERE . . . ?

**Many women were there, watching from a distance. They had
followed Jesus from Galilee to care for his needs. Among them
were Mary Magdalene, Mary the mother of James and Joses,
and the mother of Zebedee's sons (Matthew 27:55–56).**

Were you there when they crucified my Lord?
Were you there when they crucified my Lord?
O – sometimes it causes me to tremble, tremble, tremble;
Were you there when they crucified my Lord?

Were you there when they nailed him to the tree?
Were you there when they nailed him to the tree?

Were you there when they pierced him in the side?
Were you there when they pierced him in the side?

Were you there when the sun refused to shine?
Were you there when the sun refused to shine?

Were you there when they laid him in the tomb?
Were you there when they laid him in the tomb?

Were you there when he rose from out the tomb?
Were you there when he rose from out the tomb?

Negro spiritual

FOLLOWING GOD'S WILL

Test and approve what God's will is – his good, pleasing and perfect will (Romans 12:2).

Patient, meek resignation is to be exercised with regard to all outward things and occurrences of life, yet it particularly relates to our inward state, the troubles, perplexities, weaknesses, and disorders of our own souls. And to stand turned to a patient, meek, humble resignation to God, when your own impatience, wrath, and pride attack yourself, is a higher and more beneficial performance of this duty, than when you stand turned to meekness and patience, when attacked by the pride, or wrath, or disorderly passions of other people.

Resignation to the divine will signifies a cheerful approbation and thankful acceptance of everything that comes from God. It is not enough patiently to submit, but we must thankfully receive and fully approve of everything that, by the order of God's providence, happens to us. For there is no reason why we should be patient, but what is as good and as strong a reason why we should be thankful.

Whenever, therefore, you find yourself disposed to uneasiness or murmuring at any thing that is the effect of God's providence over you, you must look upon yourself as denying either the wisdom or goodness of God.

William Law, *A Serious Call to a Devout and Holy Life*

ENGULFED IN GOD

Tell him I am faint with love (Song of Songs 5:8).

As melted balm that is no longer firm or solid, the soul lets herself pass or flow into what she loves: she does not spring out of herself as by a sudden leap, nor does she cling as by a joining or union, but gently glides, as a fluid and liquid thing, into the divinity whom she loves.

She goes out by that sacred outflowing and holy liquefaction, and quits herself, not only to be united to the well-beloved, but to be entirely mingled with and steeped in him.

The outflowing of a soul into her God is a true ecstasy, by which the soul quite transcends the limits of her natural way of existence, being wholly mingled with, absorbed and engulfed in, her God.

St Francis de Sales, *Introduction to a Devout Life*

IMITATION OF CHRIST

'I am the way and the truth and the life' (John 14:6).

There is no progress in the Christian life unless you follow Christ.
Christ is the way, the truth and the life, and the gate through
which you must enter to be saved. Every spirit, therefore, that will
walk in sweetness at its ease, shunning the following of Christ, is,
in my opinion, worthless.

Your first concern must be to carefully and lovingly make it
your aim to imitate Christ in all your actions. Everything you do
must be done as our Lord himself would have done them. Every
pleasure indulged in for sensuous reason and not for God's glory
must be renounced and rejected in favour of the love of Jesus
Christ. While he was on this earth he had and followed no pleasure except doing his Father's will, which he said was his meat and
drink.

In none of your actions whatever should you take any man,
however holy he may be, for your example, because Satan is sure
to put his imperfections forward so as to attract your attention.
Rather imitate Jesus Christ, who is supremely perfect and
supremely holy. If you do this you will never go astray.

Inwardly and outwardly always live your life with the crucified
Christ, and then you will attain peace and contentment of spirit,
and in your patience you will possess your soul.

St John of the Cross, *The Dark Night of the Soul*

HOLY HUMILITY

'He has been mindful of the humble state of his servant' (Luke 1:48).

No one can attain to any knowledge or understanding of God, except through the virtue of holy humility: for the straight way upward is the straight way downward. All the perils and the great falls that have happened in this world have come about through the lifting up of the head, that is, the mind in pride. This is illustrated by the fall of the devil who was thrown out of heaven, and by the fall of our first parent, Adam, who was driven out of paradise because of the lifting up of his head, that is, through disobedience.

In the same way, all the great and good things that have ever happened in the world have occurred through the abasement of the head, that is, through the humility of the mind, which is seen through the humility of the virgin Mary, through the tax collector praying, and through the penitent thief on the cross. So we would do well to find some heavy weight to hang round our necks to force us to bow our necks in order to humble us.

A friar asked Friar Giles, 'Tell me, father, how shall we flee from this sin of pride?' Friar Giles replied, 'My brother, be persuaded of this: never hope to be able to flee from pride, unless you first put your mouth where your feet are. If you ponder God's blessings you will then know how to bow your head. Also, if you ponder your many offences against God you will have the greatest reason to humble yourself.'

The Little Flowers of St Francis

IS DEATH A MISERY?

'What good is it for a man to gain the whole world, and yet lose or forfeit his very self?' (Luke 9:25).

Penitens, a prosperous tradesman of some standing, lay dying at the age of 35. A little before his death, when the doctors could do no more for him, he said to his visiting neighbours:

'When we consider death as a misery, we think of it only as a miserable separation from the pleasures of this life. We seldom mourn over an old man who dies rich, but we lament the young who are taken away in the process of making their fortunes. You yourselves look upon me with pity, not because I am going unprepared to meet the Judge of the living and the dead, but you pity me because I am to leave a prosperous trade in the prime of my life.

'This is the wisdom of our human thoughts. Yet what stupidity of the silliest children is as great as this? For the only miserable or dreadful thing about death is the consequence of it. When a man is dead, what do worldly pleasures matter to him? All that matters is the state his soul is in.

'If I am now going into the joys of God, could there be any reason to grieve that this happened to me before I was 40 years old? Could it be a sad thing to go to heaven before I have made a few more bargains, or stood a little longer behind a counter?

'When you are as near death as I am, you will know that all the different states of life – youth and age, riches and poverty, fame and insignificance – become meaningless. The greatness of the things which follow on from death make all that precedes death sink to nothing.'

William Law, *A Serious Call to a Devout and Holy Life*

PRAISES

Let everything that has breath praise the LORD (Psalm 150:6).

'Holy, holy, holy is the Lord God Almighty, who was, and is, and is to come' (Revelation 4:8). Praise him and exalt him above all for ever (see Daniel 13:57).

Worthy art thou to receive all praise, glory, honour and blessing (see Revelation 4:11). Praise him and exalt him above all for ever.

The Lamb that was slain is worthy to receive power, and divinity, and wisdom, and strength, and honour, and glory and blessing (see Revelation 5:12).

Let us bless the Father, the Son and the Holy Spirit. Praise him and exalt him above all for ever.

'All ye works of the Lord, bless the Lord: praise and exalt him above all for ever' (Daniel 13:57).

'Give praise to our God, all ye his servants, and you that fear him little and great' (Revelation 19:5). Praise him and exalt him above all for ever.

Let heaven and earth, and 'every creature, which is in heaven, on the earth and under the earth, the sea and all that is in it, praise this glorious God' (see Revelation 5:13). Praise him and exalt him above all for ever.

St Francis of Assisi, *Prayers*

FAITH

The righteous will live by his faith (Habakkuk 2:4).

The way of faith is sound and safe, and along this souls must journey on from virtue to virtue.

The soul that travels in the light and truth of the faith is free from error, for error usually stems from our own desires, tastes and understandings. By the faith the soul is protected against the devil, its strongest and most deceitful enemy. St Peter knew of no stronger defence against him when he said, 'Resist him, standing firm in the faith' (1 Peter 5:9).

The soul that desires to come close to God and unite itself with God, must do so by not understanding rather than by understanding, and be in complete forgetfulness about created things. Outward light enables us to see so that we do not fall over, but it is different with the things of God, for in this case it is better not to see, as the soul then has greater security.

The greatest shelter of the soul is faith; for the Holy Spirit gives it light. The more pure and refined the soul is in living by perfect faith, the greater will be the degree of love in that soul and the greater use of supernatural gifts and light in his life. The soul that leans on its own understanding and feeling to travel along the correct road is most likely to be led astray and hindered, because it is not perfectly blind in faith, which is its true guide.

St John of the Cross, *The Dark Night of the Soul*

INTERNAL CONVERSATION

'The kingdom of God is within you' (Luke 17:21).

So said our blessed Redeemer. Abandon, therefore, this wretched world, and turn to the Lord with all your heart, and your soul will find rest. Learn to despise outward things, and keep your attention fixed on what goes on within yourself and you will soon perceive the coming of God's kingdom, for the kingdom of God consists in peace and joy and the Holy Spirit, which is not sensual and worldly.

Christ will come to you, showing you his consolation, if you prepare within yourself a place that is fit to receive him. All his glory and beauty come from within, and there he delights to dwell. His visits there are frequent, his conversation sweet, his comforts refreshing, and his peace passing all understanding.

O faithful soul, dispose your heart for the reception of this Bridegroom, that he may come into you, and dwell with you: for he says, 'If a man love me, he will keep my words: and my Father will love him; and we will come unto him, and make our abode with him.' Therefore, give free admission to Christ, and deny entrance to all others. When you possess Christ you are rich, and lack no other treasure. He will protect you and provide for you faithfully, so that you will no longer have any need to hope in man. Men are changeable and perishable: but Christ abideth eternally, and continueth firmly unto the end.

The Imitation of Christ, ascribed to Thomas à Kempis

INNER PEACE

'Blessed are the peacemakers, for they will be called sons of God' (Matthew 5:9).

You must first secure the peace of your own heart before you are qualified to restore peace to others. A peaceful man profiteth more than a thoroughly learned man. The angry and turbulent man, who is always ready to believe wrong, turns even good into evil; the peaceful man turns everything into good. 'The hot-tempered man stirs up dissension, but a patient man calms a quarrel' (Proverbs 15:18). The person who is not at peace in himself will not allow others to rest. He speaks what he should suppress, and suppresses what he should speak.

He watches how others carry out their duties, but neglects his own duties. Let your zeal be first applied to yourself, before it is applied in trying to reform your neighbour.

You are quick to excuse your own actions but do not allow other people to explain their actions. However, it would be more just to excuse your brother and accuse yourself.

If you wish to be borne with, you must bear with others. Think how far these people are from the love which bears all things, believes all things and hopes all things.

The Imitation of Christ, ascribed to Thomas à Kempis

A GREETING TO THE VIRTUES

'He has brought down rulers from their thrones but has lifted up the humble' (Luke 1:52).

Greetings, O wisdom, O queen, may the Lord keep thee and thy sister simplicity, holy and pure. Lady holy poverty, may the Lord keep thee and thy most holy sister obedience. May the Lord keep all of you most holy virtues. You come from the Lord, your source. No person in the world can possess a single virtue unless he first dies to himself. A person who possesses one virtue will possess all the others provided that he does not harm any of them. A person who hurts one of the virtues offends them all and does not possess any of them.

Each virtue puts vices and sins to confusion. Holy wisdom confounds Satan and all his devices. Pure and holy simplicity confounds all worldly wisdom and all human wisdom. Holy poverty confounds all covetousness, avarice and conformity to this world. Holy humility confounds pride and all worldly men and all that is in the world. Holy charity confounds all diabolical and carnal temptations and all fear of nature. Holy obedience confounds all the desires of the body and of the flesh. Holy obedience keeps the body mortified so that it can obey the spirit and its brother. Holy obedience makes a person submissive to all people in the world. Holy obedience also makes a person submissive to animals, even wild animals, which can do as they wish with him, so long as it is granted to them from above by the Lord.

St Francis of Assisi, 'Canticle'

REMEMBRANCE OF DEATH

Man is destined to die once, and after that to face judgment (Hebrews 9:27).

If a person had the remembrance of his death and of the last eternal judgment always before the eyes of his mind, he would definitely never again desire to sin against or offend God. If it was possible for someone to have lived from the beginning of the world until now, and to have endured adversity, tribulation, pain, affliction and sorrow all this time, and if he were then to die, and his soul go to receive everlasting reward in heaven, what good would all the pain he had previously endured do him? In the same way if someone who had lived from the beginning of the world had enjoyed every pleasure and consolation the world could give, and then when he died his soul should go to hell, what would all the good things he had received in the past do him?

An unstable man said to Friar Giles, 'I tell you, I long to live in this world and have great riches and an abundance of things and to be held in high honour.'

Friar Giles replied, 'My brother, even if you were ruler of the whole world, and should live for one thousand years and experience every joy and delight and pleasure and temporal delight, tell me, what reward or what merit would you expect to have from your miserable life which you have served and pleased so much! I tell you that the person who lives well in God's sight, and seeks not to offend God, he will receive from God an infinite and everlasting reward, great riches, great honour and eternal life in the glory of heaven.'

The Little Flowers of St Francis

SERVING CHRIST

'I tell you the truth, anyone who gives you a cup of water in my name because you belong to Christ will certainly not lose his reward' (Mark 9:41).

Abba Agathon, on his way to town one day, to sell a few small articles, came across a cripple on the roadside. The cripple was paralysed in his legs and he asked Abba Agathon where he was going.

Abba Agathon replied, 'I am going to town to sell a few things.'

The cripple said, 'Please do me the favour of carrying me there.' So Abba Agathon carried him to the town.

The cripple said to him, 'Put me down where you sell your goods.' Abba Agathon did so. When he had sold an article, the cripple asked, 'What did you sell it for?' and Abba Agathon told him the price.

The cripple said, 'Buy me a cake,' and Abba Agathon bought him a cake.

When Abba Agathon had sold a second article, the cripple asked, 'How much did you sell it for?' And Abba Agathon told him its price. Then the cripple said, 'Buy me this,' and Abba Agathon bought it.

When Abba Agathon, having sold all his goods, wanted to go, the cripple said to him, 'Are you returning home?'

Abba Agathon replied, 'Yes.'

Then the cripple said, 'Do me the favour of carrying me back to the place where you found me.' So Abba Agathon picked him up and carried him back to that place. Then the cripple said, 'Abba Agathon, you are filled with divine blessings, in heaven and on earth.'

Raising his eyes, Agathon saw no man; it was an angel of the Lord, who had been testing him.

Sayings of the Desert Fathers

THE HUMILITY OF MARY

'For the Mighty One has done great things for me – holy is his name' (Luke 1:49).

Behold, how completely Mary traces all to God, lays claim to no works, no honour, no fame. She conducts herself as before, when as yet she had naught of all this; she demands no higher honours than before. She is not puffed up, does not vaunt herself, nor proclaim with a loud voice that she is become the Mother of God. She seeks not any glory, but goes about her wonted household duties, milking cows, cooking meals, washing pots and kettles, sweeping out the rooms, and performing the work of a maidservant or housemother in lowly and despised tasks, as though she cared naught for such exceeding great gifts and graces. She was esteemed among other women and her neighbours no more highly than before, nor desired to be, but remained a poor townswoman, one of the great multitude.

When men accord us praise and honour, we ought to profit by the example of the Mother of God. We ought neither to reject this praise and honour as though they were wrong, nor to despise them as though they were naught; but ascribe them to him in heaven to whom they belong.

Martin Luther, 'The Magnificat'

EXPERIENCING GOD

'I know that my Redeemer lives' (Job 19:25).

Letter to Miss M. (September 3, 1776)
My Dear Miss M.,
You say: 'It never came with power and life to my soul, that he died for me.' If you mean, you never had any extraordinary sudden manifestation, something like a vision or voice from heaven, confirming it to you, I can say the same. But I know he died for sinners; I know I am a sinner; I know he invites those who are ready to perish; I am such a one; I know, upon his own invitation, that he has been with me until now, otherwise I should have been an apostate long ago; and therefore I know that he died for me; for had he been pleased to kill me (as he justly might have done), he would not have shown me such things as these.

> If I must perish, would the Lord
> Have taught my heart to love his word?
> Would he have giv'n me eyes to see
> My danger and my remedy?
> Reveal'd his name, and bid me pray,
> Had he resolv'd to say me nay?

I know that I am a child, because he teaches me to say – Abba, Father. I know that I am his, because he has enabled me to choose him for mine; for such a choice and desire never could have taken place in my heart, if he had not placed it there himself. The love I bear him is but a faint and feeble spark, but it is an emanation from himself: he kindled it, and he keeps it alive; and because it is his work, I trust many waters shall not quench it.

John Newton, *Cardiphonia*

HUMILITY VERSUS INTELLECTUAL ATTAINMENT

Knowledge puffs up (1 Corinthians 8:1).

Every man naturally desires to increase in knowledge; but what does knowledge profit, without the fear of the Lord? Better is the humble peasant, who serves God, than the proud philosopher, who, destitute of the knowledge of himself, can describe the course of the planets. He who truly knows himself, becomes vile in his own eyes, and has no delight in the praise of men. If I knew all that the world contains, and did not have love, how would that help me in God's sight, who will judge me according to my deeds?

Rest from an inordinate desire for knowledge, for it is subject to much perplexity and delusion. Learned men are fond of the notice of the world, and desire to be accounted wise. But there are many things, the knowledge of which has no tendency to promote the recovery of our first divine life. It is surely a proof of folly, to devote ourselves wholly to that, with which our supreme good has no connection.

The soul is not to be satisfied with the multitude of words; but holy life refreshes the mind, and a pure conscience is the foundation of a firm and immovable confidence in God.

The Imitation of Christ, ascribed to Thomas à Kempis

DELAYS

Yet when he [Jesus] heard that Lazarus was sick, he stayed where he was two more days (John 11:6).

Whenever the feeling of grace is withdrawn, pride is always the cause; perhaps not actual pride but potential pride, which would have arisen had not the feeling been withdrawn.

Because of this there are some silly young people who think that God is their enemy, when really he is their best friend. Sometimes it is withdrawn because of their carelessness. When this is the case, they experience a deep bitterness which eats into them. Sometimes our Lord deliberately delays the feeling of grace, because in so doing he wishes to make it grow and be more treasured, like a precious thing lost and rediscovered. One of the surest and most important ways by which a soul may know if he is called to contemplation (after such a period of long inability to contemplate) is that it returns suddenly, independently of him, and he has a burning and deep passion to do this work as never before. Often, I think, his joy at its recovery is far greater than his distress at its loss! If this is the case, then it is unmistakably a true sign that he has been called by God to become a contemplative, irrespective of his former or present state.

For it is not what you are or have been that God looks upon with merciful eyes, but what you long to be. St Gregory says that 'all holy desires grow by delays; if they fade by these delays they were never holy desires.' If a man feels increasingly less joy at new discoveries and at the upsurge of his old, deliberate, desire for good, then those passions were never holy. St Augustine speaks of these holy desires saying that 'the life of a good Christian consists of nothing else but holy desire.'

The Cloud of Unknowing

THOUGHTS ON MARTYRDOM

One of the soldiers pierced Jesus' side with a spear (John 19:34).

The endurance of the martyrs whose strength comes from Christ.
The Church does not flinch at the burning marks of the Saviour's
passion, or run away from the discoloured marks of his wounds.
The Church even takes delight in them and wishes that her own
death may be like these. The reason why the Bridegroom says to
the bride, in the Song of Songs, 'My dove in the clefts of the rock,
in the hiding-places on the mountainside, show me your face, let
me hear your voice; for your voice is sweet, and your face is
lovely' (Song of Songs 2:14) is because she dedicated herself with
single-minded devotion to the wounds of Christ and continually
meditates on them.

This is where the endurance which does not shrink from
martyrdom comes from. This is the complete confidence that she
has in the most high God. The martyr has nothing to fear if he can
lift his eyes to that discoloured and bloodless face. He is healed by
its paleness and is strengthened to become like his Master as he
faced death, even to being as pale as gold. What the Master wants
is to be seen. The Leader is full of kindness and wants his devoted
soldiers to fix their eyes on his wounds so that they can draw
strength from them. Then these soldiers will derive power from
Christ's example.

The truth of the matter is that the martyr will not feel his own
pain if he is gazing at the wounds of his Saviour. He stands
intrepid and triumphant, even though his body is a mass of
wounds. When the sword cuts into his body and he sees the sacred
blood of martyrdom pour from his body he is not only brave but
happy. Where, then, is the soul of the martyr? It is in the place of
safety, in the rock, in the heart of Jesus, and the soul enters in there
through the open door of Christ's wounds.

The voice of the martyr's witness which endures to the end
causes the Leader great joy. It is impossible that it should be
otherwise. The martyr is rewarded with this promise, 'Whoever
acknowledges me before men, I will also acknowledge him before
my Father in heaven' (Matthew 10:32).

Bernard of Clairvaux, *The Song of Songs*

HOPE

Character [produces] hope. And hope does not disappoint us, because God has poured out his love into our hearts by the Holy Spirit (Romans 5:4–5).

That which moves and overcomes God is earnest hope. In order to reach the union of love, the soul must journey in hope of God alone; for without it nothing will be achieved. A living hope in God makes the soul so courageous and so earnest in the pursuit of everlasting life that it looks on this world – which indeed it is – as dry, weak, valueless, and dead, in comparison with that hope which it hopes for hereafter.

The soul in hope strips itself of all the trappings of this world, setting the heart upon nothing, hoping for nothing in it or of it, clad in the garments of the hope of everlasting life. Through a living hope in God the heart is so raised up above the world and delivered from all its snares, that not only can it not come into contact with it, but it cannot even view it. In all your trials have recourse at once to God with confidence, and you will be comforted, enlightened, and instructed.

The soul that retains the slightest desire for earthly things, is more unseemly and impure in the way of God than if it were labouring under the heaviest and most impure temptations and darkness, provided the rational will did not consent to them; such a soul may, with greater confidence, draw near to God in obedience to the divine will; for our Lord has said: Come unto me all you who labour and are heavily burdened, and I will refresh you. Have an earnest desire that God may give you all he knows you are lacking in, for his greater honour and glory.

St John of the Cross, *The Dark Night of the Soul*

SELF-DISCIPLINE

Be clear minded and self-controlled so that you can pray (1 Peter 4:7).

An old man had been on a strict diet for fifty years. He rarely ate bread or drank wine. He even boasted, 'I have defeated fornication, greed and boasting about myself.'

When Abba Abraham heard about him he visited him and asked, 'Did you really say all that?'

The old man replied, 'Yes.'

Then Abba Abraham said to him, 'If you discovered a woman lying on your doorstep when you entered your cell, wouldn't you realise that she was a woman?'

'No,' he replied, 'But I would have to struggle against my thoughts so that I refrained from touching her.'

Then Abba Abraham said, 'In that case you have not defeated your passion. Clearly it is still alive and lives in you, even though you have it under control.'

Then Abba Abraham said, 'If you were walking along and you saw some gold among the stones and shells would your mind tell you that they were all of equal value?'

'No,' the old man replied, 'But I would wrestle with my thoughts, so that I did not pick up the gold and keep it.'

Abba Abraham said, 'This proves that avarice still lives in you, even though it is under control.'

Abba Abraham continued, 'What would happen if you heard that one of your two brothers loved you while the other hated you and spreads evil rumours about you? If they both visited you would you be able to welcome them with equal love?'

'No,' replied the old man, 'But I would struggle against my inclinations and try to be as kind to the one who hates as the one who loves me.'

Abba Abraham said to him, 'This demonstrates that passions are very much still alive in you. They are just under the control of the saints.'

Sayings of the Desert Fathers

GRACE IS FROM GOD

'Blessed are those who hunger and thirst for righteousness, for they will be filled' (Matthew 5:6).

Blessed are those who hunger for righteousness and endure work and poverty here, for this life is but a moment and will surely pass. They are blessed, though not most blessed.

Blessed are those who hunger not to be deprived of God, albeit the wonder is that man can be without him without whom he cannot be. St Augustine says it is amazing that anyone should live apart from him, apart from whom he cannot live at all. They are blessed, and yet not most blessed.

More blessed are those who so hunger that they cannot live without God; that is a fiery love which transforms their nature. As long as a man still finds anything impermanent in his desire or in hope or his love, he is not most blessed. He is blessed, but not most blessed.

Blessed, supremely blessed, are those who are installed in the eternal now, transcending time and place and form and matter, unmoved by well-being or woe or wealth or want, for to the extent that things are motionless, they are like eternity.

Meister Eckhart, *Sermons*

PRAYER

Elijah . . . prayed earnestly (James 5:17).

God does nothing but in answer to prayer: and even they who have been converted to God, without praying for it themselves (which is exceedingly rare), were not without the prayers of others. Every new victory which a soul gains is the effect of a new prayer.

On every occasion of uneasiness, we should retire to prayer, that we may give place to the grace and light of God, and then form our resolutions without being in any pain about what success that may have.

In the greatest temptations, a single look to Christ, and the bare pronouncing of his name, suffices to overcome the wicked one, so it be done with confidence and calmness of spirit.

God's command 'pray continually' (1 Thessalonians 5:17) is founded on the necessity we have of his grace to preserve the life of God in the soul, which can no more subsist one moment without it than the body can without air.

John Wesley, *A Plain Man's Guide to Holiness*

FOUR RULES OF PRAYER

'The tax collector . . . would not even look up to heaven, but beat his breast and said, "God, have mercy on me, a sinner"' (Luke 18:13).

The first rule of true prayer is to have heart and mind in the right mood for talking with God. We shall achieve this if we put aside all carnal thoughts and worries which would distract us from direct and pure contemplation of God. Our minds must be wholly concentrated on prayer and raised above themselves.

A second condition of prayer is that, in asking, we must be sincerely aware of our needs. Many people repeat prayers in a half-hearted way and following a set form, as if they were carrying out some task for God. Even though they see prayer as a necessary remedy, it still seems as though they pray out of a sense of duty, with cold hearts and not much thought. Believers should be specially careful not to come into God's presence without serious intention. So when we pray that God's name should be hallowed, we must really hunger and thirst for the answer.

The third rule of prayer is that the one who comes into God's presence to pray must get rid of all boasting and self-opinionated ideas. Self-confidence must be thrown aside and God be given all the glory. Pride always means turning away from God. The holier the servant of God, the lowlier he will bow down in the presence of the Lord.

The fourth rule of prayer is that, despite the necessary humbling, we should be spurred on to pray with real confidence of success. The two things are perfectly consistent, if we are aware that it is only the goodness of God which lifts the contrite sinner. This confidence is the privilege of those who are not worried by care, tortured with regret or alarmed by fear.

John Calvin, *The Institutes of Christian Religion*

THE HOLY FEAR OF GOD

The fear of the LORD is the beginning of wisdom (Proverbs 9:10).

The person who fears nothing demonstrates that he has nothing to lose. The holy fear of God ordains, governs, and rules the soul and makes it come to a state of grace. If anyone possesses any grace or divine virtue, holy fear is what preserves it. Anyone who has not yet gained virtue or grace can do so through holy fear. However, this holy gift of fear is given only to the perfect. For the more perfect a person is, the more godfearing and humble he is. Happy is the person who knows that he is in a dungeon in this world, and always remembers how grievously he has offended his Lord.

Everyone should stand in fear of pride, in case it attacks him and makes him fall from his state of grace. Nobody stands secure when he is surrounded by his enemies. Our enemies are the lures of this miserable world, our own sinful nature and the devil. A person needs greater fear in case his own wickedness overcomes him and defeats him more than his other enemies. It is impossible for a man to reach any divine grace, or virtue, or to persevere in it, without holy fear. Anyone who does not fear God is in danger of perishing. The fear of God makes a person humbly obey and makes him to bow his head down under the yoke of obedience. The greater a fear a person has the more fervently he worships.

The Little Flowers of St Francis

I SAW HIS PASSION

Many women were there, watching from a distance (Matthew 27:55).

I saw the red blood trickle down from under the garland of thorns, a stream of hot, fresh blood, just as it was in the time of his Passion when the crown was pressed on to the blessed head of the God-Man who suffered in this way for me. And I saw clearly, powerfully and truly, that it was none other than Jesus himself who showed this vision to me.

In that same vision, the Trinity suddenly filled my heart with the deepest joy, and I knew that all those who go to heaven will experience this joy for ever. For the Trinity is God: God is the Trinity; the Trinity is our Creator and Keeper, the Trinity is our eternal love, joy and bliss, through our Lord Jesus Christ. This was revealed to me in this first vision and indeed in all of them, for it seems to me that wherever Jesus appears the blessed Trinity is also present.

'Benedicite, Domine!' ['Welcome, O Lord!'] I cried, and I meant it in all reverence and shouted it at the top of my voice! I was overwhelmed with wonder that he, so holy and awesome, should be so at home with the likes of me – I, who am so sinful, with such a wretched earthly body.

Lady Julian of Norwich, *Revelations of Divine Love*

RUNNING AFTER BUTTERFLIES

'Provide purses for yourselves that will not wear out, a treasure in heaven that will not be exhausted, where no thief comes near and no moth destroys. For where your treasure is, there your heart will be also' (Luke 12:33–34).

Many people covet worldly riches, thinking about them during the day, and dreaming about them during the night, working out how they may acquire them. They eradicate from their minds the joys of heaven. Certainly, they are not wise. They are like children who run after butterflies, they do not take care where they are running, and they fall and break a leg. What is all the pomp and riches of this world if it is not a butterfly? It is definitely nothing else, and is even less than a butterfly.

So, I urge you, to covet the joys of heaven, where you will have riches that last for ever. For in the end, when worldly covetous men bring nothing of worth in their hands, since all their riches have disappeared, then shall those of you who have coveted heaven come into their own. For they shall be crowned as kings and ascend up with our Lord Jesus into the bliss of heaven.

Walter Hilton, *The Scale of Perfection*

MEDITATIVE READING

How sweet are your words to my taste, sweeter than honey to my mouth! I gain understanding from your precepts (Psalm 119:103–4).

Meditative reading is achieved by choosing some important practical or theoretical truth. If at all possible, you should choose the practical truth rather than the theoretical truth, and then you should proceed in this way.

Whatever truth you have chosen, only read a small part of it. Try to taste it, digest it, and extract its essence. Do not read any more while any flavour remains in the short portion you have read. When the flavour does disappear take up your book again, and proceed as before, seldom reading more than half a page at a time. It is not the quantity that is read, but the way we read that is profitable to us. Those who read fast reap no more advantage than a bee would by only skimming over the surface of the flower, instead of waiting to enter into it, and extract its nectar.

A great quantity of reading is best kept to scholastic subjects rather than divine truths. If we are to derive any benefit from spiritual books, we must read them in the way I have described. For I am certain that when that method is followed we will gradually become used to it, and so be in a better frame of mind for prayer.

Madame Guyon, *A Short and Easy Method of Prayer*

THE EYES OF THE SOUL

You have stolen my heart . . . with one glance of your eyes (Song of Songs 4:9).

There are two eyes of the soul: reason and love. By reason we may trace how mighty, how wise, and how good God is in his creatures, but we will not discover God himself. When reason fails employ love. Learn to exercise love. For through love we may feel God and find God. It is a wonderful eye, this love. Only about a loving soul can it be said that the Lord has stolen my heart with one glance of his eyes. That is to say, love, that is blind to many things, which only has eyes for the one person it seeks, when it finds the heart it seeks, it wounds that heart.

So this should, I beseech you, be the way you should live. 'Brothers, think of what you were when you were called. Not many of you were wise by human standards; not many were influential; not many were of noble birth' (1 Corinthians 1:26); 'I urge you to live a life worthy of the calling you have received' (Ephesians 4:1).

An Epistle of Discretion (14th century)

TWO ORDERS OF PEOPLE

'Some are eunuchs because they are born that way; others were made that way by men; and others have renounced marriage because of the kingdom of heaven' (Matthew 19:12).

There has been instituted in the church of Christ two ways, or manners of living. The one, raised above the ordinary state of nature and common ways of living, rejects marriage, possessions, and worldly goods, and, being completely separate and removed from the ordinary exchanges of common life, is devoted solely to the worship and service of God, through a very high degree of heavenly love.

People who belong to this order seem dead to the life of this world, and, having their bodies only on earth, are in their minds, and contemplations, dwelling in heaven. From there, like so many heavenly inhabitants, they look down upon human life, pleading and offering themselves to Almighty God for the whole race of mankind. They do this with the highest exercises of true devotion, with cleansed and purified hearts. They continually implore God for his mercy and favour for themselves and their fellow-creatures.

Christianity accepts this as the perfect way of life.

The other is of a lower form, and, suiting itself more to the condition of human nature, includes a pure marriage, the care of children and family, trade and business, and goes through all the employments of life under a sense of devotion, and fear of God.

Now those who have chosen this way of life have their set times for retreat and spiritual exercises, and particular days are set apart for listening to and learning the word of God. And this order of people is considered to be in the second state of piety.

Eusebius, *Ecclesiastical History*

UNITED TO GOD

**'Remain in me, and I will remain in you. . . . If anyone does not
remain in me, he is like a branch that is thrown away and
withers' (John 15:4, 6).**

It is impossible to become united to God solely through meditation, or by crushing the emotions, or even through the most carefully thought out prayers. There are many reasons for this, the
most important of which are as follows.

According to Scripture: the Lord said, 'no-one may see me and
live' (Exodus 33:20). All the exercises of discursive prayer, and
even the prayers of active contemplation are rated very highly.
However, they only prepare us in our approach to God since we
remain human beings who ar   God. This
that we cannot be united
stems from man must fi
it can be exalted.

St John states, 'There
Now heaven represents
majesty of God everyon
effort and even the very
ing that opposes God
increases in holiness mo
Then the barrier betwee
soul becomes united to

The soul is united to
such opposing things as
God, a great deal more
mere creature. Nothing
can ever accomplish thi

Madame Guyon, *A Short*

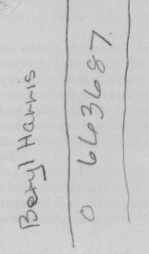

THIS PARTICULAR MOMENT

Whatever was to my profit I now consider loss for the sake of Christ. What is more, I consider everything a loss compared to the surpassing greatness of knowing Christ Jesus my Lord, for whose sake I have lost all things (Philippians 3:7–8).

The divine action, being of an all-filling plenitude, can only take hold of a soul to the extent to which that soul is emptied of all self-confidence, for such self-confidence is a pseudo-plenitude which excludes God's action. This obstacle which God's action finds in the soul herself is the one most likely to impede it.

As far as external obstacles go, the divine action can when it chooses convert them into helpful means. Everything is both equally useful and useless to it. Everything is nothing without it, and nothing becomes everything by means of it.

Whatever the value of meditation, contemplation, vocal prayers, interior silence, the acts of the soul's powers whether distinctly perceived or obscure, a life of retreat or one of action considered in themselves may be, the best of all for the soul is what God wishes at this particular moment; and the soul should look upon it all with perfect indifference as something of itself non-existent.

Jean-Pierre de Caussade, *The Sacrament of the Present Moment*

Dominus est. It is the Lord

He [Jesus] said, 'Throw your net on the right side of the boat and you will find some [fish].' When they did, they were unable to haul the net in because of the large number of fish. Then the disciple whom Jesus loved said to Peter, 'It is the Lord!' (John 21:6–7).

There is no moment at which God does not present himself under the guise of some suffering, some consolation, or some duty. All that occurs within us, around us and by our means covers and hides his divine action. His action is there, most really and certainly present, but in an invisible manner, the result of which is that we are always taken by surprise and that we only recognise his operation after it has passed away.

Could we pierce the veil and were we vigilant and attentive, God would reveal himself continuously to us and we should rejoice in his action in everything that happened to us. At every occurrence we should say: *Dominus est.* It is the Lord; and in all circumstances we should find a gift from God: we should consider creatures as very feeble instruments in the hands of an almighty worker, and we should recognise without difficulty that nothing is lacking to us and that God's constant care leads him to give us each instant what is suited to us. If we had faith, we should welcome all creatures; we should, as it were, caress them and thank them interiorly for contributing so favourably to our perfection when applied by the hand of God.

Jean-Pierre de Caussade, *The Sacrament of the Present Moment*

PRAISES OF GOD

Thanks be to God for his indescribable gift! (2 Corinthians 9:15).

Thou, Lord and God, art holy, who alone workest miracles.
Thou art strong.
Thou art great.
Thou art the most high God.
Thou art the all-powerful King, the holy Father, the Lord of heaven and earth.
Thou art the Lord God, three in one, the universal good.
Thou art goodness, universal and supreme, the true and living Lord God.
Thou art benevolence and love.
Thou art wisdom.
Thou art humility.
Thou art patience.
Thou art security.
Thou art peace.
Thou art joy and gladness.
Thou art justice and temperance.
Thou art all riches which satisfy.
Thou art beauty.
Thou art grace.
Thou art our Protector, Keeper and Defender.
Thou art our might, refreshment, hope and confidence.
Thou art immense sweetness.
Thou art eternal life, our great and adorable Lord, almighty God, merciful Saviour.

St Francis of Assisi, *Prayers*

FORTH IN MY NAME

The LORD will watch over your coming and going both now and for evermore (Psalm 121:8).

> Forth in thy name, O Lord, I go,
>   My daily labour to pursue;
> Thee, only thee, resolved to know,
>   In all I think or speak or do.
>
> The task thy wisdom hath assigned
>   O let me cheerfully fulfil;
> In all my works thy presence find,
>   And prove thy good and perfect will.
>
> Preserve me from my calling's snare,
>   And hide my simple heart above,
> Above the thorns of choking care,
>   The gilded baits of worldly love.
>
> Thee may I set at my right hand,
>   Whose eyes my inmost substance see,
> And labour on at thy command,
>   And offer all my works to thee.
>
> Give me to bear thy easy yoke,
>   And every moment watch and pray,
> And still to things eternal look,
>   And hasten to thy glorious day;
>
> For thee delightfully employ
>   Whate'er thy bounteous grace hath given,
> And run my course with even joy,
>   And closely walk with thee to heaven.
>
> Charles Wesley

THE FEAR OF GOD

Serve the LORD with fear and rejoice with trembling (Psalm 2:11).

If you have sweetness and delight, draw near to God in fear and in truth, and you will never be deceived or caught up in vanity.

Do not rejoice in temporal prosperity, because you know that it does not bring eternal life.

Even if a person should prosper in all his undertakings, and though every wish of his heart was granted, he should nevertheless fear rather than rejoice.

Blessings only increase the opportunity to forget God and it risks offending him.

How can you venture to live without fear, seeing that you must appear before God to give an account of your trivial thoughts and words?

Remember that while many are called, few are chosen. If you are not careful, your final ruin is more certain than your salvation; especially as the way that leads to eternal life is so narrow.

As in the hour of death you will certainly be sorry that you have not used all your time in God's service, why do you not now use your time in this way, as you will wish that you had done when you lie on your bed dying?

St John of the Cross, *The Dark Night of the Soul*

ALL THE VIRTUES

Love must be sincere. Hate what is evil; cling to what is good (Romans 12:9).

I think that it is best for a person to have a small amount of all the virtues. So, rise early in the morning and gain a little of each virtue and of each of God's commandments. Use great patience, along with awe and long-suffering, as you love God, with all the strength of your soul and body. Exercise great humility, put up with interior distress; be vigilant and pray frequently with reverence and with groans, with pure speech and by controlling your eyes.

When you are despised do not become angry; be at peace, and do not return evil with evil.

Pay no attention to the faults of others, and do not make comparisons about yourself with others, as you remember that you are inferior to every other created being.

Renounce all material possessions and everything that comes from your human nature.

Live by the cross, in your spiritual battles, with a poverty of spirit, engaging in voluntary spiritual asceticism, in fasting, penitence and tears, in discernment, in purity of soul, laying hold of everything that is good.

Do your work in peace. Persevere in keeping vigil, in fasting and going without drinking, in being cold and naked and in sufferings.

Close yourself up in a tomb as if you were already dead, so that you will always be aware of the closeness of death.

John the Dwarf, in *Sayings of the Desert Fathers*

THE CROSS OF ANXIETY

Do not be anxious about anything (Philippians 4:6).

The crosses of the present moment always bring their own special grace and consequent comfort with them; we see the hand of God in them when it is laid upon us. But the crosses of anxious foreboding are seen out of the dispensation of God; we see them without grace to bear them; we see them indeed through a faithless spirit which banishes grace.

So, everything in them is bitter and unendurable; all seems dark and helpless. Let us throw self aside; no more self-interest, and then God's will, unfolding every moment in everything, will console us also every moment for all that he shall do around us, or within us, for our discipline.

The crosses which we make for ourselves by a restless anxiety as to the future, are not crosses which come from God. We show lack of faith in God by our false wisdom, wishing to forestall his arrangements, and struggling to supplement his providence by our own providence.

The future is not yet ours; perhaps it never will be. If it comes, it may come wholly different from what we have foreseen. Let us shut our eyes, then, to that which God hides from us, and keeps in reserve in the treasures of his deep counsels. Let us worship without seeing; let us be silent; let us abide in peace.

Archbishop Fénelon, *Christian Perfection*

ST FRANCIS' LOVE FOR BIRDS

'Look at the birds of the air' (Matthew 6:26).

Blessed Francis, wholly wrapped up in the love of God, discerned perfectly the goodness of God not only in his own soul, but in every creature. Because of this he had a special and intimate love of creatures, especially of those which were linked to God or to his order. His favourite bird was the little bird called the lark, or as it is known to some, the cowled lark.

St Francis used to say about it, 'Sister Lark has a cowl like a religious; and she is a humble bird, because she goes willingly by the road to find food there. If she finds that it is rotting, she eats it. As she flies she praises God very sweetly like a good religious, despising earthly things, whose conversation is always in the heavens, and whose intent is always to God's praise. Her clothes are similar to the earth (that is her feathers), and she gives an example to religious that they should not have delicate and coloured clothes, but cheap and plain clothes.'

Because St Francis saw all this in the larks he looked at them happily. So it pleased the Lord, that these most holy, little birds should show some sign of affection towards Francis in the hour of his death. Late on the Sabbath, after vespers, before the night on which he passed away to the Lord, a great flock of larks came on to the roof of the house where he was lying. They flew about, circled the roof, and as they sang sweetly, they seemed to be praising the Lord.

Bonaventure, *The Mirror of Perfection*

ASCENSION DAY

He was taken up before their very eyes, and a cloud hid him from their sight (Acts 1:9).

Hail the day that sees him rise; Alleluia!
Glorious to his native skies; Alleluia!
Christ, awhile to mortals given,
Enters now the highest heaven! Alleluia!

There the glorious triumph waits; Alleluia!
Lift your heads, eternal gates! Alleluia!
Christ hath vanquished death and sin;
Take the King of glory in. Alleluia!

See! the heaven its Lord receives, Alleluia!
Yet he loves the earth he leaves: Alleluia!
Though returning to his throne,
Still he calls mankind his own. Alleluia!

See! he lifts his hands above; Alleluia!
See! he shows the prints of love: Alleluia!
Hark! his gracious lips bestow
Blessings on his Church below. Alleluia!

Still for us he intercedes; Alleluia!
His prevailing death he pleads; Alleluia!
Near himself prepares our place,
Harbinger of human race. Alleluia!

Lord, though parted from our sight, Alleluia!
Far above yon azure height, Alleluia!
Grant our hearts may thither rise,
Seeking thee beyond the skies. Alleluia!

There we shall with thee remain, Alleluia!
Partners of thine endless reign; Alleluia!
There thy face unclouded see,
Find our heaven of heavens in thee. Alleluia!

Charles Wesley and Thomas Cotterill

MOUNT, MOUNT, MY SOUL

Set your hearts on things above (Colossians 3:1).

Mount, mount, my soul, and climb, or rather fly
    With all thy force on high,
The Saviour rose not only, but ascended;
    And he must be attended
Both in his conquest and his triumph too.
    His glories strongly woo
His graces to them, and will not appear
In their full lustre, until both be there,

Where now he sits, not for himself alone,
    But that upon his throne
All his redeemed may attendants be,
    Robed, and crown'd as he.
Kings without Courtiers are lone men, they say;
    And dost thou think to stay
Behind on earth, whilst thy King reigns in heaven,
Yet not be of thy happiness bereaven?

Nothing that thou canst think worth having's here.
    Nothing is wanting there,
That thou canst wish, to make thee truly blest.
    And, above all the rest,
Thy life is hid with God in Jesus Christ,
    Higher than what is high'st.
O grovel then no longer here on earth,
Where misery every moment drowns thy mirth.

But tower, my soul, and soar above the skies,
    Where thy true treasure lies.
Though with corruption and mortality
Thou clogg'd and pinion'd be;
Yet thy fleet thoughts, and sprightly wishes, may
    Speedily glide away.
To what thou canst not reach, at least aspire,
Ascend, if not in deed, yet in desire.

George Herbert

146

HE SAT AT THE RIGHT HAND OF GOD

After the Lord Jesus had spoken to them, he was taken up into heaven and he sat at the right hand of God (Mark 16:19).

The metaphor, 'he sat at the right hand of God' comes from princes who have judges to whom they delegate the job of administration and issuing commands. So Christ, in whom the Father is pleased to reign, is said to have been received up and seated on his right hand.

It is as if he was put in control of heaven and earth and formally admitted to a position of administration until the day of judgment. The apostle implies this when he says that the Father 'seated him at his right hand in the heavenly realms, far above all rule and authority, power and dominion, and every title that can be given, not only in the present age but also in the one to come. And God placed all things under his feet and appointed him to be head over everything for the church' (Ephesians 1:20–2; 1 Corinthians 15:27).

You can see now why he is seated there: so that every creature in heaven and earth should reverence his majesty, do him homage and submit to his power. All that the apostles mean when they refer to Christ's seat at the Father's right hand, is that everything is at his disposal (Acts 2:30–6; 3:21; Hebrews 1:8). It is an error to think that it only indicates a blessed state. In Acts 7:56 we read that Stephen saw him standing. This does not refer to the position of his body but the majesty of his kingdom. Sitting simply means presiding on the judgment seat of heaven.

John Calvin, *The Institutes of Christian Religion*

GIVING YOURSELF TO GOD

What do you have that you did not receive? (1 Corinthians 4:7).

Christ loved you before you existed; he created you; he pre-destined you before the world was founded. Although you were born through the agency of your parents, Christ reared you. Your parents did not create you, even though they pass on family characteristics to you. Christ loved you, Christ created you, Christ reared you, Christ gave himself up for you. Christ listened to insults for you, he endured wounds for you, he redeemed you by his blood. You should be overwhelmed by this and respond by saying: 'How can I repay the Lord for all his goodness to me?' (Psalm 116:12). What will you give back to the Lord for all that he has given to you? Listen to what Christ said, 'Anyone who loves his father or mother more than me is not worthy of me' (Matthew 10:37). Listen to what Christ is saying, be aware of the consequences of loving Christ less than your parents.

What have you given back to the Lord for everything that he has given you? You think that you have given him back something? What? What have you given back to Christ? Have you saved him as he saved you? Have you created him, as he created you? Did you make him Lord as he made you a human being? Have you given anything back to him that doesn't come back to you? If you look at the matter carefully you will readily see that you haven't given him anything but you have merely provided yourself with it. And even this you cannot maintain that you have provided. For, 'What do you have that you do not receive?'

So why do you not find something that you can give back to the Lord. Give him back yourself, give him back what he has made. Give him back yourself, not what is yours, but what is his creation.

St Augustine, *Sermons*

CHARITY

Follow the way of love (1 Corinthians 14:1).

Charity is like a fine robe of many colours, which lends grace, beauty, and freshness, not only to the white garment of faith and the green vesture of hope, but also to all the virtues; for without charity no virtue is pleasing in the sight of God.

The strength of love does not consist in wonderful feelings, but in detachment. The strength of love is seen in having patience in all the trials God sends, so long as we love God.

This is how a person can know whether he really loves God: is he satisfied with anything less than God? The person who loves anything as much as God is making light of God, because he puts into the balance with him what is an infinite distance from him.

Study always to please God; pray that his will may be accomplished in you; love him much, for it is his due.

At the end of your life you will be judged on how loving you have been. So learn to love God in the way he desires to be loved, and give up everything you own.

The soul that seeks God wholly, must give himself wholly to God.

As a sick person is too weak to work, so the soul that is weak in loving God is also too weak to practise any perfect virtue.

To seek God selfishly is to seek for your own comfort and refreshment from God. This is contrary to the pure love of God.

The loving soul is meek, gentle, humble, and patient; the soul that is hardened in self-love hardens itself even more.

The soul that loves is neither wearied nor wearies.

St John of the Cross, *The Dark Night of the Soul*

INSTRUCTIONS FROM AN OLD MAN

There are six things the LORD hates, seven that are detestable to him: haughty eyes, a lying tongue, hands that shed innocent blood, a heart that devises wicked schemes, feet that are quick to rush into evil, a false witness who pours out lies and a man who stirs up dissension among brothers (Proverbs 6:16).

1. The monk must die to his neighbour and never judge him at all.
2. The monk must die to everything before he dies.
3. If the monk does not believe in his heart that he is a sinner God will not listen to him.

The brother asked, 'What does it mean not to believe that he is a sinner?'

The old man answered, 'When a person is so caught up with his own faults he does not see the faults of his neighbour.'

4. If a man's actions are not in line with his prayers, he works in vain.

The brother asked him, 'What is the link between practice and prayer?'

The old man answered, 'We should never do things which are contrary to what we pray about. When a person gives up his own will, then God is reconciled with him and accepts his prayers.'

The brother asked, 'What help does the monk have in all his struggles?'

The old man answered, 'It is written, "God is our refuge and strength, an ever-present help in trouble."' (Psalm 46:1).

5. The old man was asked, 'What good do fasts and watchings do?'

The old man answered, 'They make the soul humble. It is written, "Look upon my affliction and my distress and take away all my sins" (Psalm 25:18). So when the soul gives itself over to hardship, God has mercy on it.

6. The old man was asked, 'What should a person do about temptations and evil thoughts?'

The old man answered, 'He should weep and beg that the goodness of God should come to his rescue. If he prays with discernment he will receive the gift of peace. For it is written, "The Lord is with me; I will not be afraid. What can man do to me?"' (Psalm 118:6).

Moses, the Desert Father, in *Sayings of the Desert Fathers*

JOINED TO GOD

'I am the vine, you are the branches' (John 15:5).

It is a great thing, an exceeding great thing, in the time of this exile to be joined to God in the divine light by a mystical and denuded union. This takes place where a pure, humble, and resigned soul, burning with ardent love, is carried above itself by the grace of God, and through the brilliancy of the divine light shining on the mind, it loses all consideration and distinction of things, and lays aside all, even the most excellent images, and all liquefied by love, and, as it were, reduced to nothing, it melts away into God.

It is then united to God without any medium, and becomes one spirit with him, and is transformed and changed into him, as iron placed in the fire is changed into fire, without ceasing to be iron. It becomes one with God, yet not so as to be of the same substance and nature as God.

In the faculty of intellect it perceives the surpassing illumination of the Sun of Justice, and learns divine truth; and in the faculty of love it feels a certain glow of quiet love, or contact of the Holy Spirit, like a living fountain, flowing with streams of eternal sweetness; and thus it is introduced into sublime union with God. The soul, having entered the vast solitude of the Godhead, happily loses itself; and enlightened by the brightness of most lucid darkness, becomes through knowledge as if without knowledge, and dwells in a sort of wise ignorance.

Louis of Blois (Blosius), *Meditations*

DIVINE UNION

Teach me your way, O LORD, and I will walk in your truth; give me an undivided heart, that I may fear your name (Psalm 86:11).

No one can be unaware that God is the Supreme Good. To know this as a blessing in your own life you must become united with him. As Christians are united with God so they experience his glory in their own lives.

No soul can attain this divine union through her own strength. God alone reveals himself to the soul. He does this when the soul is open to God's Spirit and allows herself to be completely taken over by God. Far from being an evil activity this is the most wonderful spiritual blessing any follower of God can ever receive.

Would Jesus Christ have made this the best spiritual path to travel along if it was an evil and dangerous one? This route to God's spiritual blessing is open to everyone. Everyone is called to this. All may delight themselves in God both in this life and in the next life.

I deliberately say that we should delight in God, rather than we should take pleasure in his spiritual gifts. God's wonderful spiritual blessings do not in themselves constitute the most important blessing of all and it is for this reason that the soul will never be completely satisfied with spiritual gifts. It is God alone, the giver of all spiritual gifts, who can satisfy the soul. The divine giver of gifts must give us himself if we are to take total delight in God. It is God's will that he should give himself to every creature. God gives as much of himself as the soul can receive. So it is terribly sad to see how reluctant people are to allow themselves to be drawn to God. Our response to God's offer of divine union should be nothing short of total surrender of ourselves and humble worship of his majesty!

Madame Guyon, *A Short and Easy Method of Prayer*

CONVERSION OF JOHN WESLEY

As far as the east is from the west, so far has he removed our transgressions from us (Psalm 103:12).

On his return voyage from America John Wesley's ship hit a terrific storm. Wesley had good reason to fear that he would die that night and he was terrified at the thought. Looking at death, Wesley became a frightened man, despite all his Christian teaching and preaching.

He asked some fellow travellers who were singing hymns why they were not afraid like him. Their reply was, 'If this ship goes down we will go up to be with the Lord for ever.'

Wesley could not understand where they received such assurance of faith from. All he knew could be summed up in his now famous question, 'I came to convert the heathen, but who shall convert me?'

The ship survived the storm and Wesley attended a small chapel in Aldersgate Street in the centre of London. He heard Martin Luther's Preface to the Book of Romans being read. It described exactly what John Wesley needed to know at that moment – real faith in Jesus Christ. It spoke about trusting Jesus Christ for salvation and not trusting in any good works of our own.

John Wesley's Journal entry for that night reads: 'About a quarter before nine, while he [the preacher at the chapel] was describing the change which God works in the heart through faith in Christ, I felt I did trust in Christ, Christ alone, for salvation, and an assurance was given me that He had taken away my sins, even mine, and saved me from the law of sin and death.'

May 24, 1738 was the day that John Wesley felt that his heart had been 'strangely warmed' by God's grace.

Adapted from John Wesley's *Journal*

NEW EVERY MORNING

I cry to you for help, O LORD; in the morning my prayer comes before you (Psalm 88:13).

New every morning is the love
Our wakening and uprising prove;
Through sleep and darkness safely brought,
Restored to life, and power, and thought.

New mercies, each returning day,
Hover around us while we pray;
New perils past, new sins forgiven,
New thoughts of God, new hopes of heaven.

If on our daily course our mind
Be set to hallow all we find,
New treasures still, of countless price,
God will provide for sacrifice.

The trivial round, the common task,
Would furnish all we ought to ask,
Room to deny ourselves, a road
To bring us daily nearer God.

Only, O Lord, in thy dear love
Fit us for perfect rest above;
And help us this and every day
To live more nearly as we pray.

John Keble

WHITSUN/PENTECOST

Suddenly a sound like the blowing of a violent wind came from heaven and filled the whole house where they were sitting (Acts 2:2).

Day, startle not to hear that rushing wind,
Wherewith this place is shaken:
Attend a while, and thou shalt quickly find,
How much thou art mistaken;
If thou think here
Is any cause of fear.

Seest thou not how on those twelve rev'rend heads
Sit cloven tongues of fire?
And as the rumour of that wonder spreads,
The multitude admire
To see it: and
Yet more amazed stand.

Mock not, profane despisers of the Spirit,
At what's to you unknown:
This earnest he hath sent, who must inherit
All nations as his own:
That they may know
How much to him they owe.

To fit them for which blessed state of glory,
This is his agent here:
To publish to the World that happy story,
Always, and every where,
This resident
Ambassador is sent.

George Herbert

VENI, CREATOR SPIRITUS

All of them were filled with the Holy Spirit (Acts 2:4).

Come, Holy Ghost, our souls inspire,
And lighten with celestial fire;
Thou the anointing Spirit art,
Who dost thy sevenfold gifts impart:

Thy blessed unction from above
Is comfort, life, and fire of love;
Enable with perpetual light
The dullness of our blinded sight:

Anoint and cheer our soiled face
With the abundance of thy grace:
Keep far our foes, give peace at home;
Where thou art guide no ill can come.

Teach us to know the Father, Son,
And thee, of Both, to be but One;
That through the ages all along
This may be our endless song,

Praise to thy eternal merit,
Father, Son, and Holy Spirit. Amen

Translated by John Cosin

DISCERNING THE SPIRITS

Dear friends, do not believe every spirit, but test the spirits to see whether they are from God, because many false prophets have gone out into the world (1 John 4:1).

Because there are various kinds of spirits it is necessary to be able to distinguish different spirits. Hence St John teaches that we should not believe every spirit. Some spirits derive from a person's own imagination. David did not want to listen to his own thoughts, but said, 'I will listen to what God the LORD will say' (Psalm 85:8). It is also possible for the devil to send wicked spirits which produce evil thoughts in men. The apostle Paul refers to men who were inflated with their own pride. He warns, 'Do not let anyone who delights in false humility and the worship of angels disqualify you for the prize. Such a person goes into great detail about what he has seen, and his unspiritual mind puffs him up with idle notions' (Colossians 2:18).

There is also the Spirit which the world cannot receive. The Lord Jesus said this Spirit would be given to his disciples. This is the Holy Spirit. The apostle John records these words of Jesus about the Spirit: 'I will ask the Father, and he will give you another Counsellor to be with you for ever – the Spirit of truth. The world cannot accept him, because it neither sees him nor knows him. But you know him, for he lives with you and will be in you. I will not leave you as orphans; I will come to you' (John 14:16–18).

Discerning of Spirits (14th century)

POSSESSIONS

'Do not store up for yourselves treasures on earth, where moth and rust destroy, and where thieves break in and steal. But store up for yourselves treasures in heaven, where moth and rust do not destroy, and where thieves do not break in and steal. For where your treasure is, there your heart will be also'
(Matthew 6:19–21).

Friar Giles once said to a worldly judge, 'Do you believe that God's gifts are wonderful?' After this, Friar Giles said, 'I will demonstrate to you how unfaithful you are in your belief.' Then he said to him, 'What is the value of everything you own?'

The judge answered, 'It is worth, perhaps, a thousand pounds.'

Then said Friar Giles, 'Would you sell your possessions for ten thousand pounds?'

The judge answered immediately, 'I certainly would.'

And Friar Giles said, 'What is certain is that all the possessions in the whole world are nothing in comparison with heavenly things. So why don't you give your possessions to Christ, so that you may buy those possessions which are heavenly and eternal?'

Then the judge, wise with the foolish wisdom of the world, replied to the pure and simple Friar Giles, 'God has filled you with wise and divine foolishness. Do you think, Friar Giles, that there is a man alive whose outward deeds match up to what he believes in his heart?'

Friar Giles answered, 'Look here, my dear judge, the truth is that all the saints have laboured to fulfil through their deeds those things which they understand to be the will of God, as far as they were able. And all those things which they were not able to fulfil in their deeds, they fulfilled in the holy desire of their will. So they were not found wanting.'

The Little Flowers of St Francis

TRUSTING IN GOD

Everyone who wants to live a godly life in Christ Jesus will be persecuted (2 Timothy 3:12).

In this world we face the malice of men from without and temptations of the devil from within. Therefore no one should lull himself into a sense of false security or be so depressed on account of his own wickedness.

The inspired prophet wrote a psalm warning us about the danger of temptations that attack us in this life and teaching us how to resist them. This is how he begins: 'He who dwells in the shelter of the Most High will rest in the shadow of the Almighty' (Psalm 91:1). That is, the humble spirit knows and feels that he is weak and ignorant about how to evade temptations. Therefore he does not put his trust in himself but he seeks God's help, placing all his trust in him. He does not do this suddenly for just a moment, but throughout his life he seeks God's help. He is fully aware of his own weakness and also experiences the Lord's goodness. Truly, he rests in the shadow of the Almighty.

The person who dwells in the shelter of the Most High through grace, in this life, will live securely the endless joy of the bliss of heaven.

Walter Hilton, *The Scale of Perfection*

AS PANTS THE HART

My soul thirsts for God, for the living God. When can I go and meet with God? (Psalm 42:2).

As pants the hart for cooling streams,
    When heated in the chase;
So longs my soul, O God, for Thee,
    And Thy refreshing grace.

For Thee, my God, the living God,
    My thirsty soul doth pine;
Oh, when shall I behold Thy face,
    Thou Majesty divine?

Why restless, why cast down, my soul?
    Trust God; who will employ
His aid for thee, and change these sighs
    To thankful hymns of joy.

God of my strength, how long shall I,
    Like one forgotten, mourn;
Forlorn, forsaken, and exposed
    To my oppressor's scorn?

I sigh to think of happier days,
    When Thou, O Lord! wast nigh;
When every heart was tuned to praise,
    And none more blessed than I.

Why restless, why cast down, my soul?
    Hope still; and thou shalt sing
The praise of Him who is Thy God,
    Thy health's eternal spring.

Nahum Tate and Nicholas Brady
(paraphrase of Psalm 42)

THE MOST PERFECT PRAYERS

We do not know what we ought to pray for, but the Spirit himself intercedes for us with groans that words cannot express (Romans 8:26).

God hardly gives his Spirit even to those whom he has established in grace, if they do not pray for it on all occasions, not only once but many times.

Whether we think of, or speak of, God, whether we act or suffer for him, all is prayer when we have no other objects than his love, and the desire of pleasing him.

All that a Christian does, even in eating and sleeping, is prayer, when it is done in simplicity, according to the order of God, without either adding to or diminishing from it by his own choice.

Prayer continues in the desire of the heart, though the understanding is employed on outward things.

In souls filled with love, the desire to please God is a continual prayer.

As the furious hate which the devil bears us is termed the roaring of a lion, so our vehement love may be termed crying after God.

God requires of his adult children only that their hearts be truly purified and that they offer him continually the wishes and vows that naturally spring from perfect love. For these desires, being the genuine fruits of love, are the most perfect prayers that can spring from it.

John Wesley, *A Plain Man's Guide to Holiness*

THE DEATH OF MY OWN WILL

I do not set aside the grace of God (Galatians 2:21).

In a time of sickness once I was brought so near the gates of death that I forgot my name. Being then desirous to know who I was, I saw a mass of matter of a dull gloomy colour between the south and the east, and was told that this mass was human beings in as great misery as they could be and live, and that I was mixed with them, and that henceforth I might not consider myself as a distinct or separate being.

After several hours I heard a soft melodious voice saying, 'John Woolman is dead.' What that angelic voice could mean was a mystery to me.

I was then carried in spirit to the mines where poor oppressed people were digging rich treasures for those called Christians, and heard them blaspheme the name of Christ, at which I was grieved, for his name was precious to me. I was then told that those who oppressed them were said to be the followers of Christ, and they said among themselves, 'If Christ directed them to use us in this sort, then Christ is a cruel tyrant.'

All this time the song of the angel remained a mystery until I lay still for a time and felt a divine power make me say, 'I am crucified with Christ, nevertheless I live; yet not I, but Christ liveth in me. And the life which I now live in the flesh I live by the faith of the Son of God, who loved me and gave himself for me' (Galatians 2:20). Then the mystery was opened and I perceived there was joy in heaven over a sinner who had repented, and that the words 'John Woolman is dead' meant no more than the death of my own will.

John Woolman, *Journal*

SUFFERING WITH CHRIST

I want to know Christ and the power of his resurrection and the fellowship of sharing in his sufferings, becoming like him in his death (Philippians 3:10).

This was how I prayed: . . . I pictured Christ inside me.. . . I used to think about those times when he was most lonely. During those times he must have been most afflicted and alone, like someone in trouble, and I could come close to him.

I did many simple things like that. In particular, I used to find myself in the Garden of Gethsemane alongside him, keeping him company. I thought of the bloody sweat, and of the affliction he suffered there. I wished, if it had been possible, to wipe away that painful sweat from his face. I remember that I never dared to do that, for my sins stood too strongly before me. I used to remain with him there as long as my thoughts could concentrate on him. But many other thoughts tormented me.

For many years, before I went to sleep at night I used to meditate a little upon the mystery of this scene of Christ's prayer in the Garden. . . . It led me to pray often, without realising that I was praying, and it became my constant habit.

St Teresa of Avila, *Life*

COVET A BROKEN HEART

The sacrifice acceptable to God is a broken spirit; A broken and contrite heart, O God, thou wilt not despise (Psalm 51:17, RSV).

The broken heart is hard to bear, for soul-pain is the sorest pain. If a man is proud of his strength and manhood a broken leg will hurt him, and if a man is proud of his goodness a broken heart will hurt him. Yet a broken heart and a contrite spirit is a heaven-sent blessing. Covet a broken heart, prize a contrite spirit. It is wounding work, of course, this breaking of the heart, but without wounding there is no saving.

Conversion is not the smooth, easy-going process some men seem to think it, otherwise man's heart would never have been compared to fallow ground and God's word to a plough. The fallow ground must be ploughed and ploughed, and even after that be soundly harrowed, else there will be but slender harvest.

That other analogy of grafting is saying the same thing. For where there is grafting there is cutting, the shoot of the plant must be let in with a wound; to stick on to the outside or to tie it on with a string would be of no use. Heart must be set to heart and back to back, or there will be no sap from root to branch, and this, I say, must be done by a wound. Men are too lofty, too proud, too wild, too devilishly resolved in the ways of their own destruction. Nothing will hinder them from ruining their own precious and immortal souls but the breaking of their hearts.

John Bunyan, *Grace Abounding to the Chief of Sinners*

CLEAVE TO GOD

'You are to hold fast to the LORD your God, as you have until now' (Joshua 23:8).

Consider, O my soul, and hear, all that is within me, how much my whole being owes to him! Lord, because you have made me I owe you the whole of my love; because you have redeemed me, I owe you the whole of myself; because you have promised so much, I owe you all my being. Moreover, I owe you as much more love than myself as you are greater than I, for whom you gave yourself and to whom you promised yourself. I pray you, Lord, make me taste by love what I taste by knowledge; let me know by love what I know by understanding. I owe you more than my whole self, but I have no more, and by myself I cannot render the whole of it to you. Draw me to you, Lord, in the fullness of love. I am wholly yours by creation; make me all yours, too, in love.

Lord, my heart is before you. I try, but by myself I can do nothing; do what I cannot. Admit me into the inner room of your love. I ask, I seek, I knock. You who made me seek, make me receive; you who gave the seeking, give the finding; you who taught the knocking, open to my knock. To whom will you give, if you refuse my petition? Who finds, if this seeking is in vain? To whom is it opened, if to this knocking it is closed? What do you give to those who do not pray if you deny your love to those who do? By you I have desire; by you let me have fulfilment. Cleave to him, my soul, and never leave off. Good Lord, do not reject me; I faint with hunger for your love; refresh me with it. Let me be filled with your love, rich in your affection, completely held in your care. Take me and possess me wholly, who with the Father and the Holy Spirit are alone blessed to ages of ages. Amen.

St Anselm, *Meditations,* 'On the Miseries of this Life'

TAKING HOLY COMMUNION

The Lord Jesus, on the night he was betrayed, took bread (1 Corinthians 11:23).

When some people take Communion they struggle with all their energy to receive some kind of delight and pleasure rather than humbly giving praise and reverence to God within themselves. They are concentrating so hard on receiving sensual pleasure and delight that they believe that they have received nothing at all if they do not obtain them. This makes a mockery of God. They have failed to realise that the tangible blessings which come from the most holy sacrament are the least important ones. The most important blessings of the sacrament are the invisible graces which God gives. God often holds back the delightful and tangible blessings so that they may look to God more keenly with eyes of faith. These people try to feel and taste God as if they could fully understand him and as if he were totally accessible to them, not just in this, but in a similar way in their other spiritual devotions. All this is a serious imperfection and is completely opposed to God's nature since it is faith devoid of purity.

These people have the same shortcomings when it comes to prayer. They think of prayer as just being a time when they experience pleasure and so they seek this with all their might. But when they do not experience this kind of pleasure they are very discouraged and they think that they have accomplished nothing. This is not the way of true devotion and genuine spirituality which are made up of perseverance, patience, humility, a distrust of oneself and seeking to please only God.

St John of the Cross, *The Dark Night of the Soul*

EXAMINE YOURSELVES

A man ought to examine himself before he eats of the bread and drinks of the cup (1 Corinthians 11:28).

Dearly beloved in the Lord, ye that mind to come to the holy Communion of the Body and Blood of our Saviour Christ, must consider how Saint Paul exhorteth all persons diligently to try and examine themselves, before they presume to eat of that Bread, and drink of that Cup. For as the benefit is great, if with a true penitent heart and lively faith we receive that holy Sacrament; (for then we spiritually eat the flesh of Christ, and drink his blood; then we dwell in Christ, and Christ in us; we are one with Christ, and Christ with us;) so is the danger great, if we receive the same unworthily. For then we are guilty of the Body and Blood of Christ our Saviour; we eat and drink our own damnation, not considering the Lord's Body; we kindle God's wrath against us; we provoke him to plague us with divers diseases, and sundry kinds of death. Judge therefore yourselves, brethren, that ye be not judged of the Lord; repent you truly for your sins past; have a lively and steadfast faith in Christ our Saviour; amend your lives, and be in perfect charity with all men; so shall ye be meet partakers of those holy mysteries.

And above all things ye must give most humble and hearty thanks to God, the Father, the Son, and the Holy Ghost, for the redemption of the world by the death and passion of our Saviour Christ, both God and man; who did humble himself, even to the death upon the Cross, for us miserable sinners, who lay in darkness and the shadow of death; that he might make us the children of God, and exalt us to everlasting life.

And to the end that we should alway remember the exceeding great love of our Master and only Saviour Jesus Christ, thus dying for us, and the innumerable benefits which by his precious blood-shedding he hath obtained to us; he hath instituted and ordained holy mysteries, as pledges of his love, and for a continual remembrance of his death, to our great and endless comfort.

The Order for the Administration of The Lord's Supper, *The Book of Common Prayer*, 1662

GRACE

By grace you have been saved (Ephesians 2:5).

> Just as I am, without one plea
> But that thy blood was shed for me,
> And that thou bidd'st me come to thee,
>   O Lamb of God, I come.
>
> Just as I am, though tossed about
> With many a conflict, many a doubt,
> Fightings within, and fears without,
>   O Lamb of God, I come.
>
> Just as I am, poor, wretched, blind;
> Sight, riches, healing of the mind,
> Yea all I need, in thee to find,
>   O Lamb of God, I come.
>
> Just as I am, thou wilt receive,
> Wilt welcome, pardon, cleanse, relieve:
> Because thy promise I believe,
>   O Lamb of God, I come.
>
> Just as I am (thy love unknown
> Has broken every barrier down),
> Now to be thine, yea thine alone,
>   O Lamb of God, I come.
>
> Just as I am, of that free love
> The breadth, length, depth and height to prove,
> Here for a season then above,
>   O Lamb of God, I come.

Charlotte Elliott

INTERNAL SILENCE

'But the LORD is in his holy temple; let all the earth be silent before him'(Habakkuk 2:20).

Inward silence is absolutely indispensable, because the Word is essential and eternal, and so requires the soul to align herself with his nature. Then the soul will have the ability to receive God himself. If we really want to hear the divine voice we must open our ears to God. Christ is the eternal Word, and the soul remains dead, unenlightened and barren until Christ speaks his lifegiving words. This is why Christ requires our rapt, silent attention so that his words of life can work in our souls.

The Bible repeatedly orders us carefully to listen to and heed God's voice. There are numerous exhortations to this effect and I shall quote only a few of them: 'Listen to me, my people; hear me, my nation' (Isaiah 51:4); and again: 'Listen to me, . . . you whom I have upheld since you were conceived, and have carried since your birth' (Isaiah 46:3).

We should forget ourselves, and all self-interest, and listen and be attentive to the voice of God. These two simple actions, or rather passive approaches to God attract his love which he himself communicates. Outward silence is indispensable for the cultivation and improvement of inner silence. In fact it is impossible for us to become truly internal, without the love and practice of outward silence and retirement.

God said through the mouth of his prophet, 'I will lead her into the desert and speak tenderly to her' (Hosea 2:14), and the person who is internally engaged with God cannot also be preoccupied and concerned about the numerous trifles that surround us.

Madame Guyon, *A Short and Easy Method of Prayer*

SELF-DENIAL

'No servant can serve two masters' (Luke 16:13).

The first thing we must do is to hand ourselves over to God, and devote the total energy of our minds to his service. By service, I do not mean simply verbal obedience, but the state of mind which, stripped of carnal desires, implicitly obeys the call of God's Spirit.

This transformation, which Paul calls the renewing of the mind (Ephesians 4:23), was unknown to the philosophers of old, although it is the only way to true life. They made reason the sole ruler of man and listened only to her, as the arbiter of conduct. But Christian philosophy makes her move aside and give complete submission to the Holy Spirit, so that the individual no longer lives, but Christ lives and reigns in him (Galatians 2:20).

So follows the second principle, that we must not follow our own way but the Lord's will, and aim always to promote his glory. We are really succeeding when, almost forgetting ourselves and putting aside our own way of thinking, we genuinely try to obey God and his commandments. When Scripture tells us to put aside selfish interests, it not only removes undue desire for wealth, power or popularity from our minds, but wipes out all ambition for worldly glory, and other more secret temptations. The Christian ought to be disciplined to think that throughout his life he is dealing with God.

John Calvin, *The Institutes of Christian Religion*

THE POWER OF CHRIST'S BLOOD

To God's elect . . . who have been chosen according to the foreknowledge of God the Father, through the sanctifying work of the Spirit, for obedience of Jesus Christ and sprinkling by his blood (1 Peter 1:1–2).

Do you want to learn about the power of this blood? See where it began to flow, the spring from which it flowed down from the cross, from the Master's side. The gospel tells us that when Christ had died and was still hanging on the cross, the soldier came up to him and pierced his side with a spear, and at once water and blood came out. One was a symbol of baptism, the other of the mysteries. That soldier, piercing his side, breached the wall of the holy temple, and I got the treasure. Similarly, the Jews killed the sacrificial lamb, and I got the salvation which is the fruit of that sacrifice.

'Water and blood came out of his side.' Dearly beloved, do not pass the secret of this great mystery without reflecting on it. I can give you another secret mystical interpretation. I said that baptism and the mysteries were symbolised by that blood and water. The holy Church was born from these two 'by the washing of regeneration and the renewal of the Holy Spirit'– by baptism and the mysteries. Now these two symbols came from his side, so it was from his side that Christ formed the Church, just as he made Eve out of Adam's side.

That is why Moses, in his account of the first man, uses the words 'bone of my bone and flesh of my flesh', giving a hint of the Master's side. Just as God took a rib from Adam's side and made the woman, so now he gave the blood and water after his death.

Have you seen how Christ has united his bride to himself? Have you seen the sort of food he feeds us all with? It is by the same food that we are both formed and fed. As a woman feeds her child with her own blood and milk, so too Christ himself continually feeds those whom he has begotten with his own blood.

John Chrysostom, *Instructions to the Catechumens*

GROWING IN DEVOTION TO GOD

The righteous will flourish like a palm tree, they will grow like a cedar of Lebanon (Psalm 92:12).

My God,
    I pray that I may so know you and love you that I may rejoice in you.
And if I may not do so fully in this life, let me go steadily on to the day when I come to that fullness.
Let the knowledge of you increase in me here,
    and there let it come to its fullness.
    Let your love grow in me here, and there let it be fulfilled,
so that here my joy may be in a great hope, and there in reality.
    Lord, you have commanded, or rather advised us, to ask by your Son,
and you have promised that we shall receive, 'that our joy may be full'.
That which you counsel
    through our 'wonderful counsellor'
    is what I am asking for, Lord.
    Let me receive that which you promised through your truth,
    'that my joy may be full'.
    God of truth,
    I ask that I may receive, so that my joy may be full.
    Meanwhile, let my mind meditate on it,
let my tongue speak of it,
let my heart love it,
let my mouth preach it,
let my soul hunger for it,
my flesh thirst for it,
and my whole being desire it,
until I enter into the joy of my Lord,
who is God one and triune, blessed forever. Amen.

St Anselm, *Meditations*

THREE BEATITUDES

'Blessed are the poor in spirit: for theirs is the kingdom of heaven' (Matthew 5:3).

The poor in spirit
Many people are faithful in praying and faithful in attending the divine Office, and practise abstinence and bodily mortification. But as soon as they suffer an injury or are deprived of something they are at once offended. This is not the way to be poor in spirit. For he who is truly poor in spirit hates himself and cherishes those who strike him on the cheek (see Matthew 5:39).

Peacemakers
'Blessed are the peacemakers: for they shall be called the children of God' (Matthew 5:9). People who, in the middle of all their sufferings, in the middle of the world, preserve exterior and interior peace for the love of our Lord Jesus Christ are truly peacemakers.

Purity of heart
'Blessed are the clean of heart: for they shall see God' (Matthew 5:8). People who despise the world, seek heaven and never cease to adore and to see with a pure heart and mind the true and living God are the clean of heart.

St Francis of Assisi, *Admonitions*

THANKING GOD

'Were not all ten cleansed? Where are the other nine? Was no-one found to return and give praise to God except this foreigner?' (Luke 17:17–18).

Now thank we all our God,
With heart, and hands, and voices,
Who wondrous things hath done,
In whom His world rejoices;
Who from our mother's arms
Hath blessed us on our way
With countless gifts of love,
And still is ours today.

O may this bounteous God
Through all our life be near us,
With ever joyful hearts
And blessed peace to cheer us;
And keep us in His grace,
And guide us when perplexed,
And free us from all ills
In this world and the next.

All praise and thanks to God
The Father now be given,
The Son, and Him who reigns
With them in highest heaven,
The one eternal God,
Whom earth and heaven adore;
For thus it was, is now,
And shall be evermore.

Martin Rinkart, translated by Catharine Winkworth

THE SLOUGH OF DESPOND

He lifted me out of the slimy pit, out of the mud and mire; he set my feet on a rock and gave me a firm place to stand (Psalm 40:2).

Now I saw in my dream that they approached a very miry bog that was in the middle of the plain, and since neither of them was paying attention they suddenly fell into it. The name of the bog was the Slough of Despond. They wallowed in it for a time, badly covered with the mud and because of the burden that was on his back Christian began to sink.

Then Pliable said, 'Ha! Christian, where are you now?'

'To be honest,' said Christian, 'I don't know.'

Pliable said angrily, 'Is this the happiness you've talked about all this time? If we get out alive you can possess the brave new world all by yourself.' And with that he gave a few desperate struggles and finally got out of the bog on the side nearest to his own house. So he went away and Christian didn't see him again. Christian could not get out because of the burden on his back.

But in my dream I saw a man called Help come up to him and ask him what he was doing down there.

'Sir,' said Christian, 'I was told go this way by a man named Evangelist, who also directed me to that gate over there so that I might escape the coming disaster. As I was going there, I fell in here.'

'But why didn't you look for the steps?' asked Help.

'Fear pursued me so closely that I fled the nearest way, and fell in.'

Then Help said, 'Give me your hand.'

So Christian gave him his hand, and Help lifted him out, stood him on firm ground, and sent him on his way.

John Bunyan, *The Pilgrim's Progress*

THOUGHTS ON PRAYER

Give thanks in all circumstances (1 Thessalonians 5:18).

1. Whenever you take revenge against your brother who has harmed you, you will be reminded of this at your time of prayer.

2. Prayer is a ready remedy against depression and grief over the loss of a loved one.

3. Prayer is the absence of anger and the seed of gentleness.

4. Go, sell all your possessions and give the money to the poor, take up your cross and deny yourself, then you will be able to pray without being distracted.

5. Whatever you have borne out of love of wisdom will bear fruit for you when you turn to prayer.

6. If you want to succeed in praying properly, do not allow yourself to become upset or else you will be running in vain.

7. Do not always set your heart on everything turning out exactly as you would wish. Rather, let everything happen as pleases God; then you will have a time of undisturbed prayer.

8. A monk will be happy when he remembers that he is everybody's outcast.

9. The monk who strives to protect his interior peace will remain strong against the attacks of the enemy; but the monk who mixes with crowds of people all the time will be wounded.

Nilus, in *Sayings of the Desert Fathers*

FOUR STEPS TO FREEDOM AND PEACE

'So if the Son sets you free, you will be free indeed' (John 8:36).

'I will now teach you, my son, the way to the true liberty and peace.' Gracious Lord, do what you say, for it is most important for me to hear.

Christ says, 'Study to do the will of another, rather than your own.

Always prefer a humble state, to one of affluence.

Always choose the lowest place, and be submissive to everyone.

Always wish and pray that the will of God may be perfectly accomplished in you.

Behold, he who does this, enters into the place of peace and rest.'

Lord, this short lesson teaches great perfection. It is expressed in few words, but it is replete with truth and fruitfulness. If I could faithfully observe it, trouble would not so easily rise up within me. For as often as I find myself upset and depressed, I find that I have wandered from this, your teaching. But do thou, O Lord, who can do all things, and always loves the improvement of the soul, increase the power of your grace, that I may be enabled to fulfil your word, and to accomplish my own salvation.

The Imitation of Christ, ascribed to Thomas à Kempis

STUBBORN PRIDE

'Everyone who exalts himself will be humbled, and he who humbles himself will be exalted' (Luke 18:14).

Humility and self-contempt lead us into holiness but stubborn pride leads us in the other direction. Though God is so exalted, his eyes regard the lowly, both in heaven and on earth, and we will strive in vain to please him in any other way than by abasing ourselves.

The Son of God came down from heaven and taught us through his life and words the way to heaven, and that way is humility, as he said, 'Everyone who exalts himself will be humbled, and he who humbles himself will be exalted' (Luke 18:14).

Therefore, if you wish God to give you a new heart, you must first of all amend your deeds, and then lament your faults and accuse yourself of your sins. Do not extenuate your defects, but judge yourself justly; let not your self-love blind you, but when conscience accuses you of wrong, do not forget it, but keep it before your eyes and show it to Jesus Christ, your doctor and your saviour.

Weep for it before him, and he will comfort you without fail. No force can prevail with a Father like the tears of his child, nor is there anything which so moves God to grant us, not justice, but mercy, as our sorrow and self-accusation.

Call on the Almighty, for he will not be deaf to your cries; show him your wounded soul, for you have not to deal with someone who is blind; speak to him about your miseries, for he is merciful and he will heal them. Go to confession and Holy Communion, and when you are united to your Saviour, your soul will melt.

John of Avila, *To a Spiritual Disciple*

INNER PEACE

Peace to you from God our Father (Romans 1:7).

Luther sought to do penance for his sins as he was training to be a monk. He went without food, drink and sleep. He beat himself until he drew blood. One day, when he had been missing for some time, two monks tapped on his cell door. Getting no answer, they entered to find him unconscious on the floor, his thin body covered with blood.

When Luther visited Rome he saw the Scala Sancta, the 28 sacred steps which Jesus mounted to meet Pontius Pilate. Luther was overawed. Believing that, with every step he climbed, a soul would be released from Purgatory, he went on all fours, stopping to pray at each step for his dead brothers, grandparents and other deceased relatives. Now that he could release their sinful souls from torment, he even half wished his parents were dead. Then, at the top, he turned, looked down the stairs and asked himself, 'Is it true?'

After Luther had received his doctorate he engaged in teaching, at which he was brilliant. He made everything simple so that students could grasp the most difficult Bible passages, and his lectures were the best attended in the university. And as he taught, Luther was slowly learning the answers to all his own questions. The letters of Paul showed that God loved sinners as much as saints. His love and forgiveness could not be won or earned. God did not look for perfection but loved mankind despite its human frailties, and when Jesus Christ died on the cross, his suffering was for their sins. Luther suddenly saw God, not as a stern judge eager to punish all wrongdoers, but as the parent who loves the naughty child as much as the good one. So Luther found inner peace from God for himself.

Preserved Smith, *Life and Letters of Martin Luther*

THANKSGIVING

And be thankful (Colossians 3:15).

If anyone would tell you the shortest, surest way to all happiness and all perfection, he must tell you to make a rule to yourself, to thank and praise God for everything that happens to you. For it is certain that whatever seeming calamity happens to you, if you thank and praise God for it, you turn it into a blessing. Could you therefore work miracles, you could not do more for yourself, than by this thankful spirit, for it heals with a word of speaking, and turns all that it touches into happiness.

And although this be the highest temper that you can aim at, though it be the noblest sacrifice that the greatest saint can offer unto God, yet it is not tied to any time, or place or great occasion, but is always in your power, and may be the exercise of every day. For the common events of every day are sufficient to discover and exercise this spirit, and may plainly show you how far you are governed in all your actions by this thankful spirit.

William Law, *A Serious Call to a Devout and Holy Life*

LIVING BREAD

'I am the bread of life' (John 6:35).

> Jesu, thou joy of loving hearts,
> Thou fount of life, thou Light of men,
> From the best bliss that earth imparts
> We turn unfilled to thee again.
>
> Thy truth unchanged hath ever stood;
> Thou savest those that on thee call:
> To them that seek thee thou art good,
> To them that find thee, all in all.
>
> We taste thee, O thou living Bread,
> And long to feast upon Thee still;
> We drink of thee, the fountain-head,
> And thirst our souls from thee to fill.
>
> Our restless spirits yearn for thee,
> Where'er our changeful lot is cast, –
> Glad when thy gracious smile we see,
> Blest when our faith can hold thee fast.
>
> O Jesus, ever with us stay;
> Make all our moments calm and bright;
> Chase the dark night of sin away;
> Shed o'er the world thy holy light.
>
> Bernard of Clairvaux, translated by Ray Palmer

LIVE IN PEACE

Make every effort to live in peace with all men and to be holy (Hebrews 12:14).

Above all, see that you are followers of peace and unity, both in the church and among yourselves. Remember Hebrews 12:14. He who is not a son of peace is not a son of God. All other sins destroy the church as a result, but division and separation demolish it directly. Building the church is simply an orderly joining of the materials, so what is disjoining but pulling it down?

Many doctrinal differences must be tolerated in a church. And why, if not for unity and peace? Therefore, disunion and separation is utterly intolerable. Do not believe that people are friends of the churches if they try to cure and reform her by cutting her throat.

Those who say that no truth must be concealed for the sake of peace usually have as little of the one as of the other. Study Galatians 2:2, Romans 14:1, Acts 21:24 and 26, 1 Timothy 1:4, and Titus 3:8–9.

I hope that sad experience speaks this lesson to your hearts, even if I say nothing. Look at the state of England, and at the towns and cities where religion is prominent. Do your hearts not bleed to see how few there are that are not cut into shreds, and crumbled as to dust, by separations and divisions? To think what a wound we have given to the very name of Christianity like this! How we have hardened the ignorant, confirmed the doubting!

Richard Baxter, *The Saints' Everlasting Rest*

THE MISERIES OF LIFE

The LORD is my light and my salvation – whom shall I fear? (Psalm 27:1).

Imagine a deep and dark valley, full of all manner of torments, and spanned only by a long, narrow bridge, the width of a man's foot. A traveller is compelled to pass over this straight, high, perilous bridge; his eyes are blindfolded so that he cannot see his steps; his hands are bound behind him so that he cannot guide himself by using a stick. How great is the fear and distress of that man! Do you think he can find a place in his thoughts for cheerfulness, merriment or wantonness? I think not. Pride and vainglory have deserted him; only the darkness of death remains in his mind. Imagine, moreover, a multitude of savage birds hovering around the bridge, seeking to drag the traveller down into the abyss. Will not his fears be multiplied? And what if each plank is withdrawn as soon as he has passed over it? Is not his dread the more greatly increased?

Now, consider the significance of this image and allow a godly fear and trembling to take hold of your mind. The deep and dark valley represents hell, which is an immeasurable abyss, made terrible by the shadows of black darkness, and the multitude of torments. There is nothing in the abyss to soothe, but only those things that cause appalling distress. The perilous bridge is the present life, and the planks that are withdrawn are the days of our life, which pass away never to return, but by growing fewer press us on towards our goal. The birds that hover around the bridge are the evil spirits which endlessly seek to hurl travellers down into the abyss. We ourselves are the travellers that pass over, blindfolded by our ignorance and bound by the chain of the difficulty of doing good works, so that we cannot direct our steps freely towards God in holiness of life.

Consider, therefore, whether you should not cry out to your Creator, so that, defended by his protection, you may sing in faith among the multitude of your enemies: 'The Lord is my light and my salvation; whom shall I fear?' He is your light against blindness; your salvation against difficulty.

St Anselm, *Meditations*, 'On the Miseries of this Life'

IN THE WORLD BUT NOT OF THE WORLD

Let us throw off everything that hinders us and the sin that so easily entangles (Hebrews 12:1).

I want to advise you to leave everything – but I do not want to be presumptuous, so if you cannot abandon everything the world offers, hold the things that are of this world in such a way that you are not held by them in the world. Earthly interests must be possessed, they must not possess you.

So, use temporal possessions but desire eternal things. Temporal goods should be for use on the way, eternal goods should be desired for when you arrive at your destination. Look askance at whatever goes on in this world, but let the eyes of your mind look directly at your destination and focus on it intently.

Faults must be uprooted, torn away not only from the action but also from thinking about it. See that worldly pleasures, anxiety and the fever of ambition do not hold you back from the great supper of the Lord. Even the honourable things we do in the world should only be touched obliquely with our minds, as it were, so that the earthly things which delight us may serve our body in such a way that they hinder our heart as little as possible.

Brothers, we do not take it upon ourselves to tell you to give up everything, yet even while you hang on to things you can leave them, if you wish, provided you deal with temporal things in such a way as to strive for eternal aims with your whole mind. Use the world as if you were not using it: make use of any external things but do not not let them rule your mind, so that they are subject to you and serve you from outside. Never stop concentrating your aim on higher things. If you behave like this, you will have everything in the world for your use, and not as objects of your desire. Therefore do not let anything hold back your desire; do not let the love of anything in this world entangle you.

Gregory the Great, *Homilies on the Gospels*

GROWTH IN HOLINESS

**Forgetting what is behind and straining towards what is
ahead, I press on towards the goal to win the prize for which
God has called me heavenwards in Christ Jesus (Philippians
3:13–14).**

To her cousin (Carmel, 16 July 1894)
We have both said good-bye to the blissful days of our childhood,
and now we face life's responsibilities. The path each of us treads
is very different but it leads to precisely the same goal. You and I
must have but one aim: to grow in holiness along the road that
God in his goodness has mapped out for us.

I feel that I can talk quite openly to you, dear friend of my childhood. You understand the language of the Faith much better than
the idiom of the world, and the Lord you received in your first
holy Communion has ever remained the Master of your heart; it
is in him that you love the noble soul henceforth completely one
with your own, and it is because of him that your love is so tender
and strong.

O how glorious our Faith is! Instead of restricting hearts, as the
world fancies, it uplifts them and enlarges their capacity to love
with an almost infinite love since it will continue unbroken
beyond our mortal life. Indeed, life has been given us simply to
purchase our home in heaven, where we shall meet again the dear
ones we have loved on earth.

May Christ prolong his gift of happiness in you, and as far as
possible sweeten the bitter trials you will meet on your way.
Enjoy in peace that gladness God bestows without being anxious
about the future. I feel certain that Christ has fresh favours and
many consolations in store for you.

Your little sister in our Lord, Thérèse of the Child Jesus

Thérèse de Lisieux, *An Autobiography*

HOLY PATIENCE

If you are insulted because of the name of Christ, you are blessed, for the Spirit of glory and of God rests on you. If you suffer, it should not be as a murderer or a thief or any other kind of criminal, or even as a meddler. However, if you suffer as a Christian, do not be ashamed, but praise God that you bear that name (1 Peter 4:14–16).

The person who with steadfast humility and patience suffers and endures tribulation, through fervent love of God, will quickly attain great grace and virtue, and be lord of this world, and will have a foretaste of the next and glorious world. Everything that a person does, good or evil, he does to himself; therefore, do not be offended with the person who injures you, rather, you should show him humble patience, and only grieve within yourself for his sin, having compassion on him and praying to God earnestly for him.

The more a person is able to endure and suffer patiently injuries and tribulations, for love of God, the greater he is in God's sight. The less a person is able to endure pain and adversity, for love of God, the less he is in God's sight. If someone praises you, speaks well of you, give that praise to God alone. If anyone speaks badly about you, or reviles you, help him, speak even more badly about yourself. If you support your own cause, always put it in a bad light and support your opponent's case. Always assign guilt to yourself, but praise your neighbour.

It is of much greater consolation and much more worthy to suffer injuries and revilings patiently, without grumbling, for love of God, than to feed a hundred poor people and fast every day.

The Little Flowers of St Francis

FULL OF GRACE

We have seen his glory, the glory of the One and Only, who came from the Father, full of grace and truth (John 1:14).

> Amazing grace! how sweet the sound
> That saved a wretch like me;
> I once was lost, but now am found;
> Was blind, but now I see.
>
> 'Twas grace that taught my heart to fear,
> And grace my fear relieved;
> How precious did that grace appear,
> The hour I first believed!
>
> Through many dangers, toils and snares
> I have already come:
> 'Tis grace that brought me safe thus far,
> And grace will lead me home.
>
> The Lord has promised good to me,
> His word my hope secures;
> He will my shield and portion be
> As long as life endures.
>
> Yes, when his heart and flesh shall fail,
> And mortal life shall cease,
> I shall profess within the veil
> A life of joy and peace.
>
> When we've been there a thousand years,
> Bright shining as the sun,
> We've no less days to sing God's praise
> Than when we first begun.

John Newton

THE OVERFLOWING OF A HEART'S DEVOTION

Then Mary took about a pint of pure nard, an expensive perfume; she poured it on Jesus' feet and wiped his feet with her hair. And the house was filled with the fragrance of the perfume (John 12:3).

It is probable that in most of us the spiritual life is impoverished and stunted because we give so little place to gratitude. It is more important to thank God for blessings received than to pray for them beforehand. For that forward-looking prayer, though right as an expression of dependence upon God, is still self-centred in part, at least, of its interest; there is something which we hope to gain by our prayer. But the backward-looking act of thanksgiving is quite free from this. In itself it is quite selfless. Thus it is akin to love. . . .

To the worldly mind the acts of devotion are always foolish. God does not require our costly gifts for his honour; better spend on good works what is lavished on worship; so men often say. And there is a lurking truth. . . . Yet it is true also that where lavish expenditure expresses the overflowing of a heart's devotion, it is unspeakably precious. For love is the best thing that there is, and what represents its best moments shares that preciousness. 'The poor at all times ye have with you, but me ye have not at all times.' The Lord would soon be taken away from Mary; and it is only at moments of vivid insight that any of us perceive his presence. At those times, there is a fervour in our love for the present Lord that will not often be found in our kindly attitude towards the poor. That may be genuine enough; and what we do for them is done to him (Matthew 25:40); but it lacks the completeness of the love which is adoration. As the best thing is love itself, not the benefits which it confers, there must be no censure of its lavishness as disproportionate.

William Temple, *Readings in St John's Gospel*

SELF-ABANDONMENT

'You will seek me and find me when you seek me with all your heart' (Jeremiah 29:13).

In the state of self-abandonment the one rule is the present moment. The soul is as light as a feather, as fluid as water, simple as a child, as easily moved as a ball, so as to receive and follow all the impressions of grace.

Abandoned souls have no more hardness or consistency than melted metal. For just as metal takes all the shapes of the mould into which it is poured, these souls adapt and adjust themselves as easily to all the forms which God wishes to give them. In a word, their disposition resembles that of the air which is at the service of all who breathe it and of water which takes the form of every recipient.

They present themselves to God like a perfectly plain and simple canvas, without concerning themselves to know the subject which it may please God to paint in their souls, for they trust themselves to him, they are abandoned and wholly occupied with their duty, think neither of themselves nor of what is necessary for them, nor of how they are to procure it.

Jean-Pierre de Caussade, *The Sacrament of the Present Moment*

OBEYING GOD

But Peter and the apostles replied: 'We must obey God rather than men!' (Acts 5:29).

Mr Cobb, clerk to the Justices:
The king and the law forbids private meetings for worship, and tolerates only public meetings for worship.

John Bunyan:
Sir, said I, let me answer you in a similitude; set the case that, at such a wood corner, there did usually come forth thieves to do mischief, must there therefore a law be made, that every one that cometh out there shall be killed? May not there come out true men as well as thieves, out from thence?

Just thus is it in this case; I do think there may be many, that may design the destruction of the commonwealth. But it does not follow therefore that all private meetings are unlawful. Let those who break the law be punished. And as for your saying I may meet in public, if I may be allowed, I would gladly do it. Let me have but meetings enough in public, and I shall care the less to have them in private. I do not meet in private because I am afraid to have meetings in public. I bless the Lord that my heart is at that point, that if any man can lay anything to my charge, either in doctrine or practice, in this particular, that can be proved error or heresy, I am willing to disown it, even in the very market-place. But if it be truth, then to stand to it to the last drop of my blood.

And, sir, said I, you ought to commend me for so doing. To err, and to be a heretic, are two things. I am no heretic, because I will not stand rebelliously to defend any one thing that is contrary to the word; prove any thing which I hold to be an error, and I will recant it.

Sir, said I, Wyckliffe saith, that he who ceases to preach and hear the word of God for fear of excommunication of men, is already excommunicated by God, and shall in the day of judgment be counted a traitor to Christ.

John Bunyan, *A Relation of My Imprisonment*

DIFFERENT WAYS TO LOVE GOD

'If you obey my commands, you will remain in my love' (John 15:10).

Let Christ, who is the power of God, strengthen you so that you are not overcome by any enemies.

Let Christian love strengthen your desire to do good; let Christ's wisdom rule you and direct your life and let steadfastness make you persevere in this.

Your Christian love must not be lukewarm, timid or indiscreet. This is what is laid down in the Law, when God says, 'Love the LORD your God with all your heart and with all your soul and with all your strength' (Deuteronomy 6:5).

It seems to me that the best way to make distinctions between the different ways to love God is as follows: the love of the heart concerns your feelings, the love of the soul centres on the decisions of your mind and the love of your strength focuses on the steadfastness of your mind. So you must love God wholeheartedly, singlemindedly and sacrificially.

Bernard of Clairvaux, *The Song of Songs*

SILENCE

Be still before the LORD, all mankind (Zechariah 2:13).

To the Comtesse de Gramont

I think, Madame, that you should try hard to learn to practise silence, insofar as general good manners allow. Silence promotes the presence of God, avoids many harsh or proud words, and eradicates many dangers that come from ridiculing or rashly judging our neighbours.

Silence humbles the mind and detaches it from the world.

Silence creates a kind of solitude in the heart as you have at court.

Silence would supply a great deal of the needs your present difficulties are provoking. If you refrained from all unnecessary conversation you would have many moments to spend in silence throughout your day, even allowing for all the inevitable claims society makes on you.

The barriers to prayer which are around you are under the control of God's providential hand and will be more useful to you than any pleasure you may derive from your devotions. You know that you do not have to be on your own to experience God's love.

When God does give you time you must take it and use it. In the meantime, be patient and content that the amount of time that he gives you now is the best for you.

The thing I most fear for you is your dissipation, but you may even overcome this through silence. If you are firm about keeping silent when you do not have to speak, God will preserve you from evil when it is right for you to speak.

Archbishop Fénelon, *Christian Perfection*

RECOLLECTION

The king said to me, 'What do you want?' Then I prayed to the God of heaven, and I answered the king (Nehemiah 2:4–5).

To the Comtesse de Gramont
If you are unable to find much time for yourself, be even more vigilant for the odd moments you have for yourself, when they do come. Just a few minutes faithfully used in the middle of all your other engagements may be more useful in God's sight than complete hours given over to him, when you have more freedom in your life.

Indeed, numerous short moments during the day all mount up to a considerable length of time. You may even find that frequent short moments spent in God's presence are more profitable for you than one long period of time allocated to your devotions.

Your lot, Madame, is to love, to be silent, and to sacrifice your own desires, so that you can carry out God's will as you devote yourself to the service of others. You can be happy about this as God himself has laid this cross on you with his own caring, providential hand.

All we have to do is to give ourselves up to God each day, without looking anywhere else for help. He will carry us in his arms as a loving mother carries her child. Let us believe, hope and love with the simplicity of a child and trust our heavenly Father for every need. God has said in the Bible, 'Can a mother forget the baby at her breast and have no compassion on the child she has borne? Though she may forget, I will not forget you!' (Isaiah 49:15).

Archbishop Fénelon, *Christian Perfection*

MEDITATION

I meditate on all your works and consider what your hands have done (Psalm 143:5).

To a Lady
It is always best to bring to your mind some simple, practical subject which you can meditate on. If you do not alight on a particular subject, but are drawn into union with God in a general way, continue like this for as long as you feel drawn to God. But do not make a habit of this. Always be determined to meditate on a particular subject, one which can occupy and feed your mind as you meditate. Welcome all light and emotion which are given to you during your meditation, but do not trust any of these things which may flatter your vanity and fill you with idle self-complacency.

It is preferable to be very humble and ashamed of one's faults one has committed than to be satisfied with one's meditation and puffed up with the idea that one is very advanced in spiritual matters, just because one has experienced lots of wonderful feelings and thoughts in prayer. Accept whatever God may give you from his caring hands, but be on your guard that these gifts will turn into most dangerous illusions if you sink into self-complacency as you enjoy these divine gifts.

The great thing is to die to yourself, to obey God, to distrust yourself and to bear the cross of Christ. All the same, I am very glad that you can meditate now without that forced effort which previously hampered you so much. Your meditation is now calmer, and you are more helpful to your neighbours, but you must take care that this holy freedom never degenerates into dissipation or slackness.

Archbishop Fénelon, *Christian Perfection*

A SPIRIT OF PRAYER

Let everyone who is godly pray (Psalm 32:6).

Do everything without excitement, simply in the spirit of divine grace. As soon as you detect natural activity sliding in, recall yourself quietly into the presence of God. Listen carefully to the promptings of God's grace, and do not say anything or do anything that God's Holy Spirit does not teach you. You will discover yourself infinitely more quiet, your words will be fewer and more effective, and although you will do less, what you actually do will be more useful.

It is not a question of hopeless mental activity, but a question of acquiring a peacefulness and tranquillity in which you can easily commune with your beloved about everything you have to do. Such communion, simple and brief though it may be, will be more lasting than the bustling, restless arguments we keep within ourselves when natural energy has its way.

Once the heart has set its course on God we can easily learn to hold back the hasty actions of our nature and wait for the time when we act only under the impulse of God's grace. Constantly killing off our selfish desires awakens the life of faith. Dying to self in this way results in spiritual life because peace-giving grace takes the place of disturbing natural desires. I beg you to cultivate your inner spirit, as this gradually results in everything becoming prayer in you. You will not be free of suffering, but a peaceful suffering is twice as easy to bear as suffering in turmoil.

Archbishop Fénelon, *Christian Perfection*

THE DARK NIGHT OF CONTEMPLATION

The night will shine like the day, for darkness is as light to you (Psalm 139:12).

When God sets fire to the will we can understand some of the delightful results which the dark night of contemplation brings to the soul. Sometimes the soul is enlightened in the middle of the darkness and the light shines even though it is dark. This mystical insight is poured into the mind while the will remains dry. The will is not actually united in this love though it does receive a lesser blessing from God. So the presence of God is felt in different ways.

Sometimes God's love is a painful experience for the will, even though the fires of love are burning gently yet steadily. Sometimes the faculties of the mind and the will are so united that they receive deeper purification of their understanding. But before this happens, it is usual for the fires of God's love to be conscious in the will before the mind experiences it.

Once the flames of fire are alight in the soul it receives great power and energy and longing for him in addition to the love it already has for him. Then God gives to the soul warmth from this love so that it becomes bold and pays attention to nothing else, because it is completely overwhelmed by this love. The soul doesn't care what it does so long as it finds God who is the centre of its love.

St John of the Cross, *The Dark Night of the Soul*

IN THE DARKNESS AND YET SAFE

He made darkness his covering, his canopy around him – the dark rain clouds of the sky (Psalm 18:11).

The soul is safe in God's darkness because of the suffering it has been going through. For the way of suffering is safer and even more beneficial than the way of enjoyment and activity. This is because true suffering receives God's strength while, when the soul is merely enjoying itself, it only experiences its own weakness and imperfections. Also through suffering the soul practises and acquires virtues which make it easier and more cautious as it is purified.

There is an even more important reason why the soul is secure as it walks in this darkness, and this stems from the dark light and wisdom of contemplation which takes such a firm hold on the soul as it draws it closer to God and protects and delivers it from everything that is not of God. This soul is now going through a time of convalescence which will result in its being spiritually healthy. Almighty God puts the soul on a strict diet and removes its appetite for things it previously enjoyed. The soul is like a sick person who if he is liked by other people in the house will be looked after with care until he is cured. The lights have to be kept dimmed and the noise level has to be kept low. He is only given a small amount of nutritious and easily digestible food.

This dark contemplation causes the soul to go through all this for its own safety and benefits as it brings it closer to God. The closer the soul comes to God the more strongly the darkness presses on it and the weaker it feels itself. The soul is like a person coming close to the sun who then realises how splendid the sun is and how weak and impure he is in comparison. It is like this with the greatness of God's spiritual light. It is so far beyond any human understanding that the nearer we come to it the more we are blinded by it and left in a state of darkness.

St John of the Cross, *The Dark Night of the Soul*

THE HEIGHT OF CONTEMPLATION

Then we shall see face to face (1 Corinthians 13:12).

If we are faithful, we have already arrived at the way of faith; and if we do not abandon it, we shall without doubt arrive at not merely so great an understanding of things incorporeal and unchangeable as cannot in this life be grasped by all, but even to the height of contemplation, which the apostle calls 'face to face.'

For some of the least ones, who yet perseveringly walk in the path of faith, come to that most blessed contemplation: while others who have knowledge of what invisible, unchangeable, incorporeal nature is, but refuse to follow the path leading to the abode of such happiness, which seems folly to them, i.e. Christ crucified, are not able to come to the shrine of that quiet, although their mind is already, as at a distance, touched by the ray of its light.

St Thomas Aquinas, *Summa Theologia*

TRANQUILLITY OF MIND

**Set your minds on things above, not on earthly things
(Colossians 3:2).**

When my business is done I try to return to my inner self, but cannot, for I am driven away by vain tumultuous thoughts. It ought to be known that we do not all reach the height of contemplation, if we do not cease from the oppression of outward care.

Anger that comes from evil blinds the eye, but anger that comes from zeal disturbs it. Since necessarily, in whatever degree one is moved by a zeal for virtue, the world of contemplation, which cannot be known except by a heart in tranquillity, is broken up. For zeal for the cause of virtue in itself, in that it fills the mind with disquietude and agitation, presently dims the eye so that in its troubled state it can no longer see those objects far up above which it previously clearly saw, when it was in a state of tranquillity. Contemplation is never joined to disturbance.

Often we become angry in correcting faults and disturb our tranquil mind. Only a tranquil mind can hold itself aloft in the light of contemplation. While we pursue faults in anger we are necessarily thrown into confusion and disturbed from the contemplation of things on high.

Gregory the Great (Gregory I), *Letters*

SELF-EXAMINATION AND CONFESSION

'If you are offering your gift at the altar and there remember that your brother has something against you, leave your gift there in front of the altar. First go and be reconciled to your brother; then come and offer your gift' (Matthew 5:23–24).

Self-examination should always precede confession. For his part, God will not fail to enlighten people and enable them to see the particular nature of their faults. This examination, however, should be peaceful and tranquil; and we should depend on God for the discovery and knowledge of our sins, rather than on the diligence of our own scrutiny.

When we make half-hearted self-examination in the strength of our own insight we are easily deceived and betrayed by self-love into error. As the prophet Isaiah said: 'Woe to those who call evil good and good evil, who put darkness for light and light for darkness' (Isaiah 5:20). But when we lie fully exposed in front of the Sun of Righteousness, his divine beams reveal the smallest atoms. It follows from this that we must forsake self and abandon our souls to God, as well as in our self-examination and confession.

When souls have reached this kind of prayer, no fault escapes their notice and subsequent condemnation. Every sin of commission is instantly rebuked. The heart feels the inner burning of every sin. This soul is so thorough in her self-examination that no sin remains hidden. The soul turns to our judge and meekly bears the pain and correction he inflicts. God becomes the constant examiner of the soul. The soul can now no longer examine herself; and if she is faithful in her resignation, experience will convince her that she is a thousand times more effectively examined by its divine light, than by her own most active and vigorous inspection.

Madame Guyon, *A Short and Easy Method of Prayer*

UNION OF THE SOUL WITH GOD

'Remain in me, and I will remain in you' (John 15:4).

There are three kinds of union, the first habitual, the second virtual, the third actual.

Habitual union is when one begins an action by which one is united to God, and by virtue of that action remains one with him all the time that it continues.

Actual union is the most complete, and being entirely spiritual makes its life felt, because the soul is not asleep as in the other modes of union, but feels powerfully active, its motions alive like that of fire, more brilliant than the sun unobscured by cloud. Yet one can be deceived when feeling thus. It is not a mere expression of the heart as if one should say: 'My God, I love you with all my heart' – or other such words. It is an indescribable something of the soul, sweet, peaceful, spiritual, reverent, humble, loving and utterly simple. It lifts the soul and impels it to love God, even to lay hold of him, with emotions beyond description, and which experience alone can make us understand.

All those who aim at union with God must know that everything which can refresh the will is welcome and pleasing to it, or contains such. Everyone must admit that God is beyond understanding and that to be one with him the will must be deprived of all manner of tastes and pleasures both spiritual and bodily in order that, being thus stripped, it may be able to love God above all things. For if the will can in any fashion understand God, it can only be through love.

Brother Lawrence, *The Practice of the Presence of God*

GUARD YOUR HEART

May my heart be blameless towards your decrees, that I may not be put to shame (Psalm 119:80).

If a person does not take great care to guard his heart he is in danger of forgetting and neglecting everything that he has heard. Then his enemy will find a foothold in him and then defeat him.

It is like when a lamp is filled with oil and lit. If you forget to top up the oil, the lamp gradually goes out and eventually everything becomes dark. It is even worse if a rat manages to gnaw at the wick. A rat cannot do this while there is still oil in the lamp. But when the rat sees that the lamp is without light as well as heat, he tries to pull out the wick and brings the whole lamp crashing to the ground. If it is an earthenware pot it is smashed to pieces, but if it is made of brass, the master of the house can refill it with oil.

In the same way, when the soul is neglected, the Holy Spirit gradually withdraws until he is felt no more and the light is extinguished. Finally, the enemy devours the ardour of the soul and wickedness quickly overtakes the body as well.

But if a person perseveres in his abiding in God, and only goes away from God out of negligence, God, in his mercy, draws him back to himself. God makes the person stand in awe of him and enables him to be vigilant and to protect himself with greater prudence in the future.

Orsisius, in *Sayings of the Desert Fathers*

COMFORT IN TROUBLE

Our God is in heaven; he does whatever pleases him (Psalm 115:3).

God claims omnipotence for himself, and wants us to acknowledge it. God's omnipotence is not futile, idle and inactive as some theologians pretend, but caring, effective, energetic and always active.

It is not an omnipotence which can only serve as a general influence in uncertainty (like ordering a stream to stay inside a prescribed channel), but one which focuses on specific and definite events. The verse in the Psalms which says 'he does whatever pleases him' (see Psalm 115:3) refers to his sure and certain plan.

The believer's comfort in trouble is that everything they endure is ordained and commanded by God and that they are in his hands. If God's rule is over all his works, we would be foolish to restrict it to the natural order of things. Those who keep God's Providence within narrow limits not only deny him his glory but deprive themselves of a valuable doctrine. Nothing could be more pathetic than the thought of man at the mercy of unpredictable elements, and if it were true, God's particular goodness towards each individual would be seriously damaged. David comments (Psalm 8:2) that babies at their mothers' breasts celebrate God's glory, because, from the moment of birth, they find nourishment prepared for them by his loving care.

John Calvin, *The Institutes of Christian Religion*

PEACE

'The LORD blesses his people with peace' (Psalm 29:11).

If we forget all created things, there is then nothing to disturb our peace; nothing to excite the desires that disturb it; for, as the proverb says, What the eye has not seen, the heart does not desire.

The restless and troubled soul, the passions and desires of which are not wholly mortified, is, as such, incapacitated for spiritual good, and that enters only into the soul which is under control and ordered in peace.

Be assured of this; God reigns only in the peaceful and unselfish soul.

Keep your heart in peace; let nothing in this world disturb it: all things have an end.

In all circumstances, however hard they may be, we should rejoice, rather than be cast down, that we may not lose the greatest good, the peace and tranquillity of our soul.

It is not God's will that the soul should be troubled by anything, or that it should be afflicted; for if men are afflicted because of the adversities of this world, this results from them being weak. For the soul of the perfect rejoices in that which gives pain to the soul of the imperfect.

The heavens are steadfast, and souls who possess a heavenly nature are steadfast. They are to a certain extent like God, who never changes.

St John of the Cross, *The Dark Night of the Soul*

BE PREPARED FOR TRIALS

Perseverance must finish its work so that you may be mature and complete, not lacking anything (James 1:4).

To a spiritual disciple

If you want to be God's friend, you must prepare yourself for trials, for without them all your virtue is like an unwalled city, which falls at the first onslaught. Perseverance is the guardian of all the other virtues, and, if it fails, we may lose in one moment the labour of many days.

Our Master and Redeemer tells us, 'By standing firm you will gain life' (Luke 21:19). Without perseverance we lose control over ourselves, because anger, like wine, robs us of our reason. Prepare your heart to suffer afflictions, for without the battle there is no victory, and the crown is only for the conqueror.

Do not think that your burden is heavy; it is very light, compared with what you deserve to bear and with what Jesus Christ our Lord bore for your sake; it is slight indeed in comparison with the reward it will bring you. Remember that we will shortly leave this world, and then all the past will seem like a brief dream, and we shall see that it is better to have laboured than to have rested here.

Live here as a stranger, your body on earth, but your heart above, so that when our Lord calls you, he may not find you sleeping, but ready to go with him, and to hear the sweet words: 'Well done, good and faithful servant! You have been faithful with a few things; I will put you in charge of many things. Come and share your master's happiness!' (Matthew 25:21).

John of Avila, *Sermons*

SPIRITUAL SONG

I will be glad and rejoice in you; I will sing praise to your name, O Most High (Psalm 9:2).

The glory that I sigh for is so delightful, no one could want more. So, my soul, adorn yourself as a bride, for the King of heaven says, 'Love binds my heart with bonds that can never be broken.' And God binds my soul and holds on to it with such wonderful mastery and determination that it is more pleased to think of dying than of living. Like a flower that cannot fade away, so is God's friend burned with love, and in joy and song he prepares for death.

At the start of my conversion and the beginning of my single-mindedness, I thought I wished to be like a little bird who pines away for the love of its beloved, but which can rejoice in the midst of its longing when the loved one appears. But even in languishing, the little bird is gladdened by the coming of the one he loves, and he sings in his gladness and pines in his singing, but all with sweetness and ardour.

It is said that the nightingale spends the whole night long in song and melody so that he may please the one to whom he is united. How much more should I sing all my life with the greatest sweetness to my Jesus? This life is as night compared to the brightness to come, and Jesus is the Lover of my soul to whom I am bound, as I too languish, and in languishing faint for love. But because I faint, I shall recover and be nourished by his warmth. I shall rejoice, and in my joy sing jubilantly of the delights of love. Flute-like, I shall pour out melody in fervent devotion, raising from the heart an inward fire of songs of praise to God Most High.

Richard Rolle, *The Fire of Love*

DEATH-BED BLESSING

While they were stoning him, Stephen prayed, 'Lord Jesus, receive my spirit.' Then he fell on his knees and cried out, 'Lord, do not hold this sin against them' (Acts 7:59–60).

I bless thee, son, in all and above all: and because in thy hands the most high God has increased my brothers and my children, over thee and in thee, I bless them all. From heaven and on earth may the sovereign Lord bless thee with all things. I bless thee as much as I can and more than I can; and what I cannot do from myself, may he who can do all things grant thee. May God be mindful of thy work, and of thy trouble, and may thy share be laid up on the recompense of the just. Mayst thou find all the blessings you desire and may your just demands be granted.

Farewell, all my children, in the fear of the Lord, always live in him, for there are great trials approaching you as tribulation approaches. Happy are those who persevere in the way in which they have begun. There will be scandals in the future which will separate some of you. As for me, I hasten towards my Lord and my God. I have devoutly served him from the depths of my soul. I go to him in confidence.

St Francis of Assisi, *Letters*

THE VANITY OF HUMAN LEARNING

The fear of the LORD is the beginning of knowledge, but fools despise wisdom and discipline (Proverbs 1:7).

Be not captivated, my son, with the fair and subtle speech of man, for 'the kingdom of God is not in words, but in power' (1 Corinthians 4:20). Attend only to the truths of my word, which enlighten the understanding, and inflame the heart; which excite compunction, and bring consolations.

Read my words: not so you may seem more learned and wiser, but so that you may study how to mortify your evil passions; a knowledge, of more importance than the solution of many difficult questions.

Though you may have read, and known much, you will do well to revert to the one great principle: 'For the Lord gives true wisdom, and from his mouth come knowledge and understanding' (Proverbs 2:6). Wisdom gives 'prudence to the simple, knowledge and discretion to the young' (Proverbs 1:4). Anyone who listens to the voice of Wisdom soon makes great progress in the spirit. But woe to those who disregard the ways of Wisdom and devote their time and effort to the beguiling speculations of men.

The Imitation of Christ, ascribed to Thomas à Kempis

PRAYER

May my prayer be set before you like incense; may the lifting up of my hands be set before you like the evening sacrifice (Psalm 141:2).

Prayer, the Church's banquet, Angels' age,
   God's breath in man returning to his birth,
   The soul in paraphrase, heart in pilgrimage,
The Christian plummet, sounding heaven and earth;
Engine against the Almighty, sinner's tower,
   Reversed thunder, Christ-side-piercing spear,
   The six-days' world transposing in an hour,
A kind of tune, which all things hear and fear;
Softness, and peace, and joy, and love, and bliss,
   Exalted manna, gladness of the best,
   Heaven in ordinary, man well drest,
The milky way, the bird of Paradise,
   Church-bells beyond the stars heard, the soul's blood,
   The land of spices; something understood.

George Herbert

AN UNKNOWN PREACHER

Turn to me and be saved, all you ends of the earth; for I am God, and there is no other (Isaiah 45:22).

The minister did not come that morning; he was snowed up, I suppose. At last, a very thin-looking man, a shoemaker, or tailor, or something of that sort, went up into the pulpit to preach. He could not even pronounce his words properly.

The preacher began thus: 'My dear friends, this is a very simple text indeed. It says, "Look". Now lookin' don't take a deal of pain. It ain't liftin' your foot or your finger; it is just, "Look". Well, a man needn't go to College to learn to look. You may be the biggest fool, and yet you can look. A man needn't be worth a thousand a year to be able to look. Anyone can look; even a child can look. But then the text says, "Look unto Me". Ay!' he said, in broad Essex, 'many on ye are lookin' to yourselves, but it's no use lookin' there. You'll never find any comfort in yourselves. Some on ye say, "We must wait for the Spirit's workin'." You have no business with that just now. Look to Christ. The text says, "Look unto Me".'

Then he looked at me under the gallery. Just fixing his eyes on me, as if he knew all my heart, he said, 'Young man, you look very miserable and you always will be miserable if you don't obey my text; but if you obey now, this moment you will be saved.' Then lifting up his hands, he shouted, as only a Primitive Methodist could do, 'Young man, look to Jesus Christ. Look! Look! Look! You have nothing to do but to look and live.'

I saw at once the way of salvation. Oh, that somebody had told me before, 'Trust Christ, and you shall be saved.'

C. H. Spurgeon, *Autobiography*

ADVICE ON PRAYER

Then Jesus told his disciples a parable to show them that they should always pray and not give up (Luke 18:1).

To a noble lady (411)
You asked me to write something about prayer and now I feel it is my duty to discharge my debt and in the love of Christ meet your devout request. How much your desire pleased me as it shows your sense of a high calling.

In the darkness of this world where, as pilgrims, we stray far from our Lord, as long as we walk by faith and not by sight (see 2 Corinthians 5:6–7), the Christian soul ought to reckon itself desolate and never stop praying. Learn to fix the eye of faith on the divine word of the holy Scriptures as on 'a light shining in a dark place, until the day dawns and the morning star rises in your hearts' (2 Peter 1:19). For the ineffable source from which this lamp borrows its light is the Light that shines in darkness but that the darkness does not overcome it.

To see this light our hearts must be purified by faith: 'Blessed are the pure in heart, for they will see God' (Matthew 5:8); and 'we know that when he appears, we shall be like him, for we shall see him as he is' (1 John 3:2) – after death comes true life; after desolation, true consolation; a life which delivers our souls from death and a consolation which frees our eyes from tears.

St Augustine, *Letters*

ST MARY MAGDALENE

Mary Magdalene went to the tomb (John 20:1).

Mary Magdalene didn't let anybody get in the way of her love for Jesus. Even when she knew that Jesus was in the sealed tomb which was guarded by soldiers, she went to anoint him before dawn. 'Early on the first day of the week, while it was still dark, Mary Magdalene went to the tomb' (John 20:1).

Mary's overwhelming love is seen again when she thought the figure she saw was the gardener, and she said, 'Sir, if you have carried him away, tell me where you have put him, and I will get him' (John 20:15). Mary disregarded the foolishness of the request. For it was obvious that if the body of Jesus had been stolen this man would not tell her and he certainly would not have allowed Mary to take away the body.

The characteristics of this ardent love are that the person believes anything is possible, and that other people will think the same. The person cannot believe that other people are concerned about anything else.

This is how the beloved searched for her lover in the streets and squares thinking that everybody else was doing the same. She begged them that if they found him they would speak to him and, 'Tell him I faint with love' (Song of Songs 5:8). Mary's love was so strong that she thought that if a gardener told her where he had hidden Jesus's body, she would go and recover it no matter how hard that might be for her.

St John of the Cross, *The Dark Night of the Soul*

DEATH TO SELF

'No-one can serve two masters. Either he will hate the one and love the other, or he will be devoted to the one and despise the other' (Matthew 6:24).

What confidence will a dying person possess who has no worldly affections to tie him down to this life. But the sensual and sick soul is not capable of such thoughts, nor can the natural man conceive the power of this heaven-born freedom of spirit. When, however, he does decide to be spiritual he will have to guard himself against no one as much as against himself. It is true victory to triumph over oneself. He, whose sensual appetite is kept in subjection to the spirit, and the spirit in subjection to God's will, he is the true conqueror of himself, and the lord of the whole world. Think of the whole world as nothing: prefer the leisure which gives you time to serve God. For you will not have time to serve Christ while you are seeking delight in the transitory enjoyments of time and sense.

How few seek to obtain this divine life, which can only result from the death of self. Thus, men are chained down in animal passions, unable to rise by the spirit above the enjoyments of their sinful human nature. He who desires to walk with Christ must endeavour to put to death his depraved and inordinate affections.

The Imitation of Christ, ascribed to Thomas à Kempis

HUMAN NATURE

**You were dead in your transgressions and sins . . . we were by
nature objects of wrath (Ephesians 2:1, 3).**

My first principle in religion is what the Scripture teaches me of
the utter depravity of human nature, in connection with the
spirituality and sanction of the law of God. I believe we are by
nature sinners; by practice universally transgressors; that we are
dead in trespasses and sin; and that the bent of our natural spirit
is enmity against the holiness, government, and grace of God.
Upon this ground, I see, feel, and acknowledge the necessity of
such a salvation as the Gospel proposes, which, at the same time
that it precludes boasting, and stains the pride of all human glory,
affords encouragement to those who may be thought, or may
think themselves, the weakest or the vilest of mankind.

I believe, that whatever notions a person may take up from edu-
cation, no one ever did, or ever will, feel himself and own himself
to be such a lost, miserable sinner, unless he is supernaturally con-
victed by the Spirit of God. There is, when God pleases, a certain
light thrown into the soul, which differs not merely in degree, but
in kind, from anything that can be effected, or produced by moral
argument. But the Holy Spirit teaches or reveals no new truths but
only enables us to understand what is already revealed in the
Scripture. Here a change takes place, the person who was spiritually blind begins to see.

John Newton, *Cardiphonia*

LOVE OF OUR NEIGHBOUR

And not only do they become idlers, but also gossips and busybodies (1 Timothy 5:13).

Wisdom enters by love, silence, and mortification. It is great wisdom to know when to be silent, when to suffer, and never to regard the sayings, doings, or lives of others.

See that you do not meddle in the affairs of other people, or keep on thinking about them in your own mind, because you will not be able to concentrate on your own work.

Do not suspect evil in your brother, as that takes away the purity of your heart.

Never listen to the accounts of the frailties of others; and if anyone does complain to you about another person, humbly ask him not to speak about him at all.

Do not shrink from trouble: though it may seem to you more than you can bear. Let all men find you compassionate.

When the love and affection we give to someone is entirely spiritual and founded on God, the love of God grows with it; and the more we remember the earthly love, the more we also remember God and desire him: the one grows alongside the other.

That which is born of the flesh is flesh, and that which is born of the spirit is spirit, says our Saviour. So the love which grows out of sensuality ends in sensuality; but the love which is of the spirit ends in the spirit of God, and he makes it grow.

St John of the Cross, *The Dark Night of the Soul*

JESUS, I AM RESTING, RESTING

'Come to me, all you who are weary and burdened, and I will give you rest' (Matthew 11:28).

Jesus, I am resting, resting
    In the joy of what Thou art,
I am finding out the greatness
    Of Thy loving heart.
Here I gaze and gaze upon Thee,
    As Thy beauty fills my soul,
For by Thy transforming power,
    Thou hast made me whole.

O how great Thy loving-kindness,
    Vaster, broader than the sea;
O how marvellous Thy goodness
    Lavished all on me –
Yes, I rest in Thee, Beloved,
    Know what wealth of grace is Thine,
Know thy certainty of promise
    And have made it mine.

Ever lift thy face upon me
    As I work and wait for Thee;
Resting 'neath Thy smile, Lord Jesus,
    Earth's dark shadows flee.
Brightness of my Father's glory,
    Sunshine of my Father's face,
Let Thy glory e'er shine on me,
    Fill me with Thy grace.

Jean Sophia Pigott

PERFECT AND IMPERFECT OBEDIENCE

'This is love for God: to obey his commands' (1 John 5:3).

In the gospel, the Lord says, 'Every one of you who does not renounce all he has cannot be my disciple' (see Luke 14:33). He abandons everything that he possesses, loses his body and his soul, and gives himself up entirely to obedience in the hands of his superior. All his actions, all his thoughts, provided they are good and not opposed to the will of his superior, are fruits of true obedience. Even if the subject should see things which are more profitable for his soul than the prelate commands, let him nevertheless surrender his will to God. His duty is to aim at accomplishing the orders of his prelate. That is true and charitable obedience, and pleasing to God and one's neighbour.

If a prelate gives a command which is against the conscience of someone under him, that person may disobey the prelate, but does not have to leave him. If this results in persecution the person under the prelate's command should love his superiors all the more for God's sake. The person who prefers persecution to separation from his brothers really dwells in the true spirit of obedience, since he is sacrificing his life for his brothers. There are many religious people, who, with the excuse of knowing better than their superiors, 'look back' and return to the vomit of their own will (see Luke 9:62; Proverbs 26:11). All these people are guilty of murder and their dire examples cause many souls to be lost.

St Francis of Assisi, *Admonitions*

CHRISTIAN COURAGE AND RESOLUTION

Be strong in the Lord and in his mighty power (Ephesians 6:10).

A cowardly spirit is beneath the lowest duty of a Christian. 'Be thou strong and very courageous, that thou mayest' – what? stand in battle against those warlike nations? no, but that thou mayest 'observe to do according to all the law, which Moses my servant commanded thee' (Joshua 1:7, AV). It requires more prowess and greatness of spirit to obey God faithfully, than to command an army of men; to be a Christian than a captain. What seems less, than for a Christian to pray? yet this cannot be performed aright without a princely spirit: as Jacob is said to behave himself like a prince, when he did but pray. . . . The Christian in prayer comes up close to God, with a humble boldness of faith, and takes hold of him, wrestles with him; yea, will not let him go without a blessing, and all this in the face of his own sins, and divine justice, which let fly upon him from the fiery mouth of the law; while the other's boldness in prayer is but the child, either of ignorance in his mind, or hardness in his heart; whereby not feeling his sins, and not knowing his danger, he rushes upon duty with a blind confidence, which soon quails when conscience awakes, and gives him the alarm, that his sins are upon him, as the Philistines on Samson: alas then the poor-spirited wretch throws down his weapon, flies the presence of God with guilty Adam, and dares not look him in the face. . . . They are only a few noble-spirited souls, who dare take heaven by force, that are fit for this calling.

William Gurnall, *The Christian in Complete Armour*

DO NOT WORRY

'Consider the ravens' (Luke 12:24).

'Do not worry about your life, what you will eat or drink; or about your body, what you will wear. Is not life more important than food, and the body more important than clothes? Look at the birds of the air; they do not sow or reap or store away in barns, and yet your heavenly Father feeds them. Are you not much more valuable than they? Who of you by worrying can add a single hour to his life?

'And why do you worry about clothes? See how the lilies of the field grow. They do not labour or spin. Yet I tell you that not even Solomon in all his splendour was dressed like one of these. If that is how God clothes the grass of the field, will he not much more clothe you, O you of little faith? So do not worry, saying, 'What shall we eat?' or 'What shall we drink?' or 'What shall we wear?' For the pagans run after all these things, and your heavenly Father knows that you need them. But seek first his kingdom and his righteousness, and all these things will be given to you as well. Therefore do not worry about tomorrow, for tomorrow will worry about itself. Each day has enough trouble of its own.'

Jesus Christ, in Matthew 6:25–34

A ROUGH PATH

'Enter through the narrow gate. For wide is the gate and broad is the road that leads to destruction, and many enter through it. But small is the gate and narrow the road that leads to life, and only a few find it' (Matthew 7:13–14).

Christ's example and bearing the name Christian are sufficient motives to make us suffer adversities. The path to heaven is narrow, rough, and full of toil and can only be trodden with sweat and tears. Therefore, the people who will not learn from the witness of many thousands of saints where the correct path lies are assured of ruin.

It is enough to have Christ's example, 'who', as St Augustine said, 'calls to us and asks, "Which way are you going? I am the way. Where are you travelling to? I am the truth. Where are you staying? I am the life."' If this will not lead us through the austere and painful pathway; if this truth does not teach us humility; if this life is not achieved without a dying pilgrimage: "Woe are you who laugh, for you shall weep; and happy are those who mourn, for they will be comforted."

The truth of the matter is that the comforts of this life are really a misery and false happiness. They are guaranteed to bring sorrow and deceitful delights. They are like fair weather in winter which never lasts. They are like a calm sea, which is always prone to become turbulent again.

Robert Southwell, *Sermons*

TALKING WITH GOD

'Do not come any closer' (Exodus 3:5).

To start with, the soul learns to talk with God with greater respect and deference, which must always be present when the soul talks with Almighty God. The soul did not do this when it thrived on comfort and consolation when it was asking for special favours from God. In this kind of seeking of God the soul overstepped the mark and became too bold and lacked reverence.

This happened to Moses when he thought that God was speaking to him. Moses was carried away by enjoyment and delight and so without further thought he would have marched straight up to God, if God had not told him to stay where he was and to remove his sandals. '"Do not come any closer," God said. "Take off your sandals, for the place where you are standing is holy ground"' (Exodus 3:5).

From this incident we can learn what kind of reverence and respect a man should have when he talks with God. Moses was totally obedient in this matter and the Bible says that not only did he not dare to come near to God, but that he did not even dare to look at God. 'Moses hid his face, because he was afraid to look at God' (Exodus 3:6).

Once Moses had taken off the shoes of his appetites and pleasures he was his real miserable state before God, which was fitting for somebody about to hear the word of God.

St John of the Cross, *The Dark Night of the Soul*

TRUE WORSHIP

Love and faithfulness meet together; righteousness and peace kiss each other (Psalm 85:10).

If God is to be worshipped with prayers of thanksgiving, the person who makes it a rule to be content and thankful in every area and event of his life because it comes from God, worships God in a much higher way than the one who merely sets time aside to sing psalms. Anyone who dares not say an ill-natured word, or do an unreasonable thing, because he considers God is present everywhere, demonstrates a better devotion that the person who dares not miss going to church. To live in the world as a stranger and a pilgrim, making all our actions so many steps towards a better life, is to offer a purer sacrifice to God than any form of holy and heavenly prayers.

To content oneself with simple needs so that one may give the remainder of one's possessions to those that need it, to dare not spend money foolishly because one considers it as a gift from God which must be used according to his will, is to praise God with something that is far more glorious than songs of praise.

Bended knees, while you are clothed with pride; heavenly petitions, while you are hoarding up treasures on earth; holy devotions, while you live in stupidity of the world; prayers of meekness and charity, while your heart is the seat of spite and resentment; hours of prayer while you give up days and years to foolish, idle pleasure; these are all absurd, unacceptable services to God.

William Law, *A Serious Call to a Devout and Holy Life*

WHAT SHALL I DO TO BE SAVED?

The jailer called for lights, rushed in and fell trembling before Paul and Silas. He then brought them out and asked, 'Sirs, what must I do to be saved?' (Acts 16:29–30).

Walking through the wilderness of this world I came upon a place where there was a hollow (the gaol). There I lay down to sleep: and as I slept I dreamed a dream. I dreamed, and look! I saw a man clothed with rags. He stood with his face away from his own house, a book in his hand, and a great burden on his back. I looked, and saw him open the book, and read it. As he read he wept and trembled. Unable to contain himself, he broke down with a heartbreaking cry, calling out, 'What shall I do?' (Isaiah 64:4; Luke 14:33; Psalm 38:4; Habakkuk 2:2; Acts 2:37).

... Then I saw a man coming to him whose name was Evangelist. He asked, 'Why are you crying?'

'Sir,' he answered, 'I understand from this book I'm holding that I'm condemned to die and after that to face judgement (Hebrews 9:27); and I find that I'm not willing to do the first, nor able to do the second.'

Then Evangelist said, 'If this is your condition, why are you standing still?'

... The man said, 'Where must I flee to?'

Then Evangelist pointed with his finger over a very wide field. 'Do you see that distant wicket-gate?' he asked (Matthew 7:14).

The man said, 'No.'

'Well, do you see that shining light in the distance?' (Psalm 119:105; 2 Peter 1:19).

'I think I do.'

Then Evangelist said, 'Keep that light in your eye and go straight towards it. Then you'll see the gate. When you knock on it you'll be told what to do.'

John Bunyan, *The Pilgrim's Progress*

LORD JESUS, THINK ON ME

Then he [the other criminal] said, 'Jesus, remember me when you come into your kingdom' (Luke 23:42).

Lord Jesus, think on me,
And purge away my sin;
From earthborn passions set me free,
And make me pure within.

Lord Jesus, think on me,
With care and woe opprest;
Let me thy loving servant be,
And taste thy promised rest.

Lord Jesus, think on me,
Amid the battle's strife;
In all my pain and misery
Be thou my health and life.

Lord Jesus, think on me,
Nor let me go astray;
Through darkness and perplexity
Point thou the heavenly way.

Lord Jesus, think on me,
When flows the tempest high:
When on doth rush the enemy
O Saviour, be thou nigh.

Lord Jesus, think on me,
That, when the flood is past,
I may the eternal brightness see,
And share thy joy at last.

Synesius of Cyrene

ONLY BOAST IN THE LORD'S CROSS

May I never boast except in the cross of Christ, through which the world has been crucified to me, and I to the world (Galatians 6:14).

Consider what an excellent position the Lord has placed you in. He has created you, formed a body in the image of his well-beloved Son and a soul in his own likeness. All creatures on earth serve the Creator in their own way and they know and obey him more than you. The demons did not crucify him, for it was you who agreed with those who crucified him. Each time you delight in vice and sin you crucify him afresh. Are you able to boast about this? You might be clever and intelligent. You might possess all knowledge. You might be able to speak every language in the world and be able to search closely into heavenly problems. A single demon has known more about heavenly things and earthly things than any person, even though some men have received special knowledge from God.

You might be the richest and most beautiful person in the world. You might be able to perform miracles. You might be able to drive demons out of people. But all that would be of no advantage. However, we may boast in our infirmities and in the daily bearing of the holy cross of our Lord Jesus Christ.

St Francis of Assisi, *Admonitions*

TRANSFIGURATION OF OUR LORD

There he was transfigured before them (Matthew 17:2).

Our Lord took his three disciples with him up the mountain and showed them the transfiguration of his body by union with the Godhead – a transfiguration which we will also have in our archetypal body – and as he looked upon it, Peter at once wished to remain there always. Truly, where we find good we are loath to leave it. Where intuition finds, love follows, and memory and all the soul as well.

And knowing this, our Lord hides himself sometimes, for the soul, being the indivisible form of the body, turns as a whole to whatever she turns. If she were conscious of good, that is, of God, immediately, uninterruptedly, she would never be able to leave it to influence the body. This is what happened with Paul. Had he remained a hundred years there, where he knew the good, he would never have returned to his body, he would have forgotten it completely.

Seeing, then, that the good is wholly foreign to this life, and incompatible with it, the good God veils it when he wishes, and unveils it again when he so chooses and when he knows, like a good doctor, that it is best and most useful for you. This withdrawal is not of your making, but his, as is also the work. Let him do it or not as he wills, for he knows what is good for you. It is in his hands to reveal himself or not as you are able to endure it. God is not a destroyer of nature; he perfects it. And God does this more and more, as you are fitted for it.

Meister Eckhart, *Sermons*

FOLLOWING JESUS

'Whoever serves me must follow me; and where I am, my servant also will be' (John 12:26).

O Jesus, I have promised
    To serve thee to the end;
Be thou for ever near me,
    My Master and my Friend!
I shall not fear the battle
    If thou art by my side,
Nor wander from the pathway
    If thou wilt be my Guide.

O let me hear thee speaking
    In accents clear and still,
Above the storms of passion,
    The murmurs of self-will.
O speak to reassure me,
    To hasten or control;
O speak, and make me listen,
    Thou guardian of my soul.

O Jesus, thou hast promised
    To all who follow thee,
That where thou art in glory
    There shall thy servant be;
And, Jesus, I have promised
    To serve thee to the end;
O give me grace to follow,
    My Master and my Friend.

O let me see thy footmarks,
    And in them plant mine own:
My hope to follow duly
    Is in thy strength alone.
O guide me, call me, draw me,
    Uphold me to the end;
And then in heaven receive me,
    My Saviour and my Friend!

John Ernest Bode

CHRISTIAN PERFECTION

Therefore let us leave the elementary teachings about Christ and go on to maturity (Hebrews 6:1).

1. There is such a thing as perfection, for it is again and again mentioned in scripture.

2. It is not so early as justification, for justified people are to 'go on to maturity' ['go on unto perfection' AV] (Hebrews 6:1).

3. It is not so late as death, for St Paul speaks of living men that were perfect (see Philippians 3:15).

4. It is not absolute. Absolute perfection belongs not to man, nor to angels, but to God alone.

5. It does not make a man infallible: None is infallible, while he remains in the body.

6. Is it sinless? It is not worth while to contend for a term. It is 'salvation from sin'.

7. It is 'perfect love' (see 1 John 4:18). This is the essence of it, its properties, or inseparable fruits, are always being joyful, praying continually, and giving thanks in all circumstances (see 1 Thessalonians 5:16–18).

8. It is improvable. It is so far from lying in an indivisible point, from being incapable of increase, that one perfected in love may grow in grace far swifter than he did before.

9. It is capable of being lost, of which we have numerous instances. But we were not thoroughly convinced of this till five or six years ago.

10. It is constantly both preceded and followed by a gradual work.

John Wesley, *A Plain Man's Guide to Holiness*

THE LORD'S PRAYER

By him we cry, '*Abba,* Father' (Romans 8:15).

When we pray 'hallowed be your name', we stir up in ourselves the desire that God's name, essentially holy in itself, may also be esteemed holy by men and not be despised.

And when we pray, 'your kingdom come', we arouse a longing in our own souls for that kingdom, that it may come within ourselves, that we may be found worthy for it to reign there.

When we pray, 'your will be done on earth as it is in heaven' we beg God for the grace of obedience so that we may do his will as the angels do in the heavens.

When we pray, 'Give us today our daily bread', we use the word 'daily' about this present life and ask for necessary temporal blessings. Because bread is the most valuable food it is used to express all of our needs.

When we pray, 'Forgive us our debts, as we also have forgiven our debtors', we remind ourselves that we have to do what we are asking for. We must merit the boon of forgiveness.

When we pray, 'Lead us not into temptation', we recall how we are to plead with God not to withdraw his help from us, in case we are deceived and in our weakness give in to some temptation or be overcome by its strength.

When we pray, 'deliver us from the evil one', we reflect that we do not yet possess that bliss where no ill will be suffered. This last petition of the Lord's prayer is so comprehensive that whatever trouble he finds himself in, a Christian should use it to give vent to his tears and his groans; he should begin his prayer with this petition, use it throughout his prayers and conclude with it.

St Augustine, *Sermons*

APOSTASY

Let us not give up meeting together, as some are in the habit of doing, but let us encourage one another (Hebrews 10:25).

Christian said to Hopeful, 'Ignorance told me once that he'd resolved to go on a pilgrimage – like us now. But all of a sudden he got to know Saveself, and then he didn't want to know me.'

'Let's look into how his sudden backsliding occurred.

'1. As far as they can they stop thinking about God, death, and judgment.

'2. Then bit by bit they neglect private religious practices, like a personal prayer-time, curbing their lusts, watchfulness, sorrow for sin, and so on.

'3. Then they shun the company of lively and warm Christians.

'4. After that they become indifferent to public religious duties, like hearing and reading God's word, fellowship with other Christians, and so on.

'5. They then begin to pick holes, so to speak, in the coats of Christian people, doing it for devilish purposes so that, just because of some weakness they've spotted in other Christians, they can blacken religion behind their backs.

'6. Then they begin to associate with worldly, undisciplined, and unprincipled people.

'7. Then in secret they indulge in worldly and lewd talk and are only too glad if they can see evidence of such conduct in supposedly upright people, to encourage them in their own wrong-doing.

'8. After this they begin to play with little sins openly.

'9. And then, thoroughly hardened, they show themselves as they are. Launched once again into the chasm of misery, they for ever perish in their own deceptions, unless they are shaped by a miracle of grace.'

John Bunyan, *The Pilgrim's Progress*

LITANY TO THE HOLY SPIRIT

'And I will ask the Father, and he will give you another Counsellor to be with you for ever – the Spirit of truth' (John 14:16–17).

> In the hour of my distress,
> When temptations me oppress,
> And when I my sins confess,
> Sweet Spirit comfort me!
>
> When I lie within my bed,
> Sick in heart and sick in head,
> And with doubts discomforted,
> Sweet Spirit comfort me!
>
> When the artless Doctor sees
> No one hope but of his fees,
> And his skill runs on the lees,
> Sweet Spirit comfort me!
>
> When the Tempter me pursu'th
> With the sins of all my youth,
> And half damns me with untruth,
> Sweet Spirit comfort me!
>
> When the judgment is revealed,
> And that opened which was sealed,
> When to thee I have appealed,
> Sweet Spirit comfort me!

Robert Herrick

FRAGMENT OF THE RULE OF THE SISTERS OF ST CLARE

There will be false teachers among you (2 Peter 2:1).

The promise of St Francis to St Clare
Through divine inspiration you have become daughters and servants of the most high celestial Father, the sovereign King. You have taken the Holy Spirit as a husband by choosing a life in accordance with the perfection of the holy gospel.

I and my friars wish and promise always to show diligent care and special solicitude for you as well as for them.

The last wish St Francis wrote for St Clare
I, little Brother Francis, wish to follow the life and poverty of the most high God, our Lord Jesus Christ and his most holy mother and to persevere in this way to the end. And I beseech you, my ladies, and I counsel you to live always in this most holy life of poverty. Be on your guard against the influence of any strange teaching and advice so that you never deviate from your life of poverty in any way.

St Francis of Assisi, *Letters*

CHANCE

The lot is cast into the lap, but its every decision is from the LORD (Proverbs 16:33).

You may well ask whether anything happens by chance or is unforeseen. Basil the Great spoke the truth when he said that 'fortune' and 'chance' are heathen terms, which can have no room in the believer's mind. If all success is a blessing from God, and tragedies are his curse, there is no place left in human affairs for fortune and chance.

We ought to be influenced by Augustine's teaching that if anything is left to luck, the world moves at random. Men are controlled by Providence, since it would be absurd to believe that anything happens without God's ordination, because then it would happen at random.

For this reason, Augustine excludes any happening which depends on human will, stating that no cause must be looked for except the will of God. He certainly does not picture God sitting idly in a watch-tower, allowing anything to happen.

John Calvin, *The Institutes of Christian Religion*

TE DEUM LAUDAMUS

'Praise our God, all you his servants, you who fear him, both small and great!' (Revelation 19:5).

We praise thee, O God, we acknowledge thee to be the Lord.
All the earth doth worship thee, the Father everlasting.
To thee all angels cry aloud, the heavens and all the powers
   therein;
To thee cherubim and seraphim continually do cry,
Holy, holy, holy, Lord God of Sabaoth:
Heaven and earth are full of the majesty of thy glory.
The glorious company of the apostles praise thee.
The goodly fellowship of the prophets praise thee.
The noble army of martyrs praise thee.
The holy church throughout the world doth acknowledge thee,
The Father of an infinite majesty;
Thine adorable, true and only Son;
Also the Holy Ghost, the Comforter.

Thou art the King of glory, O Christ;
Thou art the everlasting Son of the Father.
When thou tookest upon thee to deliver man
Thou didst humble thyself to be born of a virgin.
When thou hadst overcome the sharpness of death
Thou didst open the kingdom of heaven to all believers.
Thou sittest at the right hand of God in the glory of the Father.
We believe that thou shalt come to be our judge.
We therefore pray thee help thy servants
   whom thou hast redeemed with thy precious blood.
Make them to be numbered with thy saints in glory everlasting.

Unknown author (4th century)

CHRISTIAN PERFECTION

Be perfect, therefore, as your heavenly Father is perfect (Matthew 5:48).

Christian perfection is not the strict, tiring, restrictive thing you suppose; it requires a person to give himself wholeheartedly to God. As soon as this has taken place, that person will find it easy to do whatever else God asks him to do. People who are wholly given over to God are always satisfied, for they desire to do only God's will and they are prepared to do whatever this is.

People who do this are the true children of God and they experience great happiness, even though they may be in the middle of many tribulations. This happiness consists of a clear conscience, a freedom of spirit, pleasure in handing over everything to God, the experience of God's light becoming stronger and stronger in one's life and a complete deliverance from hankering after the things that belong to this world.

God requires an undivided will. A will that desires what God desires and rejects what he rejects. This kind of person makes progress in his spiritual life because he has been delivered from his own passions. He is free from other people's judgments, their heartless mockery, their coldness and the maxims to which they slavishly adhere. From all these evils the Christian is set free. He has handed over his will to God and knows no will except God's. Happy are those who throw themselves headlong, blindfolded into the arms of the 'Father of compassion and God of all comfort' (2 Corinthians 1:3).

Archbishop Fénelon, *Christian Perfection*

IN THE FACE OF DISASTER

We fix our eyes not on what is seen, but on what is unseen. For what is seen is temporary, but what is unseen is eternal (2 Corinthians 4:18).

Despite many disasters I do not relinquish a most firm hope. I keep my mind fixed on the Pilot of all things; he does not ride the storm through humans, but with a mere nod he calms the surging sea. If he does not do this immediately he does so on purpose. He does not cut calamities short at the outset, but averts them only as they make people nearly give up hope. Only then does he display his miraculous power which he alone possesses, while he schools the sufferers in patience.

Do not lose heart then. There is only one thing to be feared, and that is sin. Everything else is beside the point, whether you talk about plots, feuds, betrayals, slanders, abuses, accusations, or universal war. Whatever you may care to mention, they are all passing away. They touch the mortal body but do not harm the watchful soul. So when blessed Paul wanted to stress the insignificance of earthly weal and woe, he summed it up in a single phrase, 'What is seen is temporary.' Why then fear the things which are temporary which will roll on in an ever-flowing stream? Whether pleasant or painful, the present does not last for ever.

Do not be upset then by what is happening. Stop running for help from this person and from that person, for all human endeavour is a mere chasing after shadows. Rather, you should incessantly invoke Jesus whom you adore, that he may but turn his face towards you. Then, in one decisive moment, all your trouble is ended.

St John Chrysostom, *Sermons*

THE LIFE OF GOD IN THE SOUL OF MAN

'How can a man be born when he is old?' Nicodemus asked (John 3:4).

For above a twelvemonth my soul longed to be acquainted with some young men called Methodists, and I was strongly pressed to follow their good example, when I saw them go through a ridiculing crowd to receive the Holy Eucharist at St Mary's. At length, God was pleased to open a door. It happened that a poor woman in one of the workhouses had attempted to cut her throat, but was happily prevented. Upon hearing of this, and knowing that both the Mr Wesleys were ready to every good work, I sent a poor apple-woman of our college to inform Mr Charles Wesley of it, charging her not to discover who sent her. She went; but, contrary to my orders, told my name. He sent an invitation to me by her, to come to breakfast with him next morning.

I thankfully embraced the opportunity; and, blessed be God! it was one of the most profitable visits I ever made in my life. My soul, at that time, was athirst for some spiritual friends to lift up my hands when they hung down, and to strengthen my feeble knees. He soon discovered it, and like a wise winner of souls, made all his discourses tend that way. And when he had put into my hands a book entitled *The Country Parson's Advice to his Parishioners,* which was wonderfully blessed to my soul, I took my leave.

In a short time he let me have another book, entitled, *The Life of God in the Soul of Man;* and, though I had fasted, watched and prayed, and received the Sacrament so long, yet I never knew what true religion was, till God sent me that excellent treatise by the hands of my never-to-be-forgotten friend.

George Whitefield, *Journals*

THIS DESERT EXPERIENCE

I will turn the darkness into light (Isaiah 42:16).

I have a great deal of experience in this matter of bodily affliction, and I know that what I say is true because I have carefully considered it and discussed it afterwards with spiritually-minded people. We are so miserable that our poor little imprisoned souls also share in the miseries of the body. So the changes in the weather and the cycles of the bodily condition often result in affecting the soul. Souls cannot do what they desire for they are constantly suffering. On these occasions, the more we force the soul, the greater will be the damage and the longer it will last. So discretion must be used in order to find out whether or not ill-health is the cause. The poor soul must not be stifled.

So let those who suffer in this way understand that they are physically ill. A change should be made in the hour of prayer, and often that change should be continued for some days afterwards. Let them suffer this desert experience as best they can. For it is a great misfortune to a soul that loves God to see that it lives in such misery. It is frustrated in its desires because it has a wretched guest as the body. . . .

It is very important that no one be distressed or afflicted over dryness or restless and distracting thoughts.

St Teresa of Avila, *The Way of Perfection*

THE BREASTPLATE

'For in him we live and move and have our being' (Acts 17:28).

> I bind unto myself today
> The power of God to hold and lead,
> His eye to watch, his might to stay,
> His ear to hearken to my need.
> The wisdom of my God to teach,
> His hand to guide, his shield to ward;
> The word of God to give me speech,
> His heavenly host to be my guard.
>
> Christ be with me, Christ within me,
> Christ behind me, Christ before me,
> Christ beside me, Christ to win me,
> Christ to comfort and restore me,
> Christ beneath me, Christ above me,
> Christ in quiet, Christ in danger,
> Christ in mouth of friend and stranger.
>
> I bind unto myself the name,
> The strong name of the Trinity;
> By invocation of the same,
> The Three in One, the One in Three,
> Of whom all nature hath creation;
> Eternal Father, Spirit, Word,
> Praise to the Lord of my salvation,
> Salvation is of Christ the Lord.
>
> St Patrick of Ireland

CORRECTION WITH LOVE

Let a righteous man strike me – it is a kindness; let him rebuke me – it is oil on my head. My head will not refuse it (Psalm 141:5).

When a person sees someone who is living a bad life, perhaps making a gift to the church, and does not correct him, he is running away in spirit. 'Running away in spirit' is being afraid. Fear is a kind of inner fright. He is frightened that the other person may take being corrected badly. However, a true shepherd cares for the sheep and does not allow him to get away with evil. With the apostle he says, 'warn those who are idle' (1 Thessalonians 5:14).

So a pastor, or anyone who acts in a pastoral way, should never think that it is a good thing to leave evil unchecked. But, of course, this has to be done from love. Because people sometimes think of those who correct them as their enemies, after, 'warn those who are idle', the apostle says, 'encourage the timid'. Perhaps, after being corrected, the person may be very upset and begin to lose heart, and this is why he needs to be encouraged. The apostle goes on to say, 'help the weak', in case they fall through weakness. If weakness makes them topple over, love should rush to their aid and hug them. In conclusion, the apostle says, 'Make sure that nobody pays back wrong for wrong, but always try to be kind to each other and to everyone else' (1 Thessalonians 5:15).

So correction, if it is offered, is not evil. So what do the good sheep say, when they are corrected by a superior? 'Let him rebuke me – it is oil on my head' (Psalm 141:5).

St Augustine, *Sermons on Psalms*

TAKING PART IN DIVINE SERVICE

They fell down on their faces before the throne and worshipped God (Revelation 7:11).

Our rule declares that nothing should take precedence over our 'Service of God'. This is the name that our father Benedict wanted to give to divine worship, which is offered daily in our oratory, thus indicating how keen he was that we should apply all our hearts to that holy work.

Therefore, Christian friends, I warn and entreat you, always be taken up with the praises of God with pure hearts and earnest minds. Be earnest to present yourself at the worship of the Lord, willingly and reverently. Do not arrive in a lazy frame of mind, sleepy and yawning. Do not truncate your words or miss some out altogether. Do not chant between your teeth or through your nose, with broken or lowered voice, in a lazy and effeminate manner, but enunciate the words of the Holy Spirit with manly, earnest voices, which correspond to the dignity of the subject they are speaking about. Also you must make sure that you are concentrating your mind on what you are chanting and that you are not allowing your thoughts to wander.

I am not just thinking about idle and vain thoughts. Thinking about your duties and your work should be out of your mind during this hour. However, as you go into the choir, I am not advising you to forget what you have read in your books, or the thoughts that have come as a result of my speaking in this lecture room of the Holy Spirit. These thoughts are for your edification, but they do not edify you when you reflect on them as you are chanting. The Holy Spirit is not pleased if you allow them to intrude during this time. Through his holy inspiration we are always able to conform our wills to the divine will.

Through the grace and mercy of him who is the Bridegroom of the Church, our Lord Jesus Christ, who is above all, may God be blessed for ever. Amen.

Bernard of Clairvaux, *The Song of Songs*

CELIA: ALIAS HOLLOWNESS

Do not grumble (1 Corinthians 10:10).

Celia is always telling everyone how provoked she is, what intolerable, shocking things happen to her, how monstrously she is treated and suffers, and what trouble she meets at every point.

She tells you that her patience is quite worn out, and she cannot bear the behaviour of people. Every party that she is at sends her home upset; something or other has been said or done that no reasonable well-bred person ought to bear. Poor people that need her charity are sent away with hasty answers, not because she hasn't the heart to part with her money, but because she is too full of her own troubles to attend to theirs.

Celia has no work other than to receive the income from a huge fortune and yet, by the depressed state of her mind, you would think she had neither food nor home. If you see her look paler than usual, if her lips tremble when she speaks to you, it is because she has just returned from a visit to Lupus, who took no notice of her at all, but talked all the time to Lucinda, who doesn't even possess wealth.

When anything might have so disordered her spirits that she is forced to send for the doctor to make her able to eat, she tells him in great anger against providence that she has never been well since she was born, and that she envies every beggar that she sees in good health.

Such is the restless life of Celia, who has nothing to torment her but her own spirit.

Yet, if one could inspire Celia with a sense of Christian humility, one need do no more to make her as happy as any person in the world. It would make her thankful to God for even half as much good health as she does possess, and help her enjoy more in the future.

William Law, *A Serious Call to a Devout and Holy Life*

HATE

If your brother sins against you, go and show him his fault, just between the two of you. If he listens to you, you have won your brother over (Matthew 18:15).

If you hate somebody else, you damage your own spirit. So, above everything else, we must not hate anybody. Then, without any beam in your own eye, you can clearly see whatever there is in your brother's eye. The light in you does not allow you to remain unconcerned about your brother's faults. But if you hate your brother how dare you correct him when you are so full of such evil hatred? This is clearly stated in scripture: 'Anyone who claims to be in the light but hates his brother is still in the darkness' (1 John 2:9). Hatred is a kind of darkness.

It is impossible to hate someone else without first harming yourself. As you try to ruin him outwardly, you are harming yourself inwardly. But in so far as our spirit is superior to our body, to that extent we should take precautions against it suffering damage. Your spirit is harmed as soon as you hate somebody else.

What are you going to do to the person you hate? Are you going to deprive him of his money? You may take his money from him but you cannot take his faith from him. You may damage his reputation, but you cannot harm his conscience. Whatever you injure, you injure outwardly; but take careful note about what damage you are doing to yourself. You are damaging yourself internally. So you are clearly your own enemy, if you hate someone else. You must not put yourself in such a position.

St Augustine, *Sermons*

ANYWHERE

By the grace of God I am what I am (1 Corinthians 15:10).

Letter to Mr B. (May 10, 1775)

My Dear Sir,

I hope you will find the Lord present at all times, and in all places. When it is so, we are at home everywhere; when it is otherwise, home is a prison, and abroad a wilderness. I know what I ought to desire, and what I do desire. I point him out to others as the all in all; I esteem him as such in my own judgment; but, alas, my experience abounds with complaints.

He is my sun; but clouds, and sometimes walls, intercept him from my view. He is my strength; yet I am prone to lean upon reeds. He is my friend; but on my part there is such coldness and ingratitude, as no other friend could bear. But still he is gracious and shames me with his repeated multiplied goodness.

O for a warmer heart, a more active zeal, a greater deliverance from the effects of this body of sin and death! However, though I cannot say I labour more abundantly than they all, I have reason to say with gratitude: 'by the grace of God I am what I am.' My poor story would be much worse, did not he support, restrain, and watch over me every minute.

John Newton, *Cardiphonia*

DISORDERLY APPETITES

Each of you should learn to control his own body in a way that is holy and honourable, not in passionate lust like the heathen, who do not know God (1 Thessalonians 4:4–5).

The passions and desires, when under control and restrained, are sources of all virtues, and also, when they have broken loose, of all the vices and imperfections of the soul. Every evil desire hurts the soul in five ways, robbing it of the Spirit of God: 1. It fatigues it. 2. Torments it. 3. Blinds it. 4. Defiles it. 5. Weakens it.

As a man dragging a cart up hill, so is that soul on its way to God, who does not throw aside the cares of this life, and does not deny itself.

He who feeds his desires is like a moth, or a fish dazzled by the light which the fishermen throw over the water, that it may not see the ruin which the fishermen have prepared for it.

As soot defiles the most beautiful and perfect face, so the unruly desires of the soul defile and pollute the soul which entertains them, and yet that soul in itself is the most beautiful and perfect image of God.

O that spiritual people knew how they are losing the blessings and fulness of the Spirit, merely because they will not raise up their desires above trifles! And how they might have the sweetness of all things in the pure food of the Spirit – of which the manna was a figure – if they would only abstain from tasting other food.

As it is necessary to till the earth that it may bring forth fruit – for otherwise it will produce nothing but weeds, – so also it is necessary to mortify our desires, that the soul may be clean.

St John of the Cross, *The Dark Night of the Soul*

THE CHRISTIAN PILGRIMAGE

These all died in faith, not having received the promises, but having seen them afar off, and were persuaded of them, and embraced them, and confessed that they were strangers and pilgrims on the earth (Hebrews 11:13, AV).

He who would valiant be
'Gainst all disaster,
Let him in constancy
   Follow the Master.
There's no discouragement
Shall make him once relent
His first avowed intent
   To be a pilgrim.

Who so beset him round
With dismal stories,
Do but themselves confound –
   His strength the more is.
No foes shall stay his might,
Though he with giants fight:
He will make good his right
   To be a pilgrim.

Since, Lord, thou dost defend
Us with thy Spirit,
We know we at the end
   Shall life inherit.
Then fancies flee away!
I'll fear not what men say,
I'll labour night and day
   To be a pilgrim.

John Bunyan

POSSESSIONS AND HEAVENLY WEALTH

As we have the opportunity, let us do good to all people, especially to those who belong to the family of believers (Galatians 6:10).

The holiness of Christianity consecrates all conditions and employments of life to God, and it requires us to aspire after complete obedience, doing and using everything as the servants of God. So we are required to observe this religious exactness in the use of our possessions and wealth.

The reason for this is quite simple. We need only consider the fact that our wealth is as much the gift of God as are our eyes or our hands. Our money is no more to be buried or thrown away at pleasure, than we are to put out our eyes, or throw away our limbs as we please.

First, because the way we spend our money or possessions involves our daily affairs. If reason and religion govern us in this, then reason and religion have a great hold on us. But if our selfish whims and fancies or our pride are the standards we employ then those standards will direct most of our living.

Secondly, our wealth is capable of great and excellent things; it is a great means of doing good. If we waste it we do not waste an insignificant trifle, we waste what could bring eyes to the blind, relief to the widow and help to the orphan. We waste not only what enables us to serve worldly comfort to those in distress, but we waste what might gain for ourselves everlasting treasures in heaven. So if we part with our money in foolish ways, we part with a great power to comfort our fellow-men, and to make ourselves for ever blessed.

William Law, *A Serious Call to a Devout and Holy Life*

NOT ALL SINGING, NOT ALL SIGHING

Jesus Christ is the same, yesterday and today and for ever (Hebrews 13:8).

Letter to Mr B (November 6, 1777)

My Dear Sir,

You say you are more disposed to cry, Lord have mercy on me, than, hallelujah. Why not both together? When the treble praise, and the heart-humiliation for the bass, the melody is pleasant, and the harmony is good. However, if both are not together, we must have them alternately; not all singing, not all sighing, but an interchange and balance, that we may be neither lifted too high nor cast down too low – which would be the case if we were very comfortable or very sorrowful for a long time.

But though we change, the Saviour changes not. All our concerns are in his hands, and therefore safe. His path is in the deep waters, his thoughts and methods of conduct are as high above ours as the heavens are high above the earth; and he often takes a course for accomplishing his purpose directly contrary to what our narrow views would prescribe. He wounds in order to heal, kills that he may make alive, casts down when he designs to raise, brings a death upon our feelings, wishes and prospects, when he is about to give us the desire of our hearts.

John Newton, *Cardiphonia*

THE LIGHT OF PEACE

Let us behave decently, as in the daytime, not in orgies and drunkenness, not in sexual immorality and debauchery, not in dissension and jealousy (Romans 13:13).

I threw myself down under a fig tree and collapsed in tears. 'How long, O Lord, how long will you be angry? For ever? Do not hold against us our former sins' – for I felt I was bound by them. 'Tomorrow, and tomorrow? Why not now? Why isn't there an end to my dirtiness here and now?'

I was talking like this and crying with most heartfelt bitterness when I heard a voice (perhaps a child's voice, I'm not sure) coming from a nearby house. It was chanting and repeating the words 'Pick it up and read it!' Immediately my face changed and I began seriously to wonder whether children used these words in any of their games, but I couldn't remember ever hearing anything like them. So, subduing my tears, I got up, thinking it must be nothing other than a command from God to open the book and read the first chapter I found.

Then I ran back to where Alypius was sitting; for, when I left him, I had left the Apostle's book lying there. I picked it up, opened it, and silently read the passage [Romans 13:13–14] I first set eyes on: 'Let us behave decently, as in the daytime, not in orgies and drunkenness, not in sexual immorality and debauchery, not in dissension and jealousy. Rather, clothe yourselves with the Lord Jesus Christ, and do not think about how to gratify the desires of the sinful nature.' I didn't want to read any further, and it wasn't necessary. As I reached the end of the sentence, the light of peace seemed to shine on my heart, and every shadow of doubt disappeared.

St Augustine, *Sermons*

THE CRUEL DEATH OF FAITHFUL

They were stoned; they were sawn in two; they were put to death by the sword. They went about in sheepskins and goatskins, destitute, persecuted and illtreated – the world was not worthy of them. They wandered in deserts and mountains, and in caves and holes in the ground (Hebrews 11:37–38).

The jury went out. Their names were Mr Blindman, Mr Nogood, Mr Malice, Mr Lovelust, Mr Liveloose, Mr Heady, Mr Highmind, Mr Enmity, Mr Liar, Mr Cruelty, Mr Hatelight and Mr Implacable. When they had talked together, each one gave in his personal verdict against the accused and then they unanimously voted to give the judge a verdict of guilty.

So Faithful was quickly condemned. So they brought him out to deal with him according to their law. First they whipped him, then they beat him, then they lanced his flesh with knives. After that they stoned him, then pierced him with their swords, and finally they burned him to ashes at the stake. So it was that Faithful came to his end.

Now I saw that behind the crowds a chariot and two horses stood waiting for Faithful. As soon as his enemies had killed him, Faithful was taken up into the chariot. Immediately he was carried through the clouds and to the sound of the trumpet was taken by the nearest way to the Celestial Gate.

John Bunyan, *The Pilgrim's Progress*

CHRIST AS MEDIATOR

For there is one God and one mediator between God and men, the man Christ Jesus (1 Timothy 2:5).

Christ's work as Mediator was unique: it was to restore us to divine favour and to make us sons of God, instead of sons of men; heirs of a heavenly kingdom instead of heirs of hell. The Son of God could only become Mediator by becoming the Son of man. He so received what is ours as to transfer to us what is his. What is his by nature can become ours by grace.

Relying on this pledge, we trust that we are the sons of God, because the Son of God took upon himself a body like our body, flesh of our flesh, bone of our bone, that he might be one with us. He did not refuse to take what was distinctive to us, so that he in turn could give us what was distinctive to him. Thus he became both Son of God and Son of man, like us.

It was essential that the one who was to be our redeemer should be truly God and truly man. He was to swallow up death, and only life could do that. He was to conquer sin, and only righteousness could do that. He was to scatter the powers of the air and earth and only a mighty power, superior to both, could do that. But God alone possesses life and righteousness, and the total rule of heaven. So God, in his infinite mercy, having resolved to redeem us, became our redeemer himself, in the person of his only begotten Son.

John Calvin, *The Institutes of Christian Religion*

MY LORD AND SAVIOUR

I have loved you with an everlasting love; I have drawn you with loving-kindness (Jeremiah 31:3).

One night as Bunyan retired to rest there came to him the quieting assurance: 'I have loved thee with an everlasting love,' and next morning it was still fresh upon his soul.

Again when doubts came as to whether the blood of Christ was sufficient to save him, there came also the words, 'He is able.' 'Methought this word able was spoke loud unto me – it showed a great word, it seemed to be writ in great letters.'

One day as he was passing into the field, still with some fears in his heart, suddenly this sentence fell into his soul, '"Thy righteousness is in heaven": and methought withal I saw with the eye of my soul, Jesus Christ at God's right hand.

'I saw, moreover, that it was not my good frame of heart that made my righteousness better, nor yet my bad frame that made my righteousness worse; for my righteousness was Jesus Christ himself, the same yesterday, today, and for ever. Now did my chains fall from my legs indeed; I was loosed from my afflictions and irons.

'Oh, methought, Christ! Christ! there was nothing but Christ that was before my eyes! Now Christ was all; all my wisdom, all my righteousness, all my sanctification, and all my redemption!'

John Brown, *John Bunyan*

MYSTIC CONTEMPLATION

The LORD will be your everlasting light (Isaiah 60:20).

Do thou, in the intent practice of mystic contemplation, leave behind the senses and the operations of the intellect, and all things that the senses or the intellect can perceive, and all things which are not and things which are, and strain upwards in unknowing, as far as may be, towards the union with him who is above all being and knowledge. For by unceasing and absolute withdrawal from thyself and all things in purity, abandoning all and set free from all, thou wilt be borne up to the ray of the divine darkness that surpasseth all being.

Unto this darkness which is beyond light we pray that we may come and through loss of sight and knowledge may see and know that which transcends sight and knowledge, by the very fact of not seeing and knowing; for this is real sight and knowledge.

The divine darkness is the unapproachable light in which God is said to dwell. In this everyone enters who is found worthy to know and to see God by not knowing or seeing him, really being him who is above sight and knowledge.

Pseudo-Dionysius

PLEASING GOD

'And when you pray, do not keep on babbling like pagans, for they think they will be heard because of their many words' (Matthew 6:7).

Daughter, you cannot please God better than to think constantly about his love. Our Lord said, 'Ponder your own wickedness and ponder my goodness.'

Daughter, if you wear a hair shirt, fast with just bread and water, and if you said one thousand Our Fathers every day, you would not please Me so well as you do when you are in silence, and allow me to speak to your soul.

Daughter, people who can do nothing else, should frequently use their rosary, but this is not the way of perfection. But it is a step along the road towards perfection. I assure you, daughter, that people who fast and do penance long for the best in life; people who give themselves to numerous devotions long for the best in life; people who give alms long for the best in life. I have frequently told you, daughter, that meditating, weeping and contemplation are the best things you can do on earth. Yet, I fear that you do not believe me, because you continue so often with your rosary. Daughter, if you knew how sweet your love is to me, you would never do anything else except love me with all your heart.

She pondered deeply that our Lord became man, suffering terrible pain, for such an unkind creature as her. Then, with many tears, she asked how she might best please him. He answered her soul, 'Ponder your own wickedness and ponder my goodness.'

Margery Kempe, *The Booke of Margery Kempe*

NEGLECT AND CARELESSNESS

Serve the LORD with fear and rejoice with trembling (Psalm 2:11).

To Gregoria, Lady-in-Waiting to Augusta (593)
When your Ladyship threatens in your letters to give me no peace until I assure you that the forgiveness of your sins has been revealed to me, you make a request that is difficult and to no purpose: difficult, in the first place, because I am unworthy of revelations; pointless, I tell you, because you are not meant to be unconcerned about your sins, except possibly on the last day of your life when you can no longer muster strength to grieve over them. But until then, your offences should always arouse compunction, and ever in fear and trembling you should daily wash them away in your tears.

Paul the apostle, as you know, was caught up to the third heaven and led into Paradise, where he heard secret words unlawful for man to utter; yet for all that, he was kept in suspense. 'I beat my body,' he declared, 'and make it my slave so that after I have preached to others, I myself will not be disqualified from the prize' (1 Corinthians 9:27). He had been carried up to heaven itself, yet he still experienced unrest, and has anyone who lives on earth any right to be free from fear?

Weigh my words well, most beloved daughter: very often security is the mother of negligence. Therefore in this world you are not meant to feel safe; that would give birth to carelessness. 'Blessed is the man who always fears the Lord' (Proverbs 28:14) says holy Writ. Your soul then must be filled with uncertainty during the brief sojourn of this life, if it is afterwards to rejoice in the happiness of safety for evermore.

May Almighty God fill your soul with the grace of his Holy Spirit, and when the tears you have shed in prayer are wiped away, may he bring you to joy everlasting.

St Gregory the Great, *Letters*

A POPE'S PROBLEMS

Therefore confess your sins to each other and pray for each other so that you may be healed (James 5:16).

Gregory to John, Bishop of Constantinople (590)
Unequal as I am to a task from which my whole soul recoils, I have been forced to take upon my shoulders the burden of the pastoral office. The more I ruminate over this and many other things, the more impossible I find it to be what I should be. This is especially so in these days, for in spite of bearing the title of Pastor, a man's time is so eaten up in external administration that it may be questioned whether he holds the office of Pastor or of worldly magnate.

As pastor, he must strive his utmost to avoid being weighed down excessively by the external cares from which no one who wields authority over his fellow men can be entirely free; but in my position so many problems have to be dealt with every day that they both overwhelm the mind and sap the strength of the body. I grow weary beneath the heavy load of pastoral care.

Therefore, venerable brother, help me by your prayerful intercession, for otherwise the burden may prove to be beyond my strength. Bearing in mind the scriptural command, 'pray for each other so that you may be healed', I also give you what I ask from you. And in giving, I shall recover the gift, for when we are linked by the power of prayer, we as it were hold each other's hand as we walk side by side along a slippery path. As it becomes harder each leans on the other and so we are bound together even closer in brotherly love.

St Gregory the Great, *Letters*

PROVED BY FIRE

These [sufferings] have come so that your faith – of greater worth than gold, which perishes even though refined by fire – may be proved genuine and may result in praise, glory and honour (1 Peter 1:7).

To start with there are many battles and a good deal of suffering for people advancing towards God; afterwards they receive joy beyond description. It is like people wanting to light a fire; at first they are choked by the smoke and cry. We must also kindle the divine fire in ourselves through tears and hard work.

Just as the most bitter medicine drives out poisonous creatures so prayer combined with fasting drives evil thoughts away.

Do not let yourself be seduced by the delights of the riches of the world, as if they contained something useful. Do not fill yourself with bread and you will not desire wine.

In answering the question, 'Is poverty a perfect good?', I reply: For the person who is capable of it, it is the perfect good. Those who can sustain it receive suffering in the body but rest in the soul, for just as one washes coarse clothes by trampling them underfoot and turning them about in all directions, so the strong soul becomes much more stable as a result of voluntary poverty.

Syncletica, in *Sayings of the Desert Fathers*

'HE MADE US'

In the beginning God created the heavens and the earth. . . .
And God saw that it was good (Genesis 1:1, 25).

But what do I love when I love thee? Not grace of bodies, nor the beauty of the seasons, nor the brightness of the light, nor inexhaustible melodies of sweet song, nor the fragrant smell of flowers, of ointments and spices. None of these love I when I love my God: and yet I love a kind of light, and of melody and of fragrance when I love my God.

And what is this? I asked the earth and it said, 'I am not he:' and whatsoever is in it confessed the same. I asked the sea and the deeps, and all that swimming or creeping live therein, and they answered 'We are not thy God, seek above us.' I asked the wandering winds; and the whole air with his inhabitants spoke: 'I am not God.' I asked the heavens, sun, moon and stars, 'Nor (say they) are we the God whom thou seekest.' And I replied unto all those things which encompass the door of my flesh, 'Ye have told me of my God, that you are not he: tell me something of him.'

And they cried all with a great voice, 'He made us.' My questioning them was my mind's desire, and their beauty was their answer.

St Augustine, *The City of God*

THE MIND AND SPIRITUAL EXPERIENCES

If any of you lacks wisdom, he should ask God, who gives generously to all without finding fault, and it will be given to him (James 1:5).

In mystical theology, the understanding stops working because God suspends it. . . . But we must not imagine that we ourselves can bring about this suspension. That must not be done. Nor must we allow the understanding to cease working, or we shall be stupid and cold and the result will be neither the one thing nor the other. But when our Lord suspends the understanding and makes it stop working, he puts before it what astonishes and occupies it. Without thinking very long, then, the mind can comprehend more than we would comprehend in all our years with all our human efforts. . . .

I repeat my advice. It is very important that we do not attempt to raise our spirits ourselves if God does not raise them for us. If he does, then there will be no mistaking it. For women this is especially wrong, because the devil can delude them. I am certain, however, that our Lord will never allow us to be hurt if we try to draw near to God in humility. On the contrary, we will derive more profit and advantage out of Satan's attempt to bring us down.

I have dwelt long upon this matter because of the importance of it.

St Teresa of Avila, *Life*

THE ORDER OF GOD

'Not everyone who says to me, "Lord, Lord," will enter the kingdom of heaven, but only he who does the will of my Father who is in heaven' (Matthew 7:21).

Perfection does not consist in knowledge of God's Order but in submission to it.

The Order of God, the good pleasure of God, the will of God, the action of God, grace, all these are one and the same thing in this life. Perfection is nothing other than the faithful cooperation of the soul with the work of God. This ultimate purpose of our life grows and increases in our souls secretly and without our knowledge.

The Order of God (which is his divine will) accepted with simplicity by a faithful soul effects this divine purpose in her without her knowledge just as a drug obediently taken by an invalid effects his recovery without it being necessary for him to know the science of medicine. Just as fire warms us, and not the philosophical analysis or knowledge of that element and its effects, so also is it the Order of God, his holy will, which produces sanctity in our souls and not intellectual speculation regarding the principle or purpose of holiness. If one wishes to quench one's thirst, one must put books on one side and drink.

We must put speculation on one side, and drink with simplicity the cup of action and suffering which the Order of God presents us. What happens to us at each moment by God's Order is precisely what for us is the holiest, the best, the most divine thing that could happen.

Jean-Pierre de Caussade, *The Sacrament of the Present Moment*

TWO FEARS

Worship God acceptably with reverence and awe (Hebrews 12:28).

Letter to Rev R. (April 15, 1776)
My Dear Sir

It is written: 'Fear not, I am with thee.' It is written again: 'Blessed is the man who feareth always.' There is perfect harmony in those seemingly different texts. May the wisdom that comes from above teach you and me to keep them both united in our view.

If the Lord be with us, we have no reason to fear. His eye is upon us, his arm over us, his ear open to our prayer; his grace sufficient, his promise unchangeable. Under his protection, though the path of duty should lie through fire and water, we may cheerfully and confidently pursue it.

On the other hand, our hearts are so deceitful, fallible, and frail, our spiritual enemies so subtle, watchful, and powerful, and they derive so many advantages from the occasions of every day, in which we are unavoidably concerned. There is so much combustible within, and so many temptations arising from without, capable of setting all in a flame. With the Psalmist we can say, 'Hold me up', and we can draw his conclusion, 'and I shall be safe'; but the moment we lean to our own understanding, we are in imminent danger of falling.

John Newton, *Cardiphonia*

LOVING GOD

Teach me, O LORD, to follow your decrees (Psalm 119:33).

Devotion consists in a certain excelling degree of charity, it not only makes us ready, active and diligent in observing all the commandments of God; but it also prompts us to do readily and heartily as many good works as we can, even though they are not actually ordered.

For just as a person who has recently recovered from some illness only walks as much as is necessary, slowly and heavily, in the same way a sinner, who has been recently healed of his iniquity, just walks where God commands him, and does so slowly and heavily, until he attains to devotion. Then he becomes like a healthy person who not only walks, but runs and leaps: 'I run in the path of your commands, for you have set my heart free' (Psalm 119:32). He makes progress and runs in the paths of heavenly counsels and inspirations. In short, charity and devotion can no longer be distinguished from each other. They become like a flame is to the fire. For charity, since it is spiritual fire, when it breaks into flame, is called devotion. So devotion adds nothing to the fire of charity, except the flame which makes charity alert, active and diligent, not only observing God's commands, but in practising the heavenly counsels and inspirations.

St Francis de Sales, *Introduction to a Devout Life*

RULES FOR A CHRISTIAN LIFE

Direct me in the path of your commands, for there I find delight (Psalm 119:35).

To an Officer (July 25th, 1700)
1. Be steadfast in your religious exercises: that is, in reading, daily meditation, regular confession and attendance at communion.
2. Let your meditation always be systematic, appropriate for your needs and with a view to mental humility and the repression of bodily sensuality.
3. Let what you glean from your reading be put into practice in your life so that your faults are corrected. Apply everything that you read to yourself.
4. Be careful about the company you keep and be especially on your guard about the women with whom you are intimate.
5. Avoid making harsh judgments about other people and let your recollection of your own faults prevent you from being fastidious and censorious.
6. Make it a habit to withhold judgment on everything on which you are not required to pass judgment.
7. Avoid the dissipation which sudden desires always bring with them.
8. Never seek to change your job out of worry, depression or an itching desire to be somebody. All careers which you have not tried have their thorns and snares which you are unable to appreciate from the outside. As Jesus Christ, our Lord, has said, 'Each day has enough trouble of its own' (Matthew 6:34). For today think only about today.
9. Endeavour to put your affairs in order without letting your heart become engrossed in them.

Archbishop Fénelon, *Christian Perfection*

A GUIDE TO DEVOTION

Seven times a day I praise you for your righteous laws (Psalm 119:164).

Prayer is the ascent of the mind to God. It is an abstract and summary of Christian religion. Prayer is an act of religion and divine worship, confessing his power and mercy; it celebrates his attributes, and confesses his glories, and reveres his person, and implores his aid, and gives thanks for his blessings.

Suppose every day to be a day of business: for your whole life is a race and a battle, a merchandise and a journey. Every day propound to yourself a set of good works to present to God at night. As you open your eyes, enter the day with some act of piety. Those parts of the Scriptures which you use in your prayers, let them not be long: a chapter at once, no more. But then what time you can afford, spend it in thinking and meditating on the holy precepts you have read.

Fasting and giving money away are the wings of prayer.

Receive the blessed sacrament as often as you can.

Confess your sins often, hear the word of God, make religion the business of your life, your study and chiefest care; and be sure that in all things a spiritual guide takes you by the hand. You will always rejoice in the evening if you have spent the day virtuously.

Jeremy Taylor, *Holy Living*

JESUS IS LORD

Who is the liar? It is the man who denies that Jesus is the Christ. Such a man is the antichrist – he denies the Father and the Son. No-one who denies the Son has the Father; whoever acknowledges the Son has the Father also (1 John 2:22–23).

I believe in thee, O Jesus, and I rejoice in thy dear name, which is so full and expressive of thy love.

Thou art Jesus our Saviour, because thou camest into the world to save us from our sins: all love, all glory, be to thee.

O be thou ever Jesus to me; O let me feel the kind force of that sweet name, in which I and all sinners do find our deliverance and our salvation and the remedy for our guilt.

I believe that thou, O Jesus, wast anointed with the Holy Spirit, that all his gifts and graces were poured out, and diffused like a sweet ointment on thy soul, without measure; thou art altogether lovely, O Christ, and of thy fullness we all receive; all love, all glory, be to thee.

By the love of thy cross, O Jesu, I live; in that I will only glory, that above all things will I study, that before all things will I value; by the love of thy cross I will take up my cross daily, and follow thee.

Thomas Ken, *Sermons*

THE CROSS OF CHRIST

No-one has ever gone into heaven except the one who came from heaven – the Son of Man. Just as Moses lifted up the snake in the desert, so the Son of Man must be lifted up, that everyone who believes in him may have eternal life (John 3:13–14).

Above everything else, our Saviour's cross is the throne of delights. That centre of eternity, that Tree of Life in the middle of God's paradise. There we are entertained with the wonder of the ages. There we enter into the heart of the universe.

'When I am lifted up,' says the Son of Man, 'I will draw all men unto me.' But by what cords? The cords of a man, the cords of love. The cross is the abyss of wonders, the centre of desires, the school of virtues, the house of wisdom, the throne of love, the theatre of joys, and the place of sorrows; it is the root of happiness and the gate of heaven. It is the ensign lifted up for all nations.

There we may see God's goodness, wisdom, and power displayed. There we may see man's sin and infinite value. It is a well of life beneath, in which we may see the face of heaven above: and the only mirror wherein all things appear in their proper colours; that is, sprinkled in the blood of our Lord and Saviour. That cross is a tree set on fire with invisible flame, that illuminates all the world. The flame is love: the love in his heart who died on it.

Thomas Traherne, *Centuries*

PRAYER

Trust in him at all times, O people; pour out your hearts to him, for God is our refuge (Psalm 62:8).

Prayer is correctly defined by Damascene as 'the ascent of the mind to God.' When the soul sets aside all other thoughts, and communicates only with God, then it is right to say that you are praying. In praying we come as close as we can to the principal end of our creation, which was to converse and enjoy communion with God, and to praise and extol his name.

But the great question is, How you and I may so perform it, that it may be acceptable to him. For we must not think that he is well pleased with everything that goes under the name of prayer among us, which I think was so much debased before, as it has been and still is in our age. For some make a long oration, seemingly directed to the great God, of what comes next to their tongues' end, and this without more ado they call by the sacred name of prayer; whereas, alas, there is nothing of all this but a man may do and yet not pray at all.

For prayer is certainly the greatest work that it is possible for creatures to be engaged in; and therefore for its correct performance is required the greatest composure of the mind, seriousness of the will, and ardency of affections, as well as the most solemn expressions of reverence and humility imaginable. So it is the hardest as well as the highest work that can be engaged in. It can never be correctly entered into without a great deal of care and study.

William Beveridge, *Meditations*

MEDITATION

One thing I ask of the LORD, this is what I seek: that I may dwell in the house of the LORD all the days of my life (Psalm 27:4).

In a religious sense, meditation is such an application of the mind to the consideration of any divine subject, as may best dispose us firmly to believe and embrace it, and stir up all the faculties of the soul to a vigorous execution of it. It consists in exciting holy movements in our souls, by virtue of those good thoughts we entertain and dwell on: and indeed without this practice the holy Scriptures and other devout books will have but little effect on us. For it is in this way that we digest what we read and turn it into nourishment for our minds.

Prepare your mind for this duty, by imploring God's assistance.

I firmly believe, O God, that thou art here, and everywhere present; that thy being and thy power is infinite. I adore thee with all humility as my sovereign Lord, and acknowledge that I am unworthy to appear before thee, because of my many sins; but for the sake of the blessed Jesus be gracious to me, and so enlighten my understanding, and influence my will and affections, that the present action may be to thy glory and for the good of my own soul.

Robert Nelson, *Meditations*

THANKSGIVING AND INTERCESSION

Jesus asked, 'Were not all ten cleansed? Where are the other nine? Was no-one found to return and give praise to God except this foreigner?' (Luke 17:17–18).

Would you know who is the greatest saint in the world? It is he who is always thankful to God, who wills everything that God wills, who receives everything as an instance of God's goodness, and has a heart always ready to praise God for it.

If anyone would tell you the shortest, surest way to all happiness and all perfection, he must tell you to make it a rule for you to thank and praise God for everything that happens to you. For it is certain that whatever seeming calamity happens to you, if you thank and praise God for it, you turn it into a blessing.

For this reason I exhort you to this method in your devotion, that every day may be a day of thanksgiving, and thus the spirit of grumbling and discontent may be unable to enter into the heart which is so often employed in singing the praises of God.

Be daily on your knees in a solemn deliberate performance of this devotion, praying for others with the same earnestness as you pray for yourself. Then you will find that all your evil passions will die away, your heart will grow great and generous, delighting in the common happiness of others, as you used to delight only in your own happiness. For you cannot possibly despise and ridicule that man whom your private prayers recommend to the love and favour of God.

William Law, *A Serious Call to a Devout and Holy Life*

FOLLOWING GOD

Whether you turn to the right or to the left, your ears will hear a voice behind you, saying, 'This is the way; walk in it' (Isaiah 30:21).

How can we come to perceive God's direct leading?

By careful looking at home, and abiding within the gates of your own soul. Therefore, let a man be at home in his own heart, and cease from his restless chasing after and searching for outward things. If he is thus at home while on earth, he will surely come to see what there is to do at home – what God commands him inwardly without means, and also outwardly by the help of means; and then let him surrender himself, and follow God along whatever path his loving Lord thinks fit to lead him: whether it be to contemplation or action, to usefulness or enjoyment; whether in sorrow or in joy, let him follow on. And if God does not give him thus to feel his hand in all things, let him still simply yield himself up, and go without, for God's sake, out of love, and still press forward.

Johann Tauler, *Sermons*

LOVED BY GOD

The eternal God is your refuge, and underneath are the everlasting arms (Deuteronomy 33:27).

Here is the heaven of heaven! This is the saint's fruition of God; it consists in these sweet, mutual, constant actions and embracings of love. To love, and to be loved: these are the everlasting arms that are underneath (Deuteronomy 33:27). His left hand is under their heads, and with his right hand doth he embrace them (Song of Songs 2:6).

Reader, stop here and think a moment what a state this is. Is it a small thing in your eyes to be loved by God – to be the son, the spouse, the love, the delight of the King of glory? Christian, believe this, and think about it: you will be eternally embraced in the arms of the love which was from everlasting, and will extend to everlasting – of the love which brought the Son of God's love from heaven to earth, from earth to the cross, from the cross to the grave, from the grave to glory – that love which was weary, hungry, tempted, scorned, scourged, buffeted, spat upon, crucified, pierced – which fasted, prayed, taught, healed, wept, sweated, bled, died. That love will eternally embrace you.

When perfect, created love and most perfect, uncreated love meet together, what a blessed meeting it will be!

Richard Baxter, *The Saints' Everlasting Rest*

FAITH, HOPE, LOVE

And now these three remain: faith, hope and love. But the greatest of these is love (1 Corinthians 13:13).

He said that only faith, hope and love need to be fed to become completely given over to God's will. Everything else is unimportant. You should stay with faith and hope, just as you quickly cross over a bridge in order to reach your final destination. Everything is possible to the person who believes, even more is possible to the person who hopes and still more to the person who possesses all three virtues: faith, hope and love. The aim set before us in this life is to worship God as perfectly as possible, as we hope to do throughout eternity.

As we set out on our spiritual pilgrimage we should reflect on what kind of people we are. Then we will quickly discover that we only deserve to be held in contempt and are unworthy to bear the name Christian. We discover that we are prone to all kinds of distress, endless circumstances which disturb us and which affect our bodily health and shatter our peace of mind as well. It is through being brought low through troubles and difficulties that God works. So we should never be surprised if troubles, opposition, temptations and difficulties cross our path. Rather, we should embrace them and submit to them and endure them for as long as God wills it, since such experiences are for our well-being. The more the soul seeks to be perfect the more it will rely on God's grace to accomplish this.

Brother Lawrence, *The Practice of the Presence of God*

MY DANCING DAY (I)

When all the people were being baptised, Jesus was baptised too. And as he was praying, heaven was opened and the Holy Spirit descended on him in bodily form like a dove (Luke 3:21–22).

Tomorrow shall be my dancing day:
    I would my true love did so chance
To see the legend of my play,
    To call my true love to my dance:

Sing O my love, O my love, my love, my love;
This have I done for my true love.

Then was I born of a virgin pure,
    Of her I took fleshly substance;
Thus was I knit to man's nature,
    To call my true love to my dance:

In a manger laid and wrapped I was,
    So very poor, this was my chance,
Betwixt an ox and a silly poor ass,
    To call my true love to my dance:

Then afterwards baptised I was;
    The Holy Ghost on me did glance,
My Father's voice heard from above,
    To call my true love to my dance:

Into the desert I was led,
    Where I fasted without substance;
The devil bade me make stones my bread,
    To call my true love to my dance:

Anonymous (15th century)

MY DANCING DAY (II)

**One of the soldiers pierced Jesus' side with a spear, bringing a
sudden flow of blood and water (John 19:34).**

The Jews on me they made great suit,
    And with me made great variance,
Because they loved darkness rather than light,
    To call my true love to my dance:

Sing O my love, O my love, my love, my love;
This have I done for my true love.

For thirty pence Judas me sold,
    His covetousness for to advance;
'Mark whom I kiss, the same do hold,'
    The same is he shall lead the dance.

Before Pilate the Jews me brought,
    Where Barabbas had deliverance;
They scourged me and set me at nought,
    Judged me to die to lead the dance:

Then on the cross hanged I was,
    Where a spear to my heart did glance;
There issued forth both water and blood,
    To call my true love to my dance:

Then down to hell I took my way
    For my true love's deliverance,
And rose again on the third day,
    Up to my true love and the dance:

Then up to heaven I did ascend,
    Where now I dwell in sure substance,
On the right hand of God, that man
    May come unto the general dance:

Anonymous (15th century)

AWAKE IN HEAVEN

Then I saw a new heaven and a new earth, for the first heaven and the first earth had passed away (Revelation 21:1).

Your enjoyment of the world is never right, till every morning you awake in heaven; see yourself in your Father's palace; and look upon the skies, the earth and the air as heavenly joys: having such a reverend esteem of all, as if you were among the angels. The bride of a monarch, in her husband's chamber, has no such causes of delight as you.

You never enjoy the world right, till the Sea itself flows in your veins, till you are clothed with the heavens, and crowned with the stars: and perceive yourself to be the sole heir of the whole world, and more than so, because men are in it who are every one sole heirs as well as you. Till you can sing and rejoice and delight in God, as misers do in gold, and kings in sceptres, you never enjoy the world.

All things were made to be yours, and you were made to prize them according to their value: which is your office and duty, the end for which you were created, and the means whereby you enjoy. The end for which you were created, is that by prizing all that God has done, you may enjoy yourself and him in blessedness.

Thomas Traherne, *Centuries*

YOUR FAULTS

. . . whenever our hearts condemn us (1 John 3:20).

Do not be discouraged at your faults; bear with yourself in correcting them, as you would with your neighbour. Lay aside this ardour of mind, which exhausts your body, and leads you to make mistakes. Accustom yourself gradually to carry prayer into all your daily occupations. Speak, move, work, in peace, as if you were in prayer, as indeed you ought to be. Do everything without excitement, by the spirit of grace. As soon as you perceive your natural impetuosity gliding in, retire quietly within, where is the kingdom of God. Listen to the leadings of grace, then say and do nothing but what the Holy Spirit shall put in your heart. You will find that you will become more tranquil, that your words will be fewer and more effectual, and that, with less effort, you will accomplish more good.

Archbishop Fénelon, *Christian Perfection*

TURNING TO GOD

In those days John the Baptist came, preaching in the Desert of Judea and saying, 'Repent, for the kingdom of heaven is near.' (Matthew 3:1–2).

Repentance itself is nothing else but a kind of circling; to return to him by repentance, from whom by sin we have turned away. This circle consists of two things. These two things need to be in two different movements. One is done with the whole heart, while the other is broken and torn. So both things cannot happen at the same time.

First of all you must turn. In this you look forward to God and with your whole heart resolve to turn to him. Then, you must turn again, and this time you look backwards to your sins, in which we have turned away from God. As we look at them our actual heart breaks. One turn is conversion from sin, and the other turn is contrition for sin. One resolves to amend what is to come while the other reflects on and is sorrowful over the past. One resists future evil while the other passes sentence on itself for the evil that it has already done. Between them, these two make up complete repentance, or a perfect revolution.

Lancelot Andrewes, *Sermons*

GOD'S PART, OUR PART

You are in Christ Jesus, who has become for us wisdom from God – that is, our righteousness, holiness and redemption (1 Corinthians 1:30).

If many books, much study, and great discernment were necessary in order to be happy, what must the poor and simple do? Yet for them especially is the Gospel designed; and few but such as these attain the knowledge and comfort of it.

The Bible is a sealed book till the heart is awakened, and then he who runs may read it. The propositions are few; I am a sinner, therefore I need a Saviour, one who is able and willing to save to the uttermost: such a one is Jesus; he is all that I want, wisdom, righteousness, sanctification, and redemption.

But will he receive me? Can I answer a prior question? Am I willing to receive him? If so, and if his word may be taken, if he meant what he said, the doubts, fears, and suspicions which would arise in my mind when I should come to know what I am, what I have done, and what I have deserved; and there he declared, before he left earth: 'Him that cometh to me I will in no wise cast out.' I have no money in my hand, no worthiness to recommend me; and I need none, for he saves freely, for his own name's sake. I have only to be thankful for what he has already shown me, and to wait upon him for more. It is my part to commit myself to him as the physician of sin-sick souls, not to prescribe to him how he shall treat me. To begin, carry on, and perfect the cure, is his part.

John Newton, *Cardiphonia*

HARVEST

The land produced vegetation: plants bearing seed according to their kinds and trees bearing fruit with seed in it according to their kinds (Genesis 1:12).

We plough the fields, and scatter
  The good seed on the land,
But it is fed and watered
  By God's almighty hand;
He sends the snow in winter,
  The warmth to swell the grain,
The breezes and the sunshine,
  And soft refreshing rain:
    All good gifts around us
      Are sent from heaven above,
      Then thank the Lord, O thank the Lord,
        For all his love.

He only is the Maker
  Of all things near and far,
He paints the wayside flower,
  He lights the evening star.
The winds and waves obey him,
  By him the birds are fed;
Much more to us, his children,
  He gives our daily bread:

We thank thee then, O Father,
  For all things bright and good;
The seed-time and the harvest,
  Our life, our health, our food.
No gifts have we to offer
  For all thy love imparts,
But that which thou desirest,
  Our humble, thankful hearts:

Matthias Claudius, translated by Jane Campbell

RESPONDING TO CHRIST'S LOVE

'Greater love has no-one than this, that he lay down his life for his friends' (John 15:13).

'Daughter, I have suffered many pains for thy love, therefore you have good reason to love me completely, for it has cost me dearly to purchase your love.'

'Dear Lord,' she said, 'I beseech you, let me never have any other joy on earth, except mourning and crying for your love; for I know, Lord, that even if I was in hell, if I could just cry and mourn there for your love as I do here, hell would not disturb me, but it would be like heaven. For your love dispels all fear of our spiritual enemy. I would rather be in hell, for as long as it pleases you, than be in this world and displease you. Therefore, good Lord, may it be done according to your will.' She often prayed the following prayer: 'Lord, on account of your great goodness, have mercy on my great wickedness.'

When she saw the crucifix, or if she saw a wounded man or animal, or if a man beat a child in front of her, or if she saw or heard a horse being whipped, she thought that she saw our Lord beaten or wounded, just as she saw the man or horse being beaten.

Margery Kempe, *The Booke of Margery Kempe*

GOD'S CHAPEL

My tongue will speak of your righteousness and of your praises all day long (Psalm 35:28).

Madame,

At table and in the middle of conversations lift your heart to God. Even when you remember him but for a brief moment pleases him. It is unnecessary to speak out aloud at such times. God is much nearer to us than we imagine.

You do not always have to be in church in order to be in God's presence. Our hearts can become a chapel where God dwells. We can withdraw there, from time to time in order to have humble, loving and gentle fellowship with God. These kinds of conversations are within the grasp of everyone, some to a greater extent, others to a lesser extent, as God knows what capacity we each have.

We must make a start. Maybe God is just waiting for us to make one wholehearted resolve. Take courage. We only have a brief life to live. You are nearly 64 and I am almost 80. We must both live and die with God. When we are with God all our sufferings are made sweet by his divine presence. Without God the greatest pleasures become the most exquisite torture. May God be blessed in us all. Amen.

So gradually become used to worshipping him and asking for his grace. Offer him your heart at different times throughout the day as you are engaged in your daily activities. Never become a slave to special rules and particular ways of worshipping God. Live and act in faith with humility and love.

Brother Lawrence, *The Practice of the Presence of God*

OUR RESURRECTION

We shall all be changed, in a moment, in the twinkling of an eye, at the last trump: for the trumpet shall sound, and the dead shall be raised incorruptible, and we shall be changed (1 Corinthians 15:51–52, AV).

Triumph now, O Christian, in these promises; you will shortly triumph in their fulfilment. For this is the day that the Lord will make; 'we shall be glad and rejoice therein' (Psalm 118:24).

The grave that could not keep our Lord cannot keep us: he arose for us, and by the same power will cause us to arise. 'For if we believe that Jesus died, and rose again; even so them also which sleep in Jesus, will God bring with him' (1 Thessalonians 4:14). Can the head live and the body and members remain dead?

Write those sweet words on your heart, Christian: 'Because I live, ye shall also live' (John 14:19). As sure as Christ lives, you shall live: and as sure as he is risen, we shall rise. Otherwise the dead perish. Otherwise what is our hope – what gain is there from all our duty or suffering? Otherwise the sensual epicure would be one of the wisest people; and what better are we than our animals? Surely our knowledge, more than theirs, would only increase our sorrows, and our dominion over them is no great happiness. The servant often has a better life than his master, because he has few of his master's cares. And our dead carcasses are no more good-looking, nor do they yield a sweeter savour, than theirs. But we have a sure ground of hope. And besides this life, we have a life that is 'hid with Christ in God'; and 'when Christ, who is our life, shall appear, then shall' we 'also appear with him in glory' (Colossians 3:3–4, AV).

Richard Baxter, *The Saints' Everlasting Rest*

THREE ENEMIES

Submit yourselves, then, to God. Resist the devil, and he will flee from you. Come near to God and he will come near to you (James 4:7–8).

You are threatened by three enemies. The devil seeks to spread evil through his malice, the world through his pride, while man stays burdened under the weight of his own corruption.

The devil wants to make you evil but does not have the power to defeat you so long as you do not give in to his wicked suggestions. So we read, 'Resist the devil, and he will flee from you' (James 4:7). It was the devil, because of his jealousy, who tempted and overthrew those who were upright in paradise, since they did not resist him, but gave way to his own evil suggestions. Through his own pride the devil threw himself down from the height of heaven without anybody else being responsible. So you must be warned that mankind is in a very serious condition and is liable to fall because of the weight which burdens his own nature.

The world also brings evil because 'the whole world is under the control of the evil one' (1 John 5:19). Everybody feels its influence, but only those who consent to go along with it in their minds and wills are overthrown by the world. I do not want to be a friend of the world in case I fall. Anybody who seeks to be a friend of the world is God's enemy and this is the most disastrous step anyone can make.

From this it seems clear that the main reason for man's downfall is himself. He can fall without anybody else being involved. But he does not have to fall if he does not want to, no matter how many other people may oppose him.

Bernard of Clairvaux, *The Song of Songs*

TWO DOCTRINES OF OUR LORD

Do not withhold your mercy from me, O LORD; may your love and your truth always protect me (Psalm 40:11).

The first doctrine of our Lord is this: 'Do you not know, daughter, who you are and who I am? If you know these two things you will be happy. You are nothing and I am he who exists. If you have this awareness in your soul, your spiritual enemy will never deceive you, but you will escape all his traps. You will also never agree with anything that opposes my commandments, but you will wholeheartedly follow grace, truth and love.'

The second doctrine of our Lord is this: 'Think about me, and I shall think about you. A soul who is truly united to God does not love herself or anyone else or any other creature, but only God. Such a soul regards herself as nothing, and is fully aware that all her goodness and all the strength of her soul belongs to her Maker. She forsakes herself and her fellow creatures utterly, and hides herself completely in her Maker, our Lord Jesus. This unity of love increases daily in such a soul. She is transformed into being like our Lord so that she does not think, or understand, or love unless it comes from God.'

Catherine of Siena, *Treatise on Divine Providence*

THE NATURE AND PRACTICE OF PRAYER

Come, let us sing for joy to the LORD; let us shout aloud to the Rock of our salvation. Let us come before him with thanksgiving and extol him with music and song (Psalm 95:1–2).

We must pray in the height, depth, length and breadth of the spirit without many words but with one word of one syllable. That word must be best suited to the nature of prayer itself, and before we can select such a word we must first understand what prayer is.

Prayer is nothing other than a devout intent directed to God in order that one may gain goodness and banish evil. Since all evil is summed up in sin, either by cause or in being, we should pray for the removing of evil. But in this prayer do not waste time thinking about the subject. Do not say much. Use only this little word 'sin'. If we pray for goodness, then let us cry, with word or thought or desire, nothing but that one word 'God'. For in God is all good; he is its beginning and its existence.

Do not be surprised, then, that I give these two words priority. If I knew any shorter words that so completely summed up good and evil as these do, or if God had taught me other words, then I would have used these instead. And that is my advice to you. Don't make a study of words, for you will never achieve your purpose or be able to contemplate that way. Contemplation is never attained by study, but by grace. And, despite what I've said, use your own words which God has led you to use for prayer. And if God directs you to use those I've given you, I advise you not to let go of them (that is, if you pray in words, not otherwise, of course).

The Cloud of Unknowing (14th century)

GOD'S FOOL

'If you want to be perfect, go, sell your possessions and give to the poor' (Matthew 19:21).

Francis underwent a reversal of a certain psychological kind; which was really like the reversal of a complete somersault, in that by coming full circle it came back, or apparently came back, to the same normal posture. In the inward sense it was a profound spiritual revolution. The man who went into the cave was not the man who came out again. He looked at the world as differently from other men as if he had come out of that dark hole walking on his hands.

It may be suspected that in that black cell or cave Francis passed the blackest hours of his life. By nature he was the sort of man who has that vanity which is the opposite of pride; that vanity which is very near to humility. He had made a fool of himself. Any man who has been young, who has ridden horses or thought himself ready for a fight, who has fancied himself as a troubadour and accepted the conventions of comradeship, will appreciate the ponderous and crushing weight of the simple phrase 'God's fool'.

The conversion of St Francis, like that of Paul, involved being in some sense flung suddenly from a horse; but in a sense it was an even worse fall; for it was a war-horse. Anyhow, there was not a rag of St Francis left that was not ridiculous. Everybody knew that at the best he had made a fool of himself.

When Francis came out of his cave of vision, he was wearing the same word 'fool' as a feather in his cap; as a crest or even a crown. He would go on being a fool: he would become more and more of a fool; he would be the court fool of the King of Paradise.

G. K. Chesterton, *St Francis of Assisi*

THE USE OF TIME

My times are in your hands (Psalm 31:15).

As far as business and all external duties are concerned, we shall use time correctly as soon as we recall that all our days are ordered by God's providential hands. As all such duties are a result of his plans, all we have to do is to accept God's plans and submit our own inclinations, self-will, restless anxiety and all our natural impulses to do everything we like in the way we like, to God's will. Take care not to allow yourself to become overwhelmed by outer things, or to be completely immersed in external interests, however important they may be.

Everything you do should begin with a definite view of God's glory, should continue quietly and should end without excitement or impatience.

The time that is spent with others in society or in general amusement is very dangerous for you although it may be very useful to others. Be on your guard, that is, be more faithful in remembering God's presence during these times. In particular, you need to cultivate the watchfulness which our Lord spoke about so often. Lift up your heart to Jesus Christ since he is your only source of strength and safety, or else you will be of little use to others and are most likely to fall prey to the subtle venom which so often lurks in the world and among its pleasures. This is particularly necessary for people in powerful positions whose words can do great good or great harm.

Spare time for oneself is often the most pleasant and useful thing one can have. It can never be spent in a more profitable way than in renewing our physical and our mental strength through secret communion with God. Prayer is so necessary as it is the source of so much blessing. Once the soul has realised the gifts it brings it is unlikely to fail to seek them again and again, as frequently as it is free to do so.

Archbishop Fénelon, *Christian Perfection*

TWO BIRTHS

'Flesh gives birth to flesh, but Spirit gives birth to spirit' (John 3:6).

Man has two births: one in the world, the other one out of the world and spiritual, in God. Do you wish to know if your child is born and if he is naked – that is to say, whether you have been made God's son? If your heart is heavy, for any reason other than sin, your child is not born. In your anguish you are not yet a mother: you are in labour and your hour is near. Do not doubt it: if you are labouring for yourself or for your friend, no birth has taken place, though birth is close at hand. The birth is not over till your heart is free from care. Then he has the essence and nature and substance and wisdom and joy of all that God has. Then the very being of the Son of God is ours and in us, and we attain to actual deity.

Christ says, 'If anyone would come after me, he must deny himself and take up his cross and follow me' (Matthew 16:24). That is: cast away care and let perpetual joy reign in your heart. Thus the child is born. And when the child is born in me, the sight of friends or of father dead before my eyes will leave my heart untouched. If my heart were moved, the child would not be born in me, though its birth could be close. I maintain that God and his angels take such keen delight in every act a good man does that there is no joy like it. And accordingly, I say, the birth of this child in you gives you the keenest delight, a continuous, never-ending joy, in all good deeds. Hence the words: 'No-one will take away your joy' (John 16:22).

Meister Eckhart, *Sermons*

FILLED BY GOD

'The wind blows wherever it pleases' (John 3:8).

In the Revelation of St John it is written that our Lord offers himself to men: 'Here I am! I stand at the door and knock. If anyone hears my voice and opens the door, I will come in and eat with him, and he with me' (Revelation 3:20). You do not need to seek him here or there, he is no further off than the door of your heart. There he stands lingering, waiting for whoever is ready to open and let him in. You do not need to call to him in the distance. He is waiting much more impatiently than you, for you to open to him. He is longing for you a thousand times more urgently than you are for him. It is instantaneous: the opening and the entering.

You will perhaps say: 'How can that be? I have no inkling of him.'

It is not in your power to find him, but in his. He reveals himself when he chooses, and he hides himself, too, when he wills. This is what Christ meant when he said to Nicodemus, 'The wind blows wherever it pleases. You hear its sound, but you cannot tell where it comes from or where it is going' (John 3:8). This is a paradox: 'You hear its sound, but you cannot tell where it comes from.' Yet it is by hearing that we know. What Christ meant is that it is imbibed or absorbed through hearing, that is to say, you receive it unconsciously. God cannot leave anything void and unfilled. Nature's God cannot endure anything to be empty. If, therefore, you seem not to find him, and to be wholly empty of him, that is nevertheless not the case. For were there any emptiness under heaven, whatever it might be, however great or small, the heavens must either draw it up to them or, bending downwards, fill it with themselves. On no account will God, who is nature's Lord, permit anything to remain empty. Therefore stand still and do not waver, in case turning away from God for a moment, you never turn back to him again.

Meister Eckhart, *Sermons*

ADVICE TO YOUNG PEOPLE

How can a young man keep his way pure? By living according to your word (Psalm 119:9).

Letter to Miss F. (October 3, 1778)
Dear Madam,

You would have me tell you what are the best means to be used by a young person, to prevent the world, with all its opening and ensnaring scenes, from drawing the heart away from God.

In the first place, I would observe, that though it be our bounden duty, and the highest privilege we can propose to ourselves, to have our hearts kept close to the Lord, yet we must not expect it absolutely or perfectly, much less all at once. The Lord permits us to feel our weakness, for though we are ready in words to confess that we are weak, we do not so properly know it, till that secret is brought to the trial, and fails us. To be humble, and like a little child, afraid of taking a step alone, and so conscious of dangers around us, as to cry to him continually to hold us up that we may be safe, is the sure, the infallible, the only secret of walking closely with him.

There are means to be observed on our part. The first is prayer; and here, above all things, we should pray for humility. It may be called both the guard of all other graces, and the soil in which they grow. The second is attention to the Scripture. Your question is directly answered in Psalm 119:9. The precepts are our rule and delight, the promises our strength and encouragement.

John Newton, *Cardiphonia*

MEDITATION ON CREATION

O LORD, our Lord, how majestic is your name in all the earth! (Psalm 8:1).

1. Consider that but a few years ago you were not in the world at all, and that you did not exist. Where were we, O my soul, at that time? The world had already lasted such a long time, and it had no news of us.

2. God has brought you forth out of this nothingness, to make you what you are, merely of his goodness, for he had no need of you.

3. Consider the being that God has given you; for it is the highest form of being on the earth, capable of living eternally and of being perfectly united to his divine majesty.

4. God has not placed you in this world for any need that he has of you, for you are of no use at all to him, but solely to show his goodness in you, giving you his grace and his glory. And for this reason he has given you an understanding to know him, a memory to be mindful of him, a will to love him, eyes to behold his wonderful creation, and a tongue to praise him.

5. Humble yourself profoundly before God, saying from your heart with the Psalmist: 'O Lord I am nothing before thee' (Psalm 39:7).

6. Give thanks to God. 'Bless thy God, O my soul, and let all that is within me bless his holy name' (Psalm 103:1), for his goodness has drawn me from nothingness, and his mercy has created me.

St Francis de Sales, *Introduction to a Devout Life*

MEDITATION ON GOD'S BLESSINGS

You, O Lord, are a compassionate and gracious God, slow to anger, abounding in love and faithfulness (Psalm 86:15).

1. Consider the bodily gifts which God has bestowed on you; your body with all that it can accomplish. Compare yourself with so many other people who are more worthy than you, who have not been endowed with such blessings. Some people are disabled in mind or in body; others are held in contempt; others are living a life of poverty, and God has spared you from such a miserable life.

2. Consider your gifts of mind. Reflect on how many people in this world are mentally ill, or completely insane. Why are you not numbered among them? God has favoured you. So many people have been brought up in complete ignorance about God, while in God's providence you have been taught about God as you grew up.

3. Consider your spiritual graces: O Philothea, you are a child of the church; God has taught you to know him from your youth.

How many times has he given you his sacraments?

How many times has he given you inspirations, interior lights, reproaches for your correction?

How many times has he pardoned your faults?

How many times has he delivered you from the occasions of spiritual ruin, to which you have been exposed?

And during these past years have you not had leisure and opportunity to make progress to the good of your soul?

Consider a little in detail how sweet and gracious God has been to you.

St Francis de Sales, *Introduction to a Devout Life*

MEDITATION ON SIN

Hide your face from my sins and blot out all my iniquity (Psalm 51:9).

1. Consider how long it is since you began to sin, and see how, since you started, sins have multiplied in your heart. See how you have added to these every day by sins against God, against yourself, against your neighbour, by deed, by word, by desire and thought.

2. Consider your evil inclinations, and how far you have followed them. Then you will realise that on these two matters your sins are more than the hairs on your head (see Psalm 40:12).

3. Consider by itself the sin of ingratitude to God, which is a general sin, that spreads itself over all the others and makes them infinitely worse: see then how many benefits God has conferred on you, and how you have misused them all against the Giver; in particular, how many inspirations have been unheeded, how many good movements of the Spirit have been made unprofitable.

More than anything else, think how many times you have failed to produce fruit from all the times you have received the sacraments. What has become of the precious jewels with which your dear Spouse adorned you? They have all been buried in your sins. Reflect on this ingratitude, how, when God was pursuing you so unceasingly to save you, you were always running away from him to lose yourself.

St Francis de Sales, *Introduction to a Devout Life*

MEDITATION ON DEATH

If the dead are not raised, 'Let us eat and drink, for tomorrow we die' (1 Corinthians 15:32).

1. Imagine yourself to be lying ill on your bed of death, without any hope of recovery.

2. Consider the uncertainty of the day of your death. O my soul, you must one day quit this body. When will it be? Will it be in winter or in summer? In a town or in the country? In the day or in the night? Will it be without any warning, or with warning? Will it be the result of some disease or of some accident? Alas, we know nothing at all about any of these things. We only know that we shall die, and always sooner than we expect.

3. Consider that the world will then come to an end, as far as you are concerned, and that there will be no more of it for you; it will turn upside down before your eyes. Yes, for then pleasures, vanities, worldly joys, vain affections will appear as phantoms and shadows. Oh, how wretched I am, for the sake of what trifles and unrealities have I offended my God? You will see that you have forsaken God for the sake of nothing. On the other hand, devotion and good works will seem to you then so desirable and sweet; and why have I not followed this beautiful and pleasant path? Then the sins which used to seem very little will appear as big as mountains, and your devotion very small.

4. Consider with what haste your body will be removed and hidden in the earth, and how, when that is done, the world will scarcely give another thought about you, and will not remember you any more than you have remembered others: God rest his soul, they will say, and that is all. O death, how important you are, how pitiless you are!

St Francis de Sales, *Introduction to a Devout Life*

HUMBLE BOLDNESS

Taste and see that the LORD is good (Psalm 34:8).

Exercise yourself in the knowledge and deep consideration of our Lord God, calling humbly to mind how excellent he is. You must endeavour to acquire this knowledge through devout prayer, rather than through study and outward deeds. It is the special gift of God, and certainly very precious.

The Lord does not want us to wrestle alone with our burdens but wants us to load them on to him. Now the desires which are breathed in prayer are, as it were, the heart unloading its burdens. Each request carries with it part of the burden and lays it on God.

If you would be rich in all grace, be much in prayer. Conversing with God assimilates the soul to him, beautifies it with the beams of his holiness, as Moses' face shined when he returned from the mount.

'In heaven.' There indeed his Majesty should humble us as we approach him, but this should not stop us from coming to him. For although God is in heaven and we are on earth, yet he is our Father. So we should link the two together, and hold them firmly in our mind as we pray with humble boldness.

Robert Leighton, *Sermons*

NOTHING BUT GOD'S HOLY WILL

'What shall I do, Lord?' I [Saul] asked. 'Get up,' the Lord said, 'and go into Damascus. There you will be told all that you have been assigned to do' (Acts 22:10).

Seeing nothing but God in everything the soul should accept and abandon all things at his will in order to be nourished, to live and hope in his will only, and not rely on things which have no force or virtue but what they derive from him. The soul should say at each moment and in reference to everything, like St Paul, 'Lord, what dost thou wish me to do?' And she should add not this or that request, but, 'All that thou wishest!' The mind loves this, the body loves that, but, Lord, I wish nothing but your holy will.

Prayer, action, vocal or mental prayers in activity or silence, in faith or in sight, lost in your general grace or precisely and specifically distinct, all distinctions, Lord, are nothing, for it is your will that makes the real and one and only virtue of them all. Your will alone is the aim of the sharp point of my devotion, and not these things, however elevated and sublime they may be: for the fulfilment of grace is the perfection of the heart and not of the mind.

Jean-Pierre de Caussade, *The Sacrament of the Present Moment*

EMBRACE THE CROSS

Who shall separate us from the love of Christ? Shall trouble or hardship or persecution or famine or nakedness or danger or sword? . . . No, in all these things we are more than conquerors through him who loved us (Romans 8:35, 37).

No foundation was made without trouble. What it is to have to contend against many minds. I have never refrained from making a foundation for fear of trouble, though I felt a great dislike for journeys, especially long ones.

It was my lack of health that most frequently wearied me. The weather was severe, and I, so old and sickly! My health is generally weak, but I saw clearly that our Lord gives me strength.

Inwardly ill at ease, my soul was in very great dryness and darkness.

The soul must be virile, not like those soldiers who lie down on their stomachs to drink when they are being led into battle. It must not dream of sweetness and enjoyments at the beginning of its career. Manna does not fall in the first habitations – we must press on further if we want to gather it. Then alone will the soul find all things to its taste, when it has learned to will only what God wills.

How comic our pretensions are! We are still immersed in difficulties and imperfections, we have virtues that can barely toddle, others hardly born; and we are not ashamed to demand sweetness in prayer, we grumble at dryness! May you never behave like that, sisters. Embrace the cross – the rest is a mere extra. If God gives it you, thank him humbly.

St Teresa of Avila, *The Interior Castle*

October 16th

MEDITATION AND THE BIBLE

Open my eyes that I may see wonderful things in your law (Psalm 119:18).

To an Officer
Beware of turning up passages from the Bible for meditation at random. You are tempting God when you do this. While it remains true that all holy Scripture has been given to us for our instruction, its direct and definite teachings are not spread evenly throughout its pages. Some passages are more ideally suited to an individual's present needs than other passages. So choose parts of the Bible which are most appropriate for your circumstances and for the correction of your faults. Choose those passages which will stimulate watchfulness, trust in God, strength to master yourself and faithfulness to carry out the duties God has given you.

In addition to this meditation, do some spiritual reading. Francis de Sales would instruct you, help you in the details of your meditation, give you spiritual exercises to do and teach you that free love from the heart, which enables us to serve God cheerfully.

The greatness and goodness of God should be a constant theme of your meditation. As your mind is unused to abiding calmly in God's presence you should choose some special words to fix in your mind as you meditate; otherwise you will just waste your time and not strengthen your heart. You should always have a definite, plain subject on which simply to reflect. Above all, ask God to draw you close to him through your emotions, for God does not win souls through intellectual arguments, but through the heart's coming alive and through the spirit's being humbled.

Archbishop Fénelon, *Christian Perfection*

WILD BEASTS

Persecuted, but not abandoned (2 Corinthians 4:9).

Pray for me that God would give me strength both inwardly and outwardly, that I may not only say, but do; that I may not only be called a Christian, but be found one.

I write to all the churches; and signify to them all that I am willing to die for God, unless you hinder me. Suffer me to be the food of wild beasts; whereby I may attain unto God. I am the wheat of God, and I am to be ground by the teeth of the wild beasts, that I may be found the pure bread of God.

Remember in your prayers the church which is in Syria, which now enjoys the Lord for its shepherd, instead of me; the Lord who said, 'I am the Good Shepherd.' He alone, together with your love for him, will be their bishop. My spirit salutes you, and the love of the churches which have received me, for the name of Jesus Christ, and not as a passenger only. For even those churches that did not belong to me, conducted me in the way from city to city.

Fare ye well, unto the end, in the patience of Jesus Christ.

St Ignatius, *Letters*

JACOB'S LADDER

'Surely the LORD was in this place, and I was not aware of it'
(Genesis 28:16).

Contemplate the ladder of Jacob, for it is a true picture of the devout life. The two sides between which one ascends, and to which the rungs are fastened, represent prayer which obtains the love of God and the sacraments which confer it; the rungs represent the various levels of charity by which one goes on from one virtue to the next virtue, either descending by action to the support and succour of one's neighbour, or ascending by contemplation to loving union with God.

Now look, I beseech you, at those who are on the ladder; they are people who have angelic hearts, or angels who have human bodies; they are not young, though they seem to be so, because they are full of vigour and spiritual agility; they have wings to fly, and they soar up towards God by holy prayer, but they have also feet to walk with people by a holy and amiable friendship with them. Their faces are beautiful and cheerful, because they receive all things with sweetness and delight. Their legs, their arms, and their affections, and their actions have no other design or motive than to please God. The rest of their body is covered, but with a beautiful and light robe, because they do indeed make use of this world and of worldly things, but in a fashion which is altogether pure and sincere, since they only take but sparingly what is necessary for their life. Such are the devout.

St Francis de Sales, *Introduction to a Devout Life*

PRAYER AND MEDITATION

'To him who knocks, the door will be opened' (Luke 11:10).

God knows all things. He knows what we wish even before we ask for it. Yet we must pray, for many reasons. But first because Christ set us an example: he went up into the mountains alone at night to pray. And also because the apostles tell us to pray: 'Pray continually' (1 Thessalonians 5:17), and men ought always to pray and not give up (see Luke 18:1). But we ought to pray to acquire grace for this life and glory in the next. So we are told, 'For everyone who asks receives; he who seeks finds; and to him who knocks, the door will be opened' (Luke 11:10). Again, we pray because angels offer our prayers to God to help their fulfilment.

Thoughts and desires are indeed naked and open to God alone. Yet angels know when saints think worthy and holy things. They know when they are inflamed by the love of eternal life; God reveals it to them, and our outward acts display who serves God alone. That is why the angel said to Daniel, 'You are a man of strong desires' (Daniel 9:23, Vulgate). We should also pray because in constant prayer the soul is ignited with the fire of divine love. Our Lord speaks truly through the prophet, 'Is not my word like fire . . . and like a hammer that breaks a rock in pieces?' (Jeremiah 23:29). And the psalmist says, 'Your speech is a burning fire' (Psalm 119:140 Vulgate).

Richard Rolle, *The Fire of Love*

THE BELOVED BLOOD OF OUR LORD JESUS CHRIST

By his wounds we are healed (Isaiah 53:5).

As I looked I saw the body bleeding heavily, apparently from the flogging. The smooth skin was gashed and all over his body I saw deep weals in the tender flesh caused by many sharp blows. The blood flowed so hot and thick that neither the wounds nor the skin could be seen: it was all covered in blood. The blood flowed all down his body, but at the point of falling to the ground, it disappeared. The bleeding continued for a while, giving me time to see it and think about it. It was so heavy that I thought that if it had been real the whole bed and everything around would have been soaked in blood.

Then the idea came to me that out of his tender love for us God has created a vast supply of water for us to use to make ourselves comfortable on this earth. Yet he would rather that we make ourselves at home with him by using his holy blood to wash ourselves clean from our sin: for no liquid has been made which he would prefer to give. It is as plentiful as it is precious because it is divine. It is part of us, and is most blissfully ours because of his precious love.

The beloved blood of our Lord Jesus Christ is truly as plentiful as it is precious. Look and see for yourself. It flows over the whole world ready to wash every human being from all sin, present, past and future, if they are willing.

Lady Julian of Norwich, *Revelations of Divine Love*

FAITH IN CHRIST

For though I am absent from you in body, I am present with you in spirit and delight to see how orderly you are and how firm your faith in Christ is (Colossians 2:5).

It is because Christ shows mercy to the vilest that Satan rages so strongly, and as he can do nothing with Christ he assails Christ's people. He holds our hands while the world buffets us; he puts bearskins upon us, and then sets the dogs at us. He daubs us with his own slime and then tempts us to believe that that slime comes from ourselves. Let the tempted think much of Christ's mercy; for the tempted wherever he dwells always thinks himself the biggest sinner.

This is Satan's master argument. I say this is his maul, his club, his masterpiece. He uses this as some use their most enchanting songs, singing them everywhere. Resist him steadfast in the faith. There is nothing like faith to help at a pinch. Faith must be always in exercise. Only put not in the place thereof presumption.

I have observed that as there are herbs and flowers in our gardens, so there are counterfeits in the field. They are only distinguishable from the others by the names of the wild ones. Why, there is faith, and wild faith; and wild faith is this presumption. I call it wild faith because God never placed it in his garden – his church: it is only to be found in his field – his world. I also call it wild faith, because it only grows up and is nourished where other wild notions abound. Wherefore take heed of this and all may be well. But let a true faith always be at work. Faith is the eye, is the mouth, is the hand, and one of these is of use all day long. Faith is to see, to receive, to work, or to eat; and a Christian should be seeing, or receiving, or working, or feeding all day long. Let it rain, let it blow, let it thunder, let it lighten, a Christian must still believe. At whatever time, said the good man, I am afraid I will trust in thee.

John Bunyan, *Grace Abounding to the Chief of Sinners*

WHERE AND WHEN TO PRAY

'When you pray, go into your room, close the door and pray to your Father, who is unseen' (Matthew 6:6).

Solitariness of place is the most appropriate place for meditation. Retire from other people, if you want to talk with profit with yourself. So Jesus meditates alone on the mount; Isaac, in the fields; John the Baptist, in the desert; David, on his bed; Chrysostom, in the bath: each, in different places; but all solitary. Nowhere is free of God's presence, he is not tied to any single place. Some people find their own room best, since their eyes can wander no further than the walls and so help to keep in check their wandering thoughts. Other people find their souls are more free as they behold God's heaven above them and around them. So long as you are alone and quiet it does not matter where you are.

No one time for praying can be prescribed for everyone; neither is God limited to set times and people differ among themselves when they find it best to pray. Some people find the golden hours of the morning the best for meditation. Then the body is fresh and calm from resting, and the soul has not yet had time to be distracted by outward things. Other people find that they can best learn wisdom at night. Like Job, they hope that their bed will bring them comfort in their meditation. They are tired of earthly cares and are ready to appreciate and love heavenly things. I, personally, have found Isaac's time best, when he went out in the evening to meditate. But no habit belonging to another is necessarily best suited to another person. All that matters is that we set ourselves a time to pray and then set apart that time, when we are best able to serve God in this way.

Joseph Hall, *Sermons*

'MY GREAT DELIVERANCE'

God was reconciling the world to himself in Christ, not counting men's sins against them (2 Corinthians 5:19).

I went to bed that night in my usual security and indifference; but was awakened from a sound sleep by the force of a violent sea, which broke on board us. It was astonishing that any of us survived to relate the story. Some of us set to bailing but the water increased against all our efforts. Almost every passing wave broke over my head. We made ourselves fast with ropes, that we might not be washed away. Although I dreaded death now, I thought, if the Christian religion was true, I could not be forgiven.

The next day I began to pray. My prayer was like the cry of the ravens, which yet the Lord does not disdain to hear. I now began to think of that Jesus whom I had so often derided: I recollected the particulars of his life, and of his death; a death for sins not his own, but, as I remembered, for the sake of those who in their distress should put their trust in him.

My companions were either quite unaffected, or soon forgot it all: but it was not so with me; not that I was any wiser or better than they, but because the Lord was pleased to vouchsafe me peculiar mercy. I had a New Testament and was struck particularly by the Prodigal, Luke chapter 15. Before we arrived in Ireland I had a satisfactory evidence in my own mind of the truth of the Gospel, as considered in itself, and its exact suitableness to answer all my needs. I saw that, by the way there pointed out, God might declare, not his mercy only, but his justice also, in the pardon of sin, on the account of the obedience and sufferings of Jesus Christ. My judgement at that time embraced the sublime doctrine of 'God manifest in the flesh, reconciling the world to himself.'

John Newton, *Cardiphonia*

FREELY GIVE

'Whoever acknowledges me before men, I will also acknowledge him before my Father in heaven' (Matthew 10:32).

As you go, preach this message: 'The kingdom of heaven is near.' Heal the sick, raise the dead, cleanse those who have leprosy, drive out demons. Freely you have received, freely give. Do not take along any gold or silver or copper in your belts; take no bag for the journey, or extra tunic, or sandals or a staff; for the worker is worth his keep.

Whatever town or village you enter, search for some worthy person there and stay at his house until you leave. As you enter the home, give it your greeting. If the home is deserving, let your peace rest on it; if it is not, let your peace return to you. If anyone will not welcome you or listen to your words, shake the dust off your feet when you leave that home or town. I tell you the truth, it will be more bearable for Sodom and Gomorrah on the day of judgement than for that town. I am sending you out like sheep among wolves. Therefore be as shrewd as snakes and as innocent as doves.

Be on your guard against men; they will hand you over to the local councils and flog you in their synagogues. On my account you will be brought before governors and kings as witnesses to them and to the Gentiles. But when they arrest you, do not worry about what to say or how to say it. At that time you will be given what to say, for it will not be you speaking, but the Spirit of your Father speaking through you.

Jesus Christ, in Matthew 10:7–20

SPEAKING TO GOD

Cast your cares on the LORD and he will sustain you (Psalm 55:22).

Put off the hour of prayer for nothing of your own; so as not to make a stroke more with the pen.

Bustle hurts the mind and soul, and benefits nothing.

Have some arrow prayers to pray during the day, or a psalm.

A good watchmaker is one who makes watches and prays: a good housemaid is one who sweeps and prays.

Prayer may be equally with words or without: it may be 'Jesu,' 'my God and my all.' Like the Samians throwing their empty sack in front of the Spartans and saying the word 'flour'; which they said was a word too much, since if they only saw the empty sack it was enough; so if we bring our emptiness only before God, he will fill it.

It would be a very good prayer to offer God your whole being, with a full earnest wish to do all to his honour and praise; that is, to seek to please him in everything; and to agree that every time the clock strikes you renew this with great intensity.

Speak to God as a child to One it may freely speak to.

Always choose some special thing to ask for at Holy Communion, and make it your earnest aim afterwards. After Holy Communion, make acts of the mind to recall it. 'Abide with me.' 'Leave me not.' Never mind their being formal at first, till collectedness is gained as a thing of course.

Be thankful for everything: especially for what is against your will.

St Catherine of Siena made a cell in her heart. Afterwards, in a most busy life she could keep quite close to God and without the least distraction.

Edward Bouverie Pusey, *Tracts for the Times*

LISTENING TO GOD

Listen to me, you islands; hear this, you distant nations (Isaiah 49:1).

God is the true Friend who always gives us the counsel and comfort we need. Our problem is that we tend to resist him, so it is essential that we make a habit of listening to his voice, of keeping silence before him so that we do not miss anything he has to say to us. We are familiar enough with keeping a verbal, exterior silence, but we know so little about interior silence. It comes from quietening our idle, restless, wandering imaginations, keeping in check the desires of our worldly mind and suppressing the countless unhelpful thoughts which excite and disturb the soul.

When we pray, we should confine ourselves to a few simple heartwarming thoughts about God, in which we should delight in our souls, rather than constantly turn over in our minds. Employing our minds in isolation to God tires, disappoints and exhausts us. But using the mind in conjunction with the heart does not tire us in the same way. The spirits of faith and love never stop flowing as long as we do not forsake their heavenly source.

If you persevere and have the correct intention in your heart, you will discover that there are times of prayer, which even though they are spent in the middle of distractions, bear inner fruit and strengthen you against temptations.

Archbishop Fénelon, *Christian Perfection*

WHEN TEMPTATION KNOCKS

Put on the full armour of God so that you can take your stand against the devil's schemes (Ephesians 6:11).

Here is a rule about how we should behave during a time of temptation. When temptation arises in us, we should never debate with it or ask it questions. For that is the precise trap the devil longs for you to fall into. He has great faith in his own cunning and expects to defeat us with his clever arguments. So a soul should never ask questions, or answer the devil's questions. Rather, the soul should turn to devout prayer and commit herself to our Lord so that she does not give in to the devil's tricks. Through devout prayer and steadfast faith, we may overcome all the subtle temptations of the devil.

Sometimes, the devout longing of a soul who loves our Lord Jesus, grows cool because of a particular sin or as a result of some new subtle temptation. Some people become devoid of all the spiritual comfort that they had been used to and so stop praying, meditating and reading. In this way they become an even easier prey for the devil. The devil desires nothing more than that Christ's knights throw away their armour by means of which they defeat all their enemies. A wise Christian knight would never take off his armour. Rather, the more he experiences dullness and spiritual sloth and emptiness in his devotions, the more he continues with his spiritual exercises. He increases them rather than decreasing them.

Catherine of Siena, *Treatise on Divine Perfection*

JESUS OUR TRUE MOTHER

'As a mother comforts her child, so will I comfort you' (Isaiah 66:13).

God is as truly our Mother as he is our Father.

Our great Father, almighty God, who is being, knew and loved us before time began. In that knowledge, out of his wonderful deep love, and with the foresight and counsel of the blessed Trinity, he willed that the second person become our Mother.

Our Father willed it, our Mother accomplished it, our good Lord the Holy Spirit established it. So we must love our God in whom we have our being. We must reverently thank and praise him for our creation, fervently ask our Mother for mercy and compassion, and our Lord the Holy Spirit for help and grace.

From nature, mercy and grace – from these three – comes our life. From them we have humility and gentleness and pity. From them, too, we get our hatred of sin and wickedness, for it is in the nature of virtue to hate these.

So Jesus is our true Mother in nature because of our first creation, and he is our true Mother in grace because he took our created nature. In the second person there is all the loving service and sweet spontaneous care that belongs to beloved motherhood, and in him our will for God is always whole and safe, both naturally and by grace, because of his own innate goodness.

I saw that the motherhood of God can be looked at in three ways. The first is his creation of our human nature; the second his assumption of nature – from which stems the motherhood of grace; and the third is the practical outworking of motherhood, as a result of which, and by that same grace, it spreads out in endless height, breadth, length, and depth. And all is one here.

Lady Julian of Norwich, *Revelations of Divine Love*

THE WAY OF PURIFICATION

Then Jesus was led up by the Spirit into the desert to be tempted by the devil (Matthew 4:1).

Let thy conduct be drawn inward, and break not forth either in words or conduct.

He who helps himself too much shall not be helped by truth.

God wills not to deprive us of desire; he wills that we desire allness, that is, he wills to give us all desire.

In the strongest subjection is the highest arising.

He who wishes to be in the most inward, must cast off all that is multifarious. Put yourself in deprivation of all that is not the One.

What is the practice of a well-composed man? It is dis-becoming.

If you would be of use to all creatures, turn away from all creatures.

If a man cannot grasp a thing, let him be idle, and the thing will grasp him.

Deprivation strengthens more than possession.

The submergence of the senses is the emergence of truth.

For God's friends, to lose the victory is to have won.

Ah! how blessed is he who remains constant in the face of multifariousness! What does he not sense of secret heavenly ingress!

Johann Joseph von Görres, *Meditations*

SPIRITUAL WARFARE

I know that you are pleased with me, for my enemy does not triumph over me (Psalm 41:11).

Our life is a warfare. For our encouragement the apostle calls it a good warfare. We are engaged in a good cause, fight under a good Captain, the victory is sure beforehand, and the prize is a crown, – a crown of life. Such considerations might make even a coward bold. But then we must be content to fight: and, considering the nature, number, situation, and subtlety of our enemies, we may expect sometimes to receive a wound; but there is a medicinal tree, the leaves of which are always at hand to heal us.

We cannot be too attentive to the evil which is always working in us, or to the stratagems which are employed against us; yet our attention should not be wholly confined to these things. We are to look upwards likewise to him who is our head, our life, our strength. One glance of Jesus will convey more effective assistance than poring over our own hearts for a month. The one is to be done, but the other should upon no account be omitted.

So far as we are content to be weak, that his power may be magnified in us, so far we shall make our enemies know that we are strong, though we ourselves shall never be directly sensible that we are so; only by comparing what we are, with the opposition we stand against, we may come to a comfortable conclusion, that the Lord works mightily in us.

John Newton, *Cardiphonia*

LIGHTING A CANDLE

[They] began to stone him [Stephen] (Acts 7:58).

In prison, Hugh Latimer prayed that he might have grace to be firm to the end, that God would give him strength to suffer any kind of cruel death rather than prove false to the truth that was in his heart. He was by no means too confident of himself, knowing that he was old and weak, and shrinking from fresh bodily suffering, and so it was for strength and courage that he most earnestly and constantly prayed.

Next, he prayed for the establishment and restoration of the true gospel in England; and this he 'did so inculcate and beat into the ears of the Lord God as though he had seen God before him, and spoke unto him face to face.'

His third prayer was for Princess Elizabeth, whom he constantly brought before God by name, looking to her to be a 'comfort to the comfortless realm of England.'

At last, on 16 October, 1555, Latimer and Ridley were led out to be burnt, Cranmer, his heart sad within him, watching the little procession from his window in the prison tower. Ridley was neatly dressed in a furred black gown with a fur tippet round his neck; Latimer in his old cloak, covering a shroud.

'Be of good comfort Master Ridley, and play the man. We shall this day light such a candle, by God's grace, in England, as I trust shall never be put out.'

Adapted from John Foxe, *Acts and Monuments*

A SUN WITHOUT SUNSET

Rejoice in the Lord always. I will say it again: Rejoice! (Philippians 4:4).

Come, true Light.
    Come, eternal Life.
    Come, secret of seclusion.
    Come, preciousness.
    Come, thou eternal jubilation.
    Come, thou light without setting.
    Come, thou who art longed for by all who are in misery.
    Come, thou mighty One, who needst but beckon to create and transform and renew all things everlastingly.
    Come, thou who dwelling above all the heavens, yet comest down to visit us who are bowed and laden.
    Come, O Solitary, to visit the solitary. For solitary I am, as thou seest. Come, Thou who hast placed me on earth alone and lonely.
    Come, thou who hast become my longing.
    Come, O my breath and my life.
    Come, Joy, Glory, O my lasting refreshment.
I give thanks to thee who, without mingling and being lost in my being, hast become one spirit with me, to thee who, though remaining God high above all, hast become everything in all things for me. I give thanks to thee, who hast become for me a day without nightfall and a sun without sunset.

Symeon the New Theologian, *Prayers*

MEDITATION

I will fulfil my vows to the LORD in the presence of all his people (Psalm 116:14).

Above all things, Philothea, when you finish your meditation, bear in mind the resolutions and intentions which you have formed, in order to practise them carefully during the day. This is the great fruit of meditation, without which it is often not only useless but harmful, because virtues meditated on and not practised, sometimes puff up the spirit and the heart, making us think that we are what we have resolved to become, which is undoubtedly true if the resolutions were carried out, but they only become harmful if they are not put into practice.

Therefore we must by all means try to practise them, and to avail ourselves of the occasions, be they small or great, of putting them into practice. For example, if I have resolved to win by gentleness the hearts of those who offend me, I will seek that very day an opportunity of meeting them in order to greet them amicably; if I fail to win them, I will at least try to speak well of them and pray to God on their behalf.

When you have finished this prayer of the heart, you must take care not to give any jolt to your heart, lest you spill the balm which you have received by means of your prayer; I mean by this, that you must keep silence for a little while, if possible, and move your heart quite gently from your prayer to your occupations, retaining, for as long as possible, the feelings and the affections which you have conceived.

St Francis de Sales, *Letters*

THE CORONATION OF THE SAINTS

'You have made them to be a kingdom and priests to serve our God, and they will reign on the earth' (Revelation 5:10).

The saints will experience a solemn coronation, enthronement, and reception into God's kingdom. For, as Christ their Head is anointed both King and Priest, so under him are his people made both kings and priests before God, to reign and to offer praises for ever. The crown of righteousness, which was laid up for them, shall by the Lord the righteous Judge be given them at that day (see 2 Timothy 4:8). They have been faithful to the death, and therefore shall receive the crown of life (see Revelation 2:10).

And their rule and dignity will be extended according to the use they have made of their talents here (see Matthew 25:21, 23), so that they are not dignified with empty titles, but real dominions. For Christ will take them and set them down with himself on his own throne (see Revelation 3:21), and will give them power over the nations, even as he received of his Father (see Revelation 2:26–27), and will give them the morning star. The Lord himself will give them possession with these expressions of praise: 'Well done, good and faithful servant; thou hast been faithful over a few things, I will make thee ruler over many things: enter thou into the joy of thy lord' (Matthew 25:21, 23, AV).

And with this solemn and blessed proclamation he will enthrone them: 'Come, ye blessed of my Father, inherit the kingdom prepared for you from the foundation of the world' (Matthew 25:34, AV).

Richard Baxter, *The Saints' Everlasting Rest*

RECOGNISING GOOD AND EVIL

'A good tree cannot bear bad fruit, and a bad tree cannot bear good fruit' (Matthew 7:18).

All our meditations on the Word, who is the Bridegroom, on his glory, his greatness, his power and his grace are nothing less than words spoken by him to our souls. This is the case, not only when he speaks, but also when we eagerly reflect in our minds on God's judgments, when we meditate on his law night and day. Then we shall know for certain that the Bridegroom is present and is speaking to us in such a delightful way that we do not become weary in our work.

It is dangerous, and can even be fatal, to be deceived in this area. We must never attribute to ourselves the work which is in fact being done by God in us. We must never think that God's words speaking to our hearts are only our own thoughts. Just as good is totally different from bad so God's words to us and our thoughts are poles apart from each other. Evil can never come from the Word and good can never come from the human heart unless the Word has first planted the seed there. I believe that it is easy to recognise what is of God in our hearts and what comes from ourselves.

This shows to the enemies of grace that without grace in our hearts we are incapable of thinking anything good and that right thinking is a gift from God. So the soul concludes that the good things which it thinks are from God and not from its own thinking. So when you do hear God's voice speaking to you in your own heart recognise it for what it is. Take great care that the voice which comes from God's mouth does not return to him empty, but achieves the purpose for which it was sent.

Bernard of Clairvaux, *The Song of Songs*

MERCY AND GRACE

Grace, mercy and peace from God the Father and Christ Jesus our Lord (1 Timothy 1:2).

Mercy is that by which we are pardoned, even all the falls, faults, failings and weaknesses, that attend us, and that we are incident to, in this our day of temptation: and for this mercy we should pray, and say, 'Our Father, forgive us our trespasses.' For though mercy is free in the exercise of it towards us, yet God will have us ask, that we may have; as he also says in the text, 'Let us therefore come boldly unto the throne of grace, that we may obtain mercy' (Hebrews 4:16, AV). That is what David means when he says, 'Surely goodness and mercy shall follow me all the days of my life, and I will dwell in the house of the LORD for ever' (Psalm 23:6).

And again, 'When I said, My foot slippeth; thy mercy, O LORD, held me up' (Psalm 94:18).

This then is the conclusion, that as there is mercy to be obtained by us at the throne of grace, for the pardon of all our weaknesses; so there is also grace there to be found that will yet strengthen us more, to all good walking and living before him.

John Bunyan, *Grace Abounding to the Chief of Sinners*

THE FIRST MANSION:
PRAYER IS THE GATE

The Lord told [Ananias], 'Go to the house of Judas on Straight Street and ask for a man from Tarsus named Saul, for he is praying' (Acts 9:11).

I began to think of the soul as if it were a castle made of a single diamond or very clear crystal. Imagine that this castle contains many rooms, some above, some below, others at each side, and at its very centre, right in the middle of them all, is the most important mansion. That is where the most secret things pass between God and the soul. You must give this comparison a great deal of careful thought.

Many souls remain in the castle's outer courtyard which is the area occupied by the guards. Such souls are not interested in going farther in, and have no idea what is in that wonderful place. They don't know who dwells in it or even how many rooms it has.

As far as I can understand, the gate into this castle is prayer and meditation. I do not mean mental rather than spoken prayer. If it is prayer at all, it must be accompanied by thought. In my opinion, a person is not praying, even if he is constantly moving his lips, if he is not aware to whom he is speaking, what he is asking for, and who it is that is doing the asking. I agree that it is sometimes possible to pray without actively giving your mind to these things, but that is only when you have already thought about them.

St Teresa of Avila, *The Interior Castle*

THE SECOND MANSION: PERSEVERANCE AND THE DEVIL

Be self-controlled and alert. Your enemy the devil prowls around like a roaring lion looking for someone to devour (1 Peter 5:8).

The attacks of the devil upon these souls now come in many forms and they are all terrible. So the soul suffers more than ever. In the preceding rooms it was unable to hear or did not hear much and put up little fight, like someone who doesn't expect to win. But here, in these rooms, the soul's understanding is sharper and its faculties are more alert, and it cannot but hear the war raging, the clash of arms and noise of cannon. Here the devils once again unleash their vipers – the things of the world. Earthly pleasures appear almost eternal.

Oh, Jesus! Poor soul! What turmoil and distress the devils cause. The soul is torn, and doesn't know what to do: should it press on ahead into the castle or should it go back to the previous room?

But then the reason comes and tells the soul not to be deluded by the false glamour of worldly things; faith teaches it what to do to satisfy its longings; and memory reveals the transience of all earthly joys. The will is moved to love in return the One who has given so many indications of his love for us. The will points out how this true Lover never leaves the soul, how he sticks with it wherever it goes, giving it life and being.

The understanding then shows the soul that it could never wish for a better friend than God, that the world is full of falsehood. The intellect convinces the soul that safety and peace are not to be found outside the castle.

Above all, the soul's own Lord is the Host within, and will give it all it desires, unless, like the Prodigal Son, it wants to go off and eat pigswill.

St Teresa of Avila, *The Interior Castle*

THE THIRD MANSION:
INSECURITY IN THIS EXILE

Praise the LORD. Blessed is the man who fears the LORD, who finds great delight in his commands (Psalm 112:1).

What misery life is in this world! We live like people whose enemies press perpetually at the gates; we cannot lay down our armour even for a second, not even when eating or sleeping, for constant fear of a break-in to our fortress. Oh! my Lord and my all! How can you want us to want such a miserable existence? We could long for it to end, and beg you to take it from us, if it were not for our hope of losing our life for your sake, or devoting it completely to your service, and most of all, were it not for the fact that we know it is your will for us to live. Since this is so, 'Let us die with him' as St Thomas said (John 11:16), because to be apart from you is to live in death, haunted as we are by the dread of losing you for ever!

Daughters, that is why I say that the happiness we ought to pray for is the complete security enjoyed by the saints.

A word of warning though: do not be overconfident because you are nuns and the daughters of so great a Mother. David was holy, yet you know what became of Solomon. So don't rely on your cloistered life, or your penitence. Do not even rely on your continual practice of prayer and your constant fellowship with God, nor on the fact that you hate the world and have completely withdrawn from it. That is all very good but all that is not enough to stop us being fearful. Bear this verse in mind and meditate on it: 'Blessed is the man who fears the Lord' (Psalm 112:1).

St Teresa of Avila, *The Interior Castle*

THE FOURTH MANSION: THE PRAYER OF RECONCILIATION

You are awesome, O God, in your sanctuary (Psalm 68:35).

The prayer of recollection I believe is supernatural, for there is no dependence on anything exterior: for example, you don't first need to close your eyes or be in darkness. Instead, you suddenly find that your eyes are closing and you desire solitude. Without any human effort a temple is being built in which the soul can pray.

The best way to find God is, by his grace, to seek him within ourselves, and not look for him in his creatures. St Augustine, who sought him in many places, tells how he found God within his own soul.

Sometimes, even before the soul has begun to think about God it finds it has entered the castle. How it enters or even hears the shepherd's pipe, I don't know. Certainly the ear heard nothing. But the soul is aware that it is gently withdrawing into itself. Anyone who has experienced this favour will know what I mean. I don't know how to make it more clear.

I think I read somewhere that the soul in that state is rather like a hedgehog or tortoise which retreats into itself. These creatures, however, close up at will, whereas with us it happens only when God is pleased to give us the grace. I personally believe that this favour, when His Majesty grants it, is given to those who have already left the things of this world. They have withdrawn at least in desire, even if they are married, and so unable to do so in actual fact. He specially calls them to give all their attention to spiritual things. If they give His Majesty complete freedom in their lives, then, I believe he will grant them all this and greater graces, for he is beginning to call them to a higher life.

St Teresa of Avila, *The Interior Castle*

THE FIFTH MANSION:
THE PRAYER OF UNION

Be confident of this, that he who began a good work in you will carry it on to completion until the day of Christ Jesus (Philippians 1:6).

If you are to enjoy the riches of the fifth mansion you must keep back nothing from God, whether great or small. The blessings you receive from God will be in proportion to what you know you've given him. There is no better way of assessing whether or not we have reached the prayer of union.

In the prayer of union our souls are deeply asleep to the things of this world and to ourselves. In fact, for the brief period this state lasts, the soul is without consciousness, and without power to think even if it wanted to. At last, there is no need for the soul to struggle to stop thinking. Even if it loves, it cannot understand how or what it is that it loves, nor what it desires. In fact, it has completely died to the world so that it may live more completely in God.

This is a delicious death. It is a withdrawing from all bodily activity; it is a death full of delight, for truly the soul appears to have left the body in order to draw near to God. I don't even know if the body still has life enough in it to breathe. On reflection, I believe it has not, or at least if it does breathe, then it does so without realising it.

Here, neither the imagination, the understanding, nor the memory, has any power to prevent God's grace flowing into the soul. What riches are ours while God so works in us, hindered by no one, not even by us! What will he not give us, our God, who is so eager to give.

St Teresa of Avila, *The Interior Castle*

THE SIXTH MANSION: GREATER FAVOURS ... MORE SEVERE AFFLICTIONS

Now I know in part; then I shall know fully, even as I am fully known (1 Corinthians 13:12).

In the sixth mansion the soul has been wounded with love for its Spouse and sighs more than ever for solitude, seeking to leave behind everything that disturbs it. That sight of God which the soul had is so deeply marked within it that its only desire is to behold him again.

The soul is now determined to take no other but our Lord as her Bridegroom, but he disregards the soul's longings for the betrothal, wanting those desires to deepen and that this greatest blessing of all should be won at some cost to the soul itself.

The Spouse increases her longing for the Bridegroom by ways so delicate that the soul itself cannot discern them. These desires are subtle impulses springing from the inmost depths of the soul and I don't know of anything to which I can compare it. These graces differ immensely from anything we can achieve in human terms.

Even when the mind is not even thinking of God, the soul is awakened by His Majesty suddenly, as if by a swiftly flying comet or thunderclap though no sound is heard. Yet the soul called by God hears him well enough. Indeed, it hears so clearly that it trembles and cries out, though it feels no pain. It is aware that it has been most delightfully wounded, but cannot discover how or from whom it came, and yet it hopes that wound will never heal for the wound is most precious.

The soul complains in words of love to its Bridegroom, even crying aloud. It cannot help itself. It knows that though he is there he will not become manifest in order that the soul may enjoy him. This is painful, a sweet, sharp pain from which the soul even if it wanted to cannot be free: it is what the soul desires.

St Teresa of Avila, *The Interior Castle*

THE SEVENTH MANSION:
SUBLIME FAVOURS

Jesus replied, 'If anyone loves me, he will obey my teaching. My Father will love him, and will come to him and make our home with him' (John 14:23).

When it is the Lord's pleasure to have compassion on all suffering endured through longing for him by the soul whom he has taken spiritually for his Bride, he brings her into this mansion. It is the chamber of his presence she enters before he consummates this celestial marriage. This is the Seventh Mansion. Just as God has a place in heaven so he has a place for the soul to dwell in, where none but he can abide. We may call it a second heaven.

In this mansion the soul receives the following vision. By some mysterious revelation of truth, the three persons of the blessed Trinity reveal themselves, preceded by an illumination which shines on the spirit like a most dazzling cloud of light. These three persons are distinct from each other. Sublime knowledge infuses the soul, imbuing it with the certainty that the three are one substance, power and knowledge and are one with God. So what once was a doctrine of faith, the soul now understands by sight, as it were. Yet it does not see the blessed Trinity by the eyes of the body or the soul as this is not an imaginary vision. All three persons here communicate themselves to the soul. They speak to it and make it understand word of our Lord in the gospel: that he, and the Father and the Holy Spirit will come and make their abode with the soul who loves him and keeps his commands (John 14:23).

St Teresa of Avila, *The Interior Castle*

CHRISTIAN HOPE

He came and preached peace to you (Ephesians 2:17).

My distress of mind continued for about three months, and well might it have continued for years, since my sins were more in number than the hairs of my head; but God in infinite condescension began at last to smile upon me, and to give me a hope of acceptance with Him.

'He is not here; he has risen, just as he said' (Matthew 28:6).

In Passion Week, as I was reading Bishop Wilson on the Lord's Supper, I met with an expression to this effect – 'That the Jews knew what they did, when they transferred their sin to the head of their offering.' The thought came into my mind, What, may I transfer all my guilt to another? Has God provided an Offering for me, that I may lay my sins on His head? Then, God willing, I will not bear them on my own soul one moment longer. Accordingly I sought to lay my sins upon the sacred head of Jesus; and on the Wednesday began to have a hope of mercy; on the Thursday that hope increased; on the Friday and Saturday it became more strong; and on the Sunday morning, Easterday, April 4, I awoke early with those words upon my heart and lips, 'Jesus Christ is risen to-day! Hallelujah! Hallelujah!'

From that hour peace flowed in rich abundance into my soul; and at the Lord's Table in our Chapel I had the sweetest access to God through my blessed Saviour.

Charles Simeon, *Sermons*

HUMILITY, PERFECT AND IMPERFECT

'He has filled the hungry with good things' (Luke 1:53).

Humility is nothing more than an accurate self-assessment, an awareness of oneself as one really is. And surely, anyone seeing himself for what he really is, must be truly humble.

Two things cause humility. One is the state of degradation, wretchedness and weakness to which man has fallen because of sin, and of which he will always to some extent remain conscious in this life, however holy he may be. The other is the superabundant love and worth of God himself: all nature trembles, all scholars are fools, all saints and angels blind in the face of it. So much so, that if God had not portioned out their vision of him to correspond with their progress in grace, I could not describe what would happen to them.

This second cause, the love and worth of God, is the 'perfect' one because it is eternal. The former is 'imperfect' because it ends with this life. Often a soul which is still in his mortal body will find that his longing for God so increases, by God's grace, that, suddenly, he becomes oblivious of himself, not dwelling on whether he has been good or bad. Whether this occurs often or seldom, this longing impulse never lasts long. During this time he is perfectly humbled, for he knows no cause but the chief one, God himself. But when this longing is moved by other motives, even if God is the chief one, then humility remains imperfect. Still, this is good and should be experienced. God forbid that you should think otherwise.

The Cloud of Unknowing

'MY POOR PROGRESS'

I press on to take hold of that for which Christ Jesus took hold of me (Philippians 3:12).

My Reverend and Most Honoured Mother,

We must often keep in mind that our single aim in this life is to please God. The sum of everything else is but foolishness and vanity. For more than forty years we have lived in a religious order. Have we devoted all these years to love and serve God who in his mercy called us to this work? On the one hand, I am full of shame and confusion as I reflect on the wonderful graces God has bestowed on me and which he continues to bestow on me; on the other hand, I am greatly concerned about how little I have used them and about my poor progress along the path of perfection.

Since, through his mercy, we still have a little time, we must be in earnest and make up for lost time and return in complete trust to this father of loving-kindness, who is always ready to receive us back with love and open arms. My dear Mother, we must renounce wholeheartedly all that is not of God. God deserves more than we can ever give him. We must think about him all the time. We must place our total trust in him. I am confident that we will shortly experience the effects of placing such trust in him, and then know the abundance of that grace with which we can do all things, and without which we can only sin.

Brother Lawrence, *The Practice of the Presence of God*

MISTRUST YOUR INTELLECT

'The wisdom of the wise will perish, the intelligence of the intelligent will vanish' (Isaiah 29:14).

To the Duc de Chevreuse
We are like birds with their feet attached to a piece of string. They think that they can fly away but can only go as far as the string allows them. They are prisoners. Do you understand this parable? What I desire for you is better than everything you fear that you may lose. Be faithful about what you do know so that you may be rewarded with more knowledge. Mistrust your intellect which has so often deceived you. Be simple and be strong in your simplicity. Remember St Paul's warning, 'this world in its present form is passing away' (1 Corinthians 7:31), and be warned that we shall pass away with the world if we conform to its vain way of life. The truth of God lasts for ever and we shall be stable so long as we cling to God's truth.

People who study should treat it as a real calling of God's providence and they should labour just like men who go to market for their daily, necessary provisions. All study should be carried out in a spirit of prayer. God is both truth and love. We cannot really know the truth unless we love it. People who love God a great deal will know God intimately. Not to love God a great deal is not to know God. People who love God a great deal and who live humbly in their lack of knowledge are loved by the God of truth. God knows what wise men are ignorant about and do not even want to learn about. This is what I desire of you: a learning that is 'hidden . . . from the wise and learned, and revealed . . . to little children' (Matthew 11:25).

Archbishop Fénelon, *Christian Perfection*

EVERY GOOD GIFT

Every good and perfect gift is from above, coming down from the Father of the heavenly lights (James 1:17).

For people who give themselves to God and diligently seek to do his will, whatever God may send will be the best. As God lives, you can be sure it is the very best, and there can be no better way. Some other way may seem better, yet is not so good for you. God wills this way and not that, therefore this way is bound to be the best. Whether it be sickness or poverty, hunger or thirst, what God gives or does not give, that is the very best for you. Yes, even though, sadly, you may be lacking in fervour for God or the interior life. Whatever you have or have not, accept it all to the glory of God, and then whatever he sends you will be for the best.

One thing I often point out: it is a fact that every day we say in the Lord's Prayer, 'Lord, your will be done.' And yet when his will is done we grumble and are dissatisfied. Whatever God does, let us consider that to be the best, and like that best of all. Those who do take it as the best always stay calm. Sometimes you will say, 'Oh dear! It would be better if something else happened.' Or, 'If that hadn't happened, things would have turned out better.' As long as you think like that, you will never be at peace. Accept it all for the best.

Meister Eckhart, *Sermons*

CAUGHT BY THE DEVIL

Escape from the trap of the devil (2 Timothy 2:26).

Many are the traps of the devil. If he is not able to disturb the soul through poverty, he suggests riches as an attraction. If he has not won the victory by insults and disgrace, he suggests praise and glory. Overcome by health, he makes the body ill. Having failed to defeat it through pleasures he tries to overthrow it by involuntary suffering. He adds severe illness to this to disturb the faint-hearted in their love of God. Rejoice that God visits you and keep this blessed saying on your lips, 'The LORD has chastened me severely, but he has not given me over to death' (Psalm 118:18).

It is written, 'Be wise as serpents and innocent as doves' (Matthew 10:16, RSV). Being like serpents means not ignoring attacks and the traps of the devil.

We must arm ourselves in every way against the devil. For he attacks us from outside and also he stirs from within us. The soul is like a ship when great waves break over it, and at the same time it sinks because the hold is too full of water. We are just like that: we lose as much through the exterior faults we indulge in as through the thoughts that arise inside us. So we must keep on guard for the attacks of men that come from outside and also repel the interior onslaughts of our thoughts.

Syncletica, in *Sayings of the Desert Fathers*

THE TOUCH OF GOD

Do not put out the Spirit's fire (1 Thessalonians 5:19).

As a fire of love is infinite, so when God touches the soul somewhat sharply the burning heat within it becomes so extreme as to surpass all the fires of the world. This is why this touch of God is said to be a 'burn'; for the fire there is more intense and more concentrated, and the effect of it surpasses all other fires. When the divine fire shall have transformed the soul into itself, the soul not only feels the burn, but itself is become wholly and entirely burnt up in this vehement fire.

O delicious wound, and the more delicious the more the burn of love penetrates the inmost substance of the soul, burning all it can burn, that it may supply all the delight it can give. This burning and wound, in my opinion, are the highest condition attainable in this life; for this is the touch of the divinity without form or figure, either intellectual or imaginary. The soul feels its loving growing, being strengthened. It refines itself so much that it seems as if seas of fire were in it, filling it with love. The soul beholds itself as one immense sea of fire.

John Ruysbroeck, *The Spiritual Espousals*

A PICTURE OF HEAVEN

I looked and there before me was a great multitude that no-one could count, from every nation, tribe, people and language, standing before the throne and in front of the Lamb (Revelation 7:9).

Christian and Hopeful asked, 'What must we do in the holy place?'

And they were told, 'There you will receive comfort for all your toil, and joy for all your sorrow. You will reap what you have sown, even the fruit of all your prayers, your tears, and sufferings for the King as you came on your way' (Galatians 6:7–8). In that place you will wear crowns of gold, and always enjoy the sight and vision of the Holy One, for there you 'shall see him as he is' (1 John 3:2). There you will serve him continually with praise and shouting and thanksgiving. You will serve the One you longed to serve in the world though you found it so difficult because of the weakness of your flesh. There your eyes will be delighted with seeing, and your ears with hearing the pleasant voice of the Mighty One. There you will enjoy your friends again, who have gone before you, and there you will receive with joy everyone who follows you into the holy place.

There you will be clothed with glory and majesty, and put into a carriage fit to ride out with the King of Glory. When he comes with sound of the trumpet in the clouds, as upon the wings of the wind, you will come with him, and when he sits upon the throne of judgment you will sit by him. Yes, and when he passes sentence upon all evil-doers, be they angels or men, you will also have a voice in that judgment, because they are his and your enemies. Also, when he again returns to the city, you will go, too, with the sound of the trumpet, and be with him for ever.'

John Bunyan, *The Pilgrim's Progress*

WHY YOU? WHY YOU? WHY YOU?

But God chose the foolish things of the world to shame the wise; God chose the weak things of the world to shame the strong (1 Corinthians 1:27).

Once when St Francis returned from the wood where he had been praying, Brother Masseo met him, and wanted to find out how humble St Francis was. So Brother Masseo asked, 'Why you? Why you? Why you?'

St Francis replied, 'What do you mean, Brother Masseo?'

Brother Masseo replied, 'The whole world seems to be going after you, everyone wants to visit you, hear you speak, obey you, and yet you are not a handsome person. You do not have a store of great knowledge or wisdom. You are not of noble birth. Therefore, why does the whole world seek you out?'

When the blessed St Francis heard this, his spirit rejoiced in him, and he lifted up his head to heaven and his mind to God for a long time. Then he came to himself and fell on his knees, and as he praised and thanked God he turned warmly to Brother Masseo and said: 'You want to know why me, why me, why me. You really want to know why the whole world runs after me. The answer lies in those most holy eyes of God which see both good and evil everywhere. Those most holy eyes saw among evil men no greater sinner than me. They found no one so useless and vile as me. Therefore in order to carry out the wonderful tasks he had in mind to do, since he could not find anyone more vile than me, he chose me. For God has chosen the foolish things of the world to confound the wise. God chose the feeble and contemptible people of the world to confound the great and noble. Then people would recognise that the grandeur of goodness proceeds from God and not from his creatures. Then nobody would have any grounds for boasting in God's presence and God alone would receive all the honour and glory.'

St Francis of Assisi, *Letters*

HUMILITY

He guides the humble in what is right (Psalm 25:9).

While humility is the foundation stone of all graces and holiness, it is so delicate and sensitive a virtue that, as we speak about it or as we seek to find it, we can make it wither. Probably no really humble person ever thought of himself as being humble. While we must earnestly and prayerfully study in order to grow in holiness we must be careful not to concentrate on our own personalities.

We are told by all spiritual writers that one important point to bear in mind, as we seek to attain humility, is not to be surprised by our own faults and failures. Who am I that I should expect to be able to stand upright? Is it not expected and natural that somebody so weak and frail as I should frequently fall? I should not be mortified, disappointed and downhearted because of my faults. I should get up again and start again and try to do better. While I must not be surprised that I have done badly I can at least learn from this experience and trust myself less and trust God more.

Some of the means for seeking humility which have been suggested now follow:

1. We remember all the time the great example of our Lord who is the perfect pattern for true humility. Not only did he take a humble position in this world but he also allowed himself to be despised, to be taken for a madman and a lawbreaker and was even rejected by his own family.

2. Accept all the humiliations meekly and, even more than that, accept them lovingly.

3. Never put off making amends for one of your faults.

Archbishop Fénelon, *Christian Perfection*

THE MEMORIAL

'Now this is eternal life: that they may know you, the only true God, and Jesus Christ, whom you have sent' (John 17:3).

Fire
'God of Abraham, God of Isaac, God of Jacob',
not of the philosophers and scientists.
Certitude. Certitude. Feeling. Joy. Peace.
God of Jesus Christ.
God of Jesus Christ.
'My God and your God.'
'You shall be my God.'

Forgetting the world and all things, except God alone.
He is to be found only by the ways taught in the Gospel.
Greatness of the human soul.
'Righteous Father, the world has not known Thee, but I have known thee.'

Joy, joy, joy, tears of joy.
I have fallen away from him, I have fled from him, denied him, crucified him. May I not be separated from him for eternity.
Total submission to Jesus Christ and to my director.
Eternally in joy for one day of trial upon earth.
'I will not forget thy word'. Amen.

Blaise Pascal [On the evening of 23 November 1654 Pascal had a spiritual experience which influenced him for the rest of his life. He recorded this mystical moment in the above Memorial, on a scrap of paper, later copied onto parchment and carried with him wherever he went, until his death.]

PERSEVERE

'Brother will betray brother to death, and a father his child. Children will rebel against their parents and have them put to death. All men will hate you because of me, but he who stands firm to the end will be saved' (Mark 13:12–13).

What now remains, my dearest, is to know about the importance of perseverance. Perseverance alone ensures that a man will receive rewards for his virtues.

For without perseverance, the champion does not obtain the conquest and the conqueror does not receive his crown. The winning of virtue is the essence of courage.

Perseverance is the nurse of our merits.

Perseverance is the sister of patience.

Perseverance is the daughter of constancy.

Perseverance is the lover of peace.

Perseverance is the knot of friendship.

Perseverance is the band of agreement.

Perseverance is the bulwark of godliness.

Take away perseverance and no service has any value; no good turn any thanks; no prowess any praise. In fine, it is not the person who begins, but he who perseveres to the end who shall be saved.

Bernard of Clairvaux, *The Song of Songs*

THE SPIRITUAL LIFE

They asked each other, 'Were not our hearts burning within us while he talked with us on the road and opened the Scriptures to us?' (Luke 24:32).

Here are four practices which are essential to acquire for the spiritual life.

1. The most essential thing for the spiritual life is to practise the presence of God. You must find joy in God's company and make it a lifetime habit to speak with him humbly and lovingly throughout the day. Speak with him at every moment in the day. Do not be bound by any rules or restrictions in this matter. Talk with God especially in times of temptation, dryness, distress, and even of sin and unfaithfulness.

2. We should live in such a way that our whole lives become occasions for fellowship with God. This should spring from a pure and sincere heart.

3. Everything we do must not be done with haste or impetuosity, but with thoughtfulness and consideration. We must not work with an undisciplined spirit, but work in God's presence quietly, placidly and lovingly. Pray to God that he will approve of your work. In this way we will defeat Satan and make his weapons fall from his hands.

4. During our work, or during whatever we are doing, even during our reading and writing, and even during our formal devotions and vocal prayers, we must pause for a moment and worship God in our hearts. We must treasure this moment, even if it is but a passing moment.

Brother Lawrence, *The Practice of the Presence of God*

NO RESTRAINT IN CONTEMPLATION

Have mercy on me, O Lord, for I call to you all day long (Psalm 86:3).

If you should ask me what restraint you should exercise in this work of contemplation, I would answer, 'None whatever!' In all other matters you are bound to use restraint; for example, in the question of food and drink, sleeping, keeping warm or cool, in long prayers or time spent reading, or in conversation with fellow Christians. In all this you get the right balance. But in contemplation, be abandoned! I want you never to cease from this work as long as you live.

I am not saying that you can continue in it always with the same freshness; that cannot be. Illness or some other disorder of body or soul, or physical needs will greatly hinder you in contemplation, and pull you down. But you should always attend to your work in intention if not in actuality: there is no 'time of'! So, for the love of God, take care of yourself and try not to fall ill. Don't let illness be the cause of weakness on your part. I tell you honestly, contemplation demands great tranquillity, wholeness, and purity in both body and soul.

So, for the love of God, discipline your body and soul alike, keeping fit and healthy. If you should get ill, through circumstances beyond your control, bear it patiently and wait patiently upon God's mercy. That is all you need do. It is true to say that patience in sickness and other forms of trouble pleases God much more than any splendid devotion that you might show in health.

The Cloud of Unknowing

DENIALL

Do not withhold your mercy from me, O LORD; may your love and your truth always protect me (Psalm 40:11).

When my devotions could not pierce
    Thy silent eares;
Then was my heart broken, as was my verse:
    My breast was full of fears
        And disorder:

My bent thoughts, like a brittle bow,
    Did flie asunder:
Each took his way; some would to pleasures go,
    Some to the warres and thunder
        Of alarms.

As good go any where, they say,
    As to benumme
Both knees and heart, in crying night and day,
    Come, come, my God O come,
        But no hearing.

O that thou shouldst give dust a tongue
    To crie to thee,
And then not heare it crying! all day long
    My heart was in my knee,
        But no hearing.

Therefore my soul lay out of sight,
    Untun'd, unstrung:
My feeble spirit, unable to look right,
    Like a nipt blossome, hung,
        Discontented.

O cheer and tune my heartlesse breast,
    Deferre no time;
That so thy favours granting my request,
    They and my minde may chime,
        And mend my ryme.

George Herbert

A FISH, AN EGG AND A SCORPION

'Ask and it will be given to you; seek and you will find; knock and the door will be opened to you' (Luke 11:9).

To a noble lady (411)

You asked me, I remember to write you something on prayer.

From Luke 11:9–13 the apostle Luke commends three things.

The fish signifies faith, either because of the water of baptism, or because it remains unharmed in the middle of the tempestuous waves of this world.

In contrast with this is the serpent with its poisonous guile persuading men to disbelieve God.

The egg signifies hope, because the life of the young bird is not yet evident but is to be – it is not seen but hoped for, because 'hope which is seen is no hope at all' (Romans 8:24). In contrast with this is the scorpion, for the person who hopes for eternal life forgets the things that are behind and reaches forward to what lies ahead, since it is dangerous to look back. But the scorpion is to be feared because of what lies in its tail – its sharp, poisonous sting. Bread stands for charity, for 'the greatest of these is charity' (1 Corinthians 13:13) and bread surpasses all other food in worth; in contrast to which is the stone, for hearts that are hardened refuse to exercise charity.

Thus, when we practise faith, hope and charity with continual desire, we pray always. But at the same time, we also set aside stated hours and times devoted to explicit prayer to God according to the apostle's instruction: 'Let your petitions be made known to God' (Philippians 4:6), not as if you were giving God information, because he knows them before we say a word, but rather that in the presence of God we ourselves should realise all we need and wait patiently on him.

St Augustine, *Sermons*

GRACE ABOUNDING

He saved us . . . justified by his grace (Titus 3:5, 7).

'Thy righteousness is in heaven,' and methought withal I saw with the eye of my soul, Jesus Christ is at God's right hand. I saw, moreover, that it was not my good frame of heart that made my righteousness better, nor yet my bad frame that made my right-eousness worse; for my righteousness was Jesus Christ himself, the same yesterday, today and for ever. Now did my chains fall from my legs indeed; I was loosed from my afflictions and irons.

Oh, methought, Christ! Christ! There was nothing but Christ that was before my eyes! I could look from myself to him and should reckon that all those graces of God that now were green on me, were yet but like those crack-groats and fourpence-halfpennies that rich men carry in their purses, when their gold is in their trunk at home!

Oh, I saw my gold was in my trunk at home! In Christ my Lord and Saviour! Now Christ was all; all my wisdom, all my right-eousness, all my sanctification, and all my redemption!

John Bunyan, *Grace Abounding to the Chief of Sinners*

CALLING OF ST ANDREW

Andrew, Simon Peter's brother, was one of the two who heard what John [the Baptist] had said and who had followed Jesus (John 1:40).

Jesus calls us! O'er the tumult
Of our life's wild restless sea
Day by day his voice is sounding,
Saying, 'Christian, follow me':

As of old Saint Andrew heard it
By the Galilean lake,
Turned from home and toil and kindred,
Leaving all for his dear sake.

Jesus calls us from the worship
Of the vain world's golden store,
From each idol that would keep us,
Saying, 'Christian, love me more'.

In our days and in our sorrows,
Days of toil and hours of ease,
Still he calls, in cares and pleasures,
'Christian, love me more than these'.

Jesus calls us! By thy mercies,
Saviour, may we hear thy call,
Give our hearts to thy obedience,
Serve and love thee best of all.

C. F. Alexander

THINK OF GOD'S LOVE

This is how God showed his love among us: He sent his one and only Son into the world that we might live through him (1 John 4:9).

If you want your heart to be in heaven, let your soul concentrate on true believing thoughts of the exceeding, infinite love of God. Love attracts love.

Love is the very essence of God. The Scripture tells us that 'God is love'.

Oh, if we could only think of God as we do a friend! As one that loves us unfeignedly, even more than we do ourselves; whose very heart is set on doing us good, and who has therefore provided us with an everlasting dwelling with himself. It would not then be so hard to carry on loving him! Where we love most heartily, we shall think most sweetly, and most freely; and nothing will more bring our love to life than believing he loves us.

So get a truer idea of the loving nature of God, and store up all the experiences and discoveries of his love to you; and then see if it does not further your heavenly-mindedness. I fear most Christians think more highly of the love of a hearty friend than of the love of God; and then what wonder is it if they love their friends better than God, and would rather be with them than with God, when they take them to be better and trustier friends than God, and more merciful and compassionate!

Richard Baxter, *The Saints' Everlasting Rest*

THE KINGDOM OF GOD IS NEAR

'When you see these things happening, you know that the kingdom of God is near' (Luke 21:31).

Our Lord says, 'the kingdom of God is near'. Yes, the kingdom of God is within us, and according to St Paul, our salvation is nearer than we think. In what sense is the kingdom of God near?

A philosopher says, 'That man knows God aright who is equally aware of him in all things'; and, 'To serve God in fear is good; to serve him in love is better; but he who is apt to behold love in fear does best of all.' A life of rest and peace in God is good; a life of pain lived in patience is still better; but to have peace in a life of pain is best of all. One may go in the fields and say one's prayers and be conscious of God or go to church and be conscious of God. If we are more conscious of God when we are in a quiet place, that comes of our own imperfection and is not due to God, for God is the same in all things and all places and is just as ready to reveal himself as far as it lies in him to do so. The man who always finds God the same is the man who knows him aright.

St Bernard says, 'Why does my eye see sky, and not my foot? Because my eye is like the sky, more than my foot.' For my soul to see God, then, she must be heavenly. What makes the soul alive to God in her, and aware of how close he is to her? My answer: Heaven permits no alien intrusion. No mortal deficiency can penetrate within to do it outrage. And the soul who knows God is so firmly established in God that nothing can reach her, not hope nor fear nor joy nor grief nor good nor ill nor nothing that would bring her down to earth.

Meister Eckhart, *Sermons*

SPIRITUAL DRYNESS

Then the man said, 'Let me go, for it is daybreak.' But Jacob replied, 'I will not let you go unless you bless me' (Genesis 32:26).

If it should happen, Philothea, that you have neither relish nor consolation in your meditation, I implore you not to be in the least troubled by this. Sometimes open the door to vocal prayers: complain to our Lord, confess your unworthiness, ask him to come to your aid, kiss his image if you have it, say to him these words of Jacob: 'I will not let you go unless you bless me.' Or, say the words of the Canaanite woman, 'Yes, Lord, but even the dogs eat the crumbs that fall from their master's table' (Matthew 15:27).

At other times, take a book in your hand and read it with attention, until your spirit is awakened and restored within you; sometimes stir up your heart by some posture or movement of exterior devotion, prostrating yourself on the ground, crossing your hands on your chest, embracing a crucifix; that is, if you are in some private place.

But if after all this you obtain no consolation, do not be upset, no matter how great your dryness is, just continue to keep yourself in a devout attitude before your God. How many courtiers there are that go a hundred times a year into the prince's presence-chamber without hope of speaking to him, but only to be seen by him and to pay their respects. So also, my dear Philothea, should we come to holy prayer, purely and simply to pay our respects and give proof of our fidelity.

Francis de Sales, *Introduction to a Devout Life*

TAKE ALL CHANCES AND CROSSES
WILLINGLY

Jesus said, 'Father, forgive them for they do not know what they are doing' (Luke 23:34).

If a man ought and is willing to lie still under God's hand, he must and ought also to lie still under all things, whether they come from God, himself, or the creatures, nothing excepted. And he who would be obedient, resigned, and submissive to God, must and ought to be also resigned, obedient, and submissive to all things, in a spirit of yielding, and not of resistance; and take them in silence, resting on the hidden foundations of his soul, and having a secret inward patience, that enables him to take all the chances and crosses willingly; and, whatever befalls, neither to call for nor desire any redress, or deliverance, or resistance, or revenge, but always in a loving, sincere humility to cry, 'Father, forgive them, for they know not what they do!'

Theologia Germanica

ANXIETY AND UNREST

Why are you downcast, O my soul? Why so disturbed within me? Put your hope in God, for I will yet praise him, my Saviour and my God (Psalm 42:11).

Beware of letting your care degenerate into anxiety and unrest; tossed as you are by the winds and waves of many troubles. Keep your eyes fixed on the Lord, and say, 'Oh, my God, I look to Thee alone; be Thou my guide, my pilot'; and then be comforted. When the shore is gained, who will heed the toil and the storm? And we shall steer safely through every storm, so long as our heart is right, our intention fervent, our courage steadfast, and our trust fixed on God. If at times we are somewhat stunned by the tempest, never fear; let us take breath, and go on afresh.

Do not be disconcerted by the fits of vexation and uneasiness which are sometimes produced by the multiplicity of your domestic worries. No indeed, dearest child, all these are but opportunities of strengthening yourself in the loving forbearing graces which our dear Lord sets before us.

Francis de Sales, *Introduction to a Devout Life*

SPIRITUAL MARRIAGE

I waited patiently for the LORD; he turned to me and heard my cry. . . . You are my help and my deliverer (Psalm 40:1, 17).

The spiritual marriage is like the water that falls from the heavens and unites with the water of rivers and springs in such a way that the earthly water can no longer be distinguished from the other; or it is like a little brook that enters the ocean, and there is lost; or again it is like a strong light which, divided, streams into a house through two windows, and there forms but one light.

In that marriage the mystic butterfly dies in unspeakable joy, because Jesus Christ becomes its life.

The soul comes to know, in inmost and most living exaltation of love, that it was its God who gave it life. And ceaselessly must it call: O Life of my life, O my strength! and similar expressions.

In perfect clarity it sees that it is God, and no one else, who looses the arrows that wound it, that he is the Life of its life, and the Sun which sheds light within it, over all its powers. If a tree planted near running water is more refreshed and bears more fruit, then it should not surprise us that a soul whose higher part, or spirit, forms a perfect whole with the heavenly water, should be given so ardent a desire for the splendour of God.

St Teresa of Avila, *The Interior Castle*

FLEEING FROM THE WISDOM OF THE WORLD

'Who are my mother and my brothers?' he [Jesus] asked. Then he looked at those seated in a circle around him and said, 'Here are my mother and my brothers! Whoever does God's will is my brother and sister and mother' (Mark 3:33–34).

We must not be wise and prudent by the standards of the world, but simple, humble and pure. Let us keep our body under subjection and in contempt because we are all through our own fault corrupt and miserable and vile worms of the earth. As the Lord says through the psalmist, 'I am a worm, and no man: the reproach of men, and the outcast of the people' (Psalm 22:6).

We must never seek to dominate others but be servants and subject to other people, 'to every human creature for God's sake' (1 Peter 2:13).

May the spirit of the Lord rest on everyone who behaves and perseveres to the end in this way. May God dwell in the lives of such people. They will be the sons of the heavenly Father as they carry out his wishes. They are the husbands, wives, brothers and mothers of our Lord Jesus Christ. We are married to Christ when our soul is sanctified and united to Jesus Christ through the Holy Spirit. We are his brothers when we do the will of his heavenly Father. We are his mothers when we cherish him in our heart and in our body through pure love and a clean conscience. We do this as we do holy actions for Christ's sake which are an example to others.

Oh, what glory, what dignity and what splendour it is to have a Father in heaven! How gracious, how beautiful and how sweet it is to have a Spouse in heaven! What splendour, what charm, what happiness, what peace, what sweetness, what inner joy and what supreme fortune it is to have such a Brother!

St Francis of Assisi, *Admonitions*

MARTHA AND MARY

Martha was distracted by all the preparations that had to be made (Luke 10:40).

Martha chose a good part, but Mary the better. What Martha chose passes away. She ministered to the hungry, the thirsty, the homeless: but all these pass away – there will be a time when none will hunger nor thirst. Therefore will her care be taken from her.

Martha's part is holy and great: yet Mary has chosen the better, in that while her sister was solicitous and working and caring for many things, she was at leisure and sat still and listened. Mary's part will not be taken from her, Martha's will – for the ministering to the saints will pass away; to whom will food be given, where no one is hungry? Mary's part does not pass away, for her delight was in justice and truth, and in this same will be her delight in eternity. What Mary chose waxes greater; for the delight of the human heart – of a faithful and holy human heart – in the light of truth and the affluence of wisdom, if it be sweet now, will then be sweeter far.

In these two women, both pleasing the Lord, two lives were figured:

the present and the future,
the laborious and the quiet,
the troublous and the happy,
the temporal and the eternal.

Both are praiseworthy: but the one is laborious, the other leisured. What Martha was doing, there we are; what Mary, that we hope for. While in this life how much can we have of Mary's part? For even now we do somewhat of her work, when removed from businesses and laying aside our ordinary cares. Inasmuch as we do thus, we are like Mary.

St Augustine, *Sermons*

THREE KINDS OF LIFE

'Martha, Martha,' the Lord answered, 'you are worried and upset about many things, but only one thing is needed' (Luke 10:41–42).

Concerning the three kinds of life – the leisurely [contemplative], the busy [active], and the life which combines the two [mixed] – anyone without prejudice to his faith can spend his life in any one of them and attain to an everlasting reward, for all that matters is to hold to the love of truth and the service of love.

For no one should be so at leisure as in his leisure not to think of his neighbour's welfare; nor so busied as not to seek after the contemplation of God. In his leisure he should not find delight in an idle vacancy, but it should be a seeking and finding of the truth: so that each one may advance in this, and not grudge to others what he find.

In the life of action honour in this life is not to be loved, nor power; but the work itself which is done in virtue of the said honour and power, if it is rightly and usefully done, that is, if it work the salvation of those under us. No one is precluded from the pursuit of knowing the truth, which is the work of a leisure that is praiseworthy. Wherefore the love of truth seeks for a holy leisure; and the obligation of charity makes us undertake righteous business.

St Augustine, *Sermons*

THE TWO LIVES

'Mary has chosen what is better, and it will not be taken away from her' (Luke 10:42).

There are two lives in which almighty God by his holy word instructs us – the active and the contemplative.

The active life is: to give bread to the hungry, to teach the ignorant the word of wisdom, to correct the erring, to recall to the path of humility our neighbour when he waxes proud, to tend the sick, to dispense to all what they need, and to provide those entrusted to us with the means of substance.

But the contemplative life is: to retain indeed with all one's mind the love of God and neighbour, but to rest from exterior action, and cleave only to the desire of the Maker, that the mind may now take no pleasure in doing anything, but having spurned all cares, may be aglow to see the face of its Creator; so that it already knows how to bear with sorrow the burden of the corruptible flesh, and with all its desires to seek to join the hymn-singing choirs of angels, to mingle with the heavenly citizens, and to rejoice at its everlasting incorruption in the sight of God.

While placed in this life we taste only the beginnings of intimate contemplation; whereas the active life can be fully laid hold of. The active life ceases with this present world; but the contemplative life begins here, that it may be perfected in the heavenly country, because the fire of love which begins to burn here, when it sees him whom it loves, will in his life blaze up the more. Therefore the contemplative life is by no means taken away, for when the light of the present world is withdrawn it is perfected.

St Augustine, *Sermons*

THE ACTIVE LIFE

'And if anyone gives even a cup of cold water to one of these little ones because he is my disciple, I tell you the truth, he will certainly not lose his reward' (Matthew 10:42).

Though both the active life and the contemplative life are both gifts of God's grace, yet as long as we live among our neighbours one is by necessity, the other by choice. For who that knows God enters into his kingdom, unless he first works well? Without the contemplative life, therefore, those can enter into the heavenly kingdom who neglect not to do the good that they can; but without the active life they cannot enter, if they neglect to do the good they can. Therefore the active life is by necessity, the contemplative by choice.

The active life is to be lived first, that afterwards the contemplative may be attained to.

Perfectness of practice having been received, we come to contemplation.

Everyone that is perfect is first joined to an active life for productiveness, and afterwards united to a contemplative life for rest.

The mind should first spend itself in labour, and afterwards it may be refreshed by contemplation. We ascend to the heights of contemplation by the steps of the active life. The active life is before the contemplation in time, because by good works we tend to contemplation.

Augustine, *Sermons*

SEE YOUR NEIGHBOUR IN GOD

Serve wholeheartedly, as if you were serving the Lord, not men (Ephesians 6:7).

To a married woman. Annecy, 3 May 1604
We must see our neighbour in God who would have us show him love and consideration. Such is Paul's advice in Ephesians 6:5–8 where he instructs servants to obey God in their masters and their masters in God. We must put this love into practice by showing our neighbour visible signs of kindness. Even if this goes against the grain we should not give up because through our goodwill and the habit formed through constant repetition we will finally conquer our lower natures.

We must use our times of prayer and meditation to deal with this problem. First we must pray for the love of God, and then we must pray for our neighbour, especially for those we are not humanly attracted to.

Go to the trouble of visiting your hospital occasionally. Comfort the sick, show compassion on their illnesses, make it clear that you are moved by the sight of their suffering. Pray for them and give them practical help. In all you do, take great care not to offend your husband, family or parents by going to church too much, by constant seclusion or by neglecting your family duties.

Don't become censorious about other people's conduct, or turn up your nose at conversations which fail to match up to your lofty standards. In all such matters charity must rule and enlighten us, so that we comply graciously with our neighbour's wishes in anything that is not contrary to God's law.

St Francis de Sales, *Letters*

THE UNION OF THE TWO LIVES

'Love the Lord your God . . . Love your neighbour' (Mark 12:30–31).

Whoever opens his mind in holy works, has over and above to extend it to the secret pursuits of inward contemplation. For he is no perfect preacher who either, from devotion to contemplation, neglects works that ought to be done, or, from urgency of business, puts aside the duties of contemplation.

It is hence that the Redeemer of mankind in the daytime exhibits his miracle in cities, and spends the night in devotion to pray on the mountain, namely, that he may teach all perfect preachers, that they should neither entirely leave the active life from love of the speculative, nor wholly slight the joys of contemplation from the excess of working; but in quiet imbibe by contemplation what in employment they may pour back to their neighbours by word of mouth. For by contemplation they rise into the love of God, but by preaching they return back to the service of their neighbour.

In the sight of the eternal judge our charity should be coloured with the love both of God and of our neighbour, that the converted soul may neither so delight in repose for the sake of the love of God, as to put aside the care and service of our neighbour; nor, busying itself for the love of our neighbour, be so wedded thereto that, entirely forsaking quiet, it extinguish in itself the fire of love of the most high.

St Gregory the Great, *Sermons*

HOW CHRIST WAS REVEALED TO HOPEFUL

I didn't see him with my physical eyes, but with the eyes of my heart (Ephesians 1:18–19).

It was like this: one day I was very sad, I think sadder than at any time in my life, and this sadness was the result of a fresh sight of the greatness and vileness of my sins. I was expecting nothing but hell, and the everlasting damnation of my soul. But suddenly I thought I saw the Lord Jesus looking down from heaven on me and saying, 'Believe in the Lord Jesus, and you will be saved' (Acts 16:31).

I replied, 'Lord, I'm a great, very great sinner.'

And he answered, 'My grace is sufficient for you' (2 Corinthians 12:9).

But I said, 'But, Lord, what is believing?'

And then I understood from the words, 'He who comes to me will never be hungry, and he who believes in me will never be thirsty' (John 6:35) that believing and coming are all one. So someone who comes, that is, who runs out in his heart and feelings after salvation by Christ, is someone who believes in Christ.

Then my eyes filled with tears and I asked, 'But, Lord, will you really accept and save such a great sinner as I am?'

And I heard him say, 'whoever comes to me I will never drive away' (John 6:37).

John Bunyan, *Grace Abounding to the Chief of Sinners*

WORSHIP GOD

'God is spirit, and his worshippers must worship in spirit and in truth' (John 4:24).

To worship God in spirit and in truth means to worship God as we should worship him. God is spirit and he must indeed be worshipped in truth – that is to say by a humble and genuine worship of the spirit in the depth and centre of our soul. It is God alone who can see this worship, a worship we can so often repeat that in the end it becomes as it were natural, and as if God were one with our soul and our soul one with God. Practice makes this clear.

To worship God in truth is to recognise him for what he is and to recognise ourselves for what we are. To worship God in truth is to recognise in verity and at this moment and in spirit that God is what he is, that is to say infinitely perfect, infinitely to be adored, infinitely removed from evil and thus with every attribute divine. What man shall there be, however small the reason he may have, who will not use all his strength to render to this great God his reverence and his worship?

To worship God in truth is again to confess that we are completely separated from him, and that he greatly desires to make us like him if we will. Who will be so unwise as to turn away, even for a moment, from the honour, from the love, the service and the unending worship that we owe to him?

Brother Lawrence, *The Practice of the Presence of God*

THE CLOUD OF UNKNOWING

You, O LORD, keep my lamp burning; my God turns my darkness into light (Psalm 18:28).

Lift up your heart to God. In humble and total love for him seek God himself. Do not consider what the rewards may be. Refuse utterly to think of anything that detracts from God himself. Forget the world and everything in it, forget your own understanding of its meaning, so that your singleness of mind may not be distracted from God himself.

Your soul will be helped by God's grace when it consciously longs to be in union with God. And it can happen in no time at all, in a flash, in a moment. If it did not, the struggle would be too hard and beyond your powers. So press on. Don't give up. Work away at it until this longing to know God surges up within you.

When you first begin, you may find only darkness – a cloud of unknowing, as it were. It will seem incomprehensible, meaningless, except that in your innermost will you will feel a simple steadfast intention reaching out towards God. No matter what you do, this darkness, this cloud, will seem to remain between you and God. It will stop you seeing God in the clear light of rational understanding and from experiencing his loving mercy in your inner being. But be reconciled to the fact that you must wait in this darkness as long as necessary, and don't give up. Continue the struggle, longing to know God whom you love. For if you are ever to feel him and see him in this life, it will always be in this darkness, this cloud. But if you work at what I tell you, I believe you will arrive there. Through God's mercy you will achieve your heart's desire.

The Cloud of Unknowing

DO NOT QUENCH THE SPIRIT

Let us keep in step with the Spirit (Galatians 5:25).

I advise you to observe the movements of the Spirit and avoid quenching it, or resisting its activity. If ever your soul rises above the earth, and becomes acquainted with living in heaven, the Spirit of God must be to you as the chariot was to Elijah – the living principle by which you must move and ascend. Do not grieve your guide – do not quench your life – do not knock off your chariot wheels!

If you do, no wonder your soul is at a loss, and everything stands still or falls to the earth. You do not realise how much the life of all your graces, and the happiness of your souls, depends on your ready and hearty obedience to the Spirit. When the Spirit urges you to private prayer, and you refuse to obey; when he forbids you to indulge in some known sin, and yet you go on; when he tells you which is the way and which is not, and you disregard him – no wonder if your soul is a stranger to heaven. If you will not follow the Spirit when it would draw you to Christ, and to your duty, how can it lead you to heaven, and bring your heart into the presence of God? What supernatural help, what bold access will the soul find in approaching the Almighty, when it is accustomed to obeying the Spirit constantly!

The more of this Spirit we resist, the deeper it will wound; and the more we obey, the speedier is our pace – as the one with the wind in his face makes heaviest weather, and the one with the wind behind him goes most easily.

Richard Baxter, *The Saints' Everlasting Rest*

MENTAL PRAYER AND RECOLLECTION

You will keep in perfect peace him whose mind is steadfast, because he trusts in you (Isaiah 26:3).

Meditation, consisting of considerations on the great truths of Christianity, pious affections and manifold elevations of the soul to God, and serious resolutions of devoting one's self to him, is one of the most important exercises of the Christian life, which should be performed each day by everyone who desires to serve God.

Lay up in your mind such thoughts from your meditation which have touched you most, and during the day often reflect on them. This is equivalent to gathering a bunch of flowers, in this garden of devotion, and taking in their scent throughout the day.

People who find it difficult to meditate should help themselves by reading some good books. Read them in a leisurely way, pause and reflect on what you read, and draw helpful conclusions from such reading.

Call to mind, as often as you can in the day, the presence of God, who is in the centre of your soul. Frequently tell him how much you love him; offer him your whole being many times through the day. Give him your soul, your senses, all your faculties, all your thoughts, all your words and all your actions. Keep far from your thoughts, in so far as you are able, all vain amusements, anxious cares and unhelpful thoughts. Then your heart will easily find him, freely embrace him and quietly rest in him.

Richard Challoner, *Meditations*

THE PRESENT MOMENT

'Today salvation has come to this house' (Luke 19:9).

The present moment is always full of infinite treasures, it contains far more than you have the capacity to hold. Faith is the measure, you will find in the present moment according as you believe.

Love is also the measure. The more your heart loves, the more it desires, and the more it desires the more it finds.

The will of God presents itself at each instant like an immense ocean which the desire of your heart cannot empty, although it will receive from that ocean the measure to which it can extend itself by faith, confidence and love.

The whole of the created universe cannot fill your heart as it has a greater capacity than everything else which is not God. The mountains which alarm your eyes, are but atoms to the heart. The divine will is an abyss the opening of which is the present moment. Plunge into this abyss and you will find it even deeper than your desires.

Pay court to no one, do not worship illusions, they can neither enrich you nor deprive you of anything. The sole will of God will wholly fill you and leave you with no void; adore that will, go straight towards it, pierce through and abandon all appearances.

Jean-Pierre de Caussade, *The Sacrament of the Present Moment*

THE CANTICLE OF THE SUN

Praise the LORD from the heavens, praise him in the heights above (Psalm 148:1).

Most high, most great and good Lord, to thee belong praises, glory and every blessing; to thee alone do they belong, most high God. No one is worthy to call thee by thy name.

Blessed be thou, my Lord for the gift of all thy creatures and especially for our brother, master sun, by whom the day is enlightened. He is radiant and bright, of great splendour, bearing witness to thee, O my God.

Blessed be thou, my Lord for our sister the moon and the stars; thou hast formed them in the heavens, fair and clear.

Blessed be thou, my Lord for my brother the wind, for the air, for cloud and calm, for every kind of weather, for through them thou sustainest all creatures.

Blessed be thou, my Lord for our sister water, which is very useful, humble, chaste and precious.

Blessed be thou, my Lord for brother fire, bright, noble and beautiful, untamable and strong, by whom thou illuminest the night.

Blessed be thou, my Lord for our mother earth, who sustains and nourishes us, who brings forth all kinds of fruit, herbs and brightly coloured flowers.

Blessed be thou, my Lord for those who pardon for love of thee, and who patiently bear infirmity and tribulation.

Happy are those who abide in peace, for by thee, most high God, they will be crowned.

Blessed be thou, my Lord, for our sister death of body, from whom no living man can escape. Woe to him who dies in a state of mortal sin. Happy are those who at the hour of death are found in obedience to thy holy will, for the second death cannot hurt them.

Praise ye and bless ye my Lord; give him thanks and serve him with great humility.

St Francis of Assisi, *Canticles*

KNOWING GOD

Jesus answered [Thomas], 'I am the way and the truth and the life. No-one comes to the Father except through me' (John 14:6).

The person who feels God to be incomprehensible, unknowable, is the one who truly knows God. Nothing is fully known unless its cause, and 'how' and 'what' it is, can be understood. In this world we know and understand in part only: in the next world we shall know as completely and to our benefit as much as it is right and proper for creatures to know (1 Corinthians 13:12).

In fact, anyone seeking to know God our Maker more than is of benefit will certainly fall further away from him. If you asked, 'What is God?', I would answer: 'One as great and of such a nature that there is no other.'

If you truly wanted to know God, I would tell you that you will never find out. I do not know him, angels do not know him, archangels do not know him. How can you wish to know the unknowable, the one who cannot be taught? God himself, though almighty, cannot teach you what he is. If you knew what God is, you would be as wise as God. And that neither you nor any other creature can be. It is enough for you to know that God is. It will be to your detriment to know what God is.

So to know God perfectly is to say he is incomprehensible. Through knowing one loves, through loving one rejoices, through rejoicing one finds peace, and through inward quiet comes eternal rest. Do not be disturbed when I say 'Know God perfectly' though I have denied that he may be known. As the psalmist says, 'Continue your love to those who know you' (Psalm 36:10). If you are not to fall into error, understand this rule: 'to those who know you', is to say that God is to be loved, praised, worshipped and glorified as Creator God alone, above all things and in all things, who is blessed for ever and ever. Amen.

Richard Rolle, *The Fire of Love*

TRUE PERFECTION

[God] is able to keep you from falling and to present you before his glorious presence without fault and with great joy (Jude 24).

There are three stages which lead a person to true perfection.

Now be assured that no one can be enlightened unless he is first cleansed and purified and freed himself.

And further, no one can be united with God unless he has first been enlightened.

First, purification, second, enlightenment, third, union.

Purification belongs to those who are beginning and repenting, and takes place in three ways: by contrition and sorrow for sin, by full and free confession, and by perfect penitence.

Enlightenment belongs to those who are growing, and also takes place in three ways: by the rejection of sin, by the practice of virtue and good works, and by the willing endurance of adversity and tribulations.

Union belongs to those who are perfect, and also comes about in three ways: by pureness and singleness of heart, by godly love, and by the contemplation of God, the Creator of all things.

Theologia Germanica

EXERCISE FOR THE MORNING

**'We saw his star in the east and have come to worship him'
(Matthew 2:2).**

1. Thank God and adore him profoundly for the favour he has done you in preserving you during the past night; and if, in the course of it, you have committed any sin, ask his pardon for it.

2. Consider that the present day is given you, that in it you may gain the future day of eternity, and make a firm resolution to employ the day well for this intention.

3. Forecast what affairs, what meetings and what events you are likely to meet during the day so that you can serve God as you engage in them. Think about the temptations which may beset you, whether they come through your anger or your vanity or some other unworthy action. Make a holy resolution to prepare yourself to make good use of the means of grace which are offered you as you serve God and carry out your own devotions.

You must at the same time prepare yourself to carefully avoid, resist and overcome whatever may present itself to you which is contrary to your salvation and the glory of God.

4. Humble yourself before God, acknowledge that by yourself you cannot do any of the things you have been praying over, whether it is to avoid evil or to do good. Then, as if you were holding your heart in your hands, offer it together with your good intentions to the divine Majesty, imploring him to take it under his protection, and to strengthen it that it may be very successful in his service.

St Francis de Sales, *Treatise on the Love of God*

A PURE INTENTION

'The kingdom of heaven is like a merchant looking for fine pearls. When he found one of great value, he went away and sold everything he had and bought it' (Matthew 13:45–46).

Divine love is for souls who give themselves wholly to it, the principle of all good. And in order to acquire this inestimable good it is sufficient to will it firmly.

Yes, dear souls, God asks for your heart only; if you are seeking this treasure, this kingdom in which God reigns alone, you will find it. For if your heart is wholly devoted to God, it forthwith becomes his treasure, this very kingdom that you are desiring and seeking. From the moment that we put our will with God and his will, we enjoy God and his will, and our enjoyment corresponds to the ardour of our desire. To love God is to desire sincerely to love him; because we love him, we wish to be the instrument of his action, so that his life may exercise itself in and through us.

It is not to the cleverness of the simple and holy soul that the degree of the divine action corresponds; it corresponds to the purity of her intention and not to the wisdom of the measures she adopts, or the projects that she forms or the means she chooses. The soul may be deceived in all this, and it not infrequently happens that she is so deceived, but her upright and good intention never deludes her. Provided that God sees this good disposition, he forgives her all the rest, and he accepts as done what she would be certain to do, if sounder views were at the service of her good will.

Jean-Pierre de Caussade, *The Sacrament of the Present Moment*

SALUTE THE HAPPY MORN

The time came for the baby to be born, and she gave birth to her firstborn, a son. She wrapped him in cloths and placed him in a manger (Luke 2:6–7).

Christians awake! salute the happy morn
Whereon the Saviour of the world was born;
Rise to adore the mystery of love
Which hosts of angels chanted from above;
With them the joyful tidings first begun
Of God incarnate and the Virgin's Son.

Then to the watchful shepherds it was told,
Who heard the angelic herald's voice, 'Behold,
I bring you tidings of a Saviour's birth
To you and all the nations on the earth:
This day hath God fulfilled his promised word,
This day is born a Saviour, Christ the Lord.'

He spake; and straightway that celestial choir
In hymns of joy, unknown before, conspire;
The praises of redeeming love they sang,
And heaven's whole orb with alleluyas rang:
God's highest glory was their anthem still,
Peace on earth, and unto men goodwill.

Like Mary let us ponder in our mind
God's wondrous love in saving lost mankind;
Trace we the Babe, who hath retrieved our loss,
From his poor manger to his bitter cross;
Then may we hope, angelic hosts among,
To sing, redeemed, a glad triumphal song.

John Byrom

THE FIRST CHRISTIAN MARTYR

They saw that his face was like the face of an angel (Acts 6:15).

Now Stephen, a man full of God's grace and power, did great wonders and miraculous signs among the people. Opposition arose, however, from members of the Synagogue of the Freedmen. These men began to argue with Stephen, but they could not stand up against his wisdom or the Spirit by whom he spoke.

Then they secretly persuaded some men to say, 'We have heard Stephen speak words of blasphemy against Moses and against God.'

So they stirred up the people and the elders and the teachers of the law. They seized Stephen and brought him before the Sanhedrin. They produced false witnesses, who testified, 'This fellow never stops speaking against this holy place and against the law. For we have heard him say that this Jesus of Nazareth will destroy this place and change the customs Moses handed down to us.'

All who were sitting in the Sanhedrin looked intently at Stephen, and they saw that his face was like the face of an angel. Then the high priest asked him, 'Are these charges true?'

To this Stephen replied: '. . . You are just like your fathers: You always resist the Holy Spirit! Was there ever a prophet your fathers did not persecute? They even killed those who predicted the coming of the Righteous One. And now you have betrayed and murdered him – you who have received the law that was put into effect through angels but have not obeyed it.'

When they heard this, they were furious and gnashed their teeth at him. But Stephen, full of the Holy Spirit, looked up to heaven and saw the glory of God, and Jesus standing at the right hand of God. 'Look,' he said, 'I see heaven open and the Son of Man standing at the right hand of God.'

At this they covered their ears and yelling at the top of their voices, they all rushed at him, dragged him out of the city and began to stone him. . . .

While they were stoning him, Stephen prayed, 'Lord Jesus, receive my spirit.' Then he fell on his knees and cried out, 'Lord, do not hold this sin against them.' When he had said this, he fell asleep.

Dr Luke, in Acts 6:8–7:2; 7:51–60

ST JOHN THE EVANGELIST

He [Jesus] saw two other brothers, James son of Zebedee and his brother John. They were in a boat with their father Zebedee, preparing their nets. Jesus called them, and immediately they left the boat and their father and followed him (Matthew 4:21–22).

Word supreme, before creation
   Born of God eternally
Who didst will for our salvation
   To be born on earth, and die;
Well thy saints have kept their station,
   Watching till thine hour drew nigh.

Now 'tis come, and faith espies thee:
   Like an eagle in the morn,
John in steadfast worship eyes thee,
   Thy belov'd, thy latest born:
In thy glory he descries thee
   Reigning from the tree of scorn.

He first hoping and believing
   Did beside the grave adore;
Latest he, the warfare leaving,
   Landed on the eternal shore;
And his witness we receiving
   Own thee Lord for evermore.

Much he asked in loving wonder,
   On thy bosom leaning, Lord!
In that secret place of thunder,
   Answer kind didst thou accord,
Wisdom for thy Church to ponder
   Till the day of dread award.

John Keble

SHALL I BE SILENT?

An angel of the Lord appeared to them [the shepherds], and the glory of the Lord shone around them (Luke 2:9).

The shepherds sing; and shall I be silent?
    My God, no hymn for thee?
My soul's a shepherd too; a flock it feeds
    Of thoughts, and words and deeds.
The pasture is thy word: the streams thy grace
    Enriching all the place.
Shepherd and flock shall sing, and all my powers
    Out-sing and day-light hours.
Then we will chide the sun for letting night
    Take up his place and right:

We sing one common Lord; wherefore he should
    Himself the candle hold.
I will go searching, till I finde a sun
    Shall stay, till we have done;
A willing shiner, that shall shine as gladly,
    As frost-nipt suns look sadly.
Then we will sing, and shine all our own day,
    And one another pay:
His beams shall cheer my breast, and both so twine,
Till ev'n his beams sing, and my music shine.

George Herbert

A GIFT FOR JESUS

They bowed down and worshipped him. Then they opened their treasures and presented him with gifts of gold and of incense and of myrrh (Matthew 2:11).

Lord Jesus,
I give you my hands to do your work,
I give you my feet to go your way,
I give you my eyes to see as you do.
I give you my tongue to speak your words,
I give you my mind that you may think in me,
I give you my spirit that you may pray in me.

Above all, I give you my heart that you may love in me, your Father, and all mankind.
I give you my whole self that you may grow in me, so that it is you, Lord Jesus, who live and work and pray in me.

I hand over to your care, Lord my soul and body, my mind and thoughts, my prayers and hopes, my health and my work, my life and my death, my parents and my family, my friends and my neighbours, my country and all men. Today and always.

Lancelot Andrewes, *Private Prayers*

THE BIRTH OF JESUS

**'Where is the one who has been born king of the Jews?'
(Matthew 2:2).**

Now note where this birth occurs. This birth falls in the soul exactly as it does in eternity, neither more nor less, for it is the same birth. This birth falls in the ground and essence of the soul.

Certain questions, then, arise. Given that God is in all things as intelligence (or mind), and is more innate and natural in things than things are in themselves, and given that God is at work no matter where he is, knowing himself and speaking his Word, given these things, then note in what respects the soul is better fitted for this divine work than other rational creatures in which God works.

God is in all things as being, as activity, as power. But God gives birth in the soul alone, for though every creature bears God's mark, the soul is the natural image of God. This image is perfected and adorned in this birth.

If you nurture this birth in yourself, you will experience all good, all comfort, all happiness, all being and all truth. Whatever comes to you in this way brings true being, and stability. Whatever else you may seek and grasp without this, it will perish, no matter how you possess it. This alone gives life; all else corrupts. And further, through this birth you participate in the divine influx and its gifts.

To find the newborn King in you, all else you might find must be passed by and left behind. May we outstrip and leave behind those things that are not pleasing to the newborn King. So help us, Jesus, who became the child of man that we might become the children of God. Amen.

Meister Eckhart, *Sermons*

THE PILLAR OF THE CLOUD

I will instruct you and teach you in the way you should go; I will counsel you and watch over you (Psalm 32:8).

> Lead, Kindly Light, amid the encircling gloom,
>   Lead Thou me on!
> The night is dark, and I am far from home –
>   Lead Thou me on!
> Keep Thou my feet; I do not ask to see
> The distant scene; one step enough for me.
>
> I was not ever thus, nor pray'd that Thou
>   Shouldst lead me on.
> I loved to choose and see my path, but now
>   Lead Thou me on!
> I loved the garish day, and, spite of fears,
> Pride ruled my will: remember not past years.
>
> So long Thy power hath blest me, sure it still
>   Will lead me on,
> O'er moor and fen, o'er crag and torrent, till
>   The night is gone;
> And with the morn those angel faces smile
> Which I have loved long since, and lost awhile.
>
> John Henry Newman

BIOGRAPHICAL NOTES & INDEX OF SOURCES

Butler, Joseph (1692–1752) English royal chaplain and Bishop of Durham, who defended revealed religion against the rationalist ideas of the Deists *Jan 14*

Byrom, John (1691–1763) English shorthand teacher, friend of the Wesleys and disciple of William Law *Dec 25*

Calvin, John (1509–64) French-born Reformation theologian who settled in Geneva as political and religious leader; many of his sermons and Bible commentaries survive *Apr 30; May 18; Jun 10; Jul 13; Aug 12, 30*

Campbell, Jane (translator) *Sep 27*

Catherine of Siena (1347–80) Italian mystic noted for her ecstatic prayer and her gift of reconciliation *Feb 25; Oct 2, 27*

Caussade, Jean-Pierre de (1675–1751) French Jesuit writer and travelling preacher who promoted mysticism *Mar 14; May 8, 9; Jun 29; Sep 8; Oct 14; Dec 19, 24*

Challoner, Richard (1691–1781) English Roman Catholic bishop, devotional writer and Biblical scholar *Dec 18*

Chesterton, G. K. (1874–1936) English Roman Catholic essayist *Oct 4*

Chrysostom *see* John Chrysostom

Claudius, Matthias (1743–1815) German poet *Sep 27*

Cloud of Unknowing, The (14th century) *Jan 3; Apr 24; Oct 3; Nov 14, 26; Dec 16*

Cosin, John (translator) *May 27*

Cotterill, Thomas (1779–1823) Sheffield vicar who pioneered the use of hymns in the Church of England *May 16*

Cowper, William (1731–1800) English poet who contributed to the collection of *Olney Hymns* edited by his friend John Newton *Jan 14*

De Foucauld, Charles (1858–1916) French soldier, explorer and desert ascetic *Mar 13*

Discerning of Spirits (14th century) *May 28*

Dream of the Rood, The (8th century) *Mar 11–12*

Eckhart, Meister (?1260–1327) German mystic and Dominican preacher *Apr 28; Aug 5; Oct 6, 7; Nov 17; Dec 2, 30*

Edwards, Jonathan (1703–58) US Calvinist philosopher and revival preacher who wrote about conversions which took place in religious revivals *Jan 9*

Elliott, Charlotte (1789–1871) English hymn-writer; friend of evangelical leaders *Jun 8*

Epistle of Discretion (14th century) *Mar 3; May 5*

Epistle of Prayer (14th century) *Feb 6*

Eusebius (?265–340) Bishop of Caesarea; church historian *May 6*

Everest, Charles (1814–77) hymn-writer *Apr 4*

Fénelon, François (1651–1715) Archbishop of Cambrai, France; author of many letter of spiritual guidance *Jan 2; May 14; Jul 2, 3, 4, 5; Aug 14; Sep 11, 24; Oct 5, 16, 26; Nov 16, 22*

Foxe, John (1516–87) English author of the *Acts and*

Foxe, John – *continued*
Monuments, about the English
Protestant martyrs of Mary's
reign *Mar 7–8; Oct 31*

Francis de Sales (1567–1622)
Bishop of Geneva; French
theologian who opposed
Calvinism *Jan 5, 24; Apr 10; Sep
10; Oct 9, 10, 11, 12, 18; Nov 2;
Dec 3, 5, 12, 23*

Francis of Assisi (1181–1226)
Italian founder of the
Franciscan order of friars *Jan 6;
Feb 11–12; Apr 14, 18; May 10,
15; Jun 13; Jul 17, 27; Aug 4, 11;
Nov 21; Dec 7, 20*

Gerhardt, Paul (c. 1607–76)
German Lutheran hymn-writer
Mar 15

Görres, Johann Joseph von
(1776–1848) German Roman
Catholic political journalist and
literary historian; also author of
a four-volume work on
Christian mysticism *Oct 29*

Gregory the Great (540–604)
Pope (Gregory I), who
organised the papal estates to
help starving people; founder of
monasteries and writer of the
standard textbook for medieval
bishops *Jun 24; Jul 9; Sep 3, 4;
Dec 13*

Gurnall, William (1616–79)
English Puritan minister *Jul 28*

**Guyon, Madame Jeanne-Marie
Bouvier de le Motte**
(1648–1717) French Quietist
author *Feb 3, 16; May 4, 7, 23;
Jun 9; Jul 10*

Hall, Joseph (1574–1656) Bishop
of Exeter (and later, briefly, of
Norwich); writer and moral
philosopher who Christianised
Stoicism *Oct 22*

Herbert, George (1593–1633)
English clergyman and religious
poet *Feb 27–28; Mar 17–26;
Apr 6; May 17, 26; Jul 19;
Nov 27; Dec 28*

Herrick, Robert (1591–1674)
English clergyman and poet
Mar 1, 28–29; Aug 10

Hilton, Walter (?–1396) English
Augustinian canon and mystic
Jan 30; Feb 9; May 3, 30

Ignatius of Loyola (1491/5–1556)
Spanish founder of the Society
of Jesus (Jesuits) *Mar 4–5; Oct
17*

Imitation of Christ, The (15th
century) *Jan 29; Feb 29; Mar 9;
Apr 16, 17, 23; Jun 17; Jul 18, 23*

John Chrysostom (?347–407)
Bishop of Constantinople who
was noted for his preaching (his
title means 'John Golden-
Mouth') *Jan 27; Jun 11; Aug 15*

John of Avila (1499/1500–1569)
Spanish preacher, author and
spiritual director; known for his
evangelism in Andalusia *Jun 18;
Jul 15*

John of the Cross (1542–91)
Spanish Carmelite mystic *Jan
16–23; Feb 15, 26; Mar 2; Apr
11, 15, 26; May 12, 20; Jun 6; Jul
6, 7, 14, 22, 25, 31; Aug 24*

Julian of Norwich (?1342–)
English anchoress whose
Revelations of Divine Love was
the first book to be written in
English by a woman *Jan 7; May
2; Oct 20, 28*

Keble, John (1792–1866) Oxford
poetry professor and Tractarian
May 25; Dec 27

Kempe, Margery (?1313–?1440)
English housewife and mystic
Sep 2, 28

Ken, Thomas (1637–1711) English bishop and hymn-writer *Sep 13*

Law, William (1686–1761) English clergyman and spiritual writer *Feb 1, 13; Mar 6; Apr 9, 13; Jun 20; Aug 1, 21, 26; Sep 17*

Lawrence, Brother (1605–91) French Carmelite lay brother and mystic *Jan 14; Jul 11; Sep 20, 29; Nov 15, 25; Dec 15*

Leighton, Robert (1611–84) Scottish Presbyterian minister and devotional writer, influenced by the *Imitation of Christ* and the Jansenists *Oct 13*

Lewis, C. S. (1898–1963) English literary scholar and author of many popular books about Christian belief *Introduction*

Little Flowers of St Francis, The (14th century) *Apr 12, 19; May 1, 29; Jun 26*

Louis of Blois *see* Blosius, Ludovicus

Luther, Martin (1483–1546) German monk and theologian who led the Protestant Reformation and translated the Bible into German *Jan 15; Apr 21; Jun 19*

Lyra Davidica (1708) *Apr 7*

Meditations on the Life of Christ (14th century) *Apr 3*

Milman, Henry Hart (1791–1868) English clergyman, and Professor of Poetry at Oxford University *Apr 1*

Newman, John Henry (1801–90) English clergyman who led the Oxford revival of Anglican worship and later became a Roman Catholic cardinal *Dec 31*

Newton, John (1725–1807) English evangelical clergyman and hymn-writer *Apr 22; Jun 27; Jul 24; Aug 23, 27; Sep 9, 26; Oct 8, 23, 30*

Palmer, Ray (translator) *Jun 21*

Pascal, Blaise (1623–62) French mathematician and theologian *Mar 30; Nov 23*

Patrick, St (c.372–466) missionary to Ulster and Armagh *Aug 18*

Piggott, Jean Sophia *Jul 26*

Pseudo-Dionysius (c. AD 500) anonymous Syrian monk (?) who wrote under the pseudonym Dionysius the Areopagite; his philosophical and mystical writings were very influential in medieval times *Sep 1*

Pusey, Edward Bouverie (1800–82) English theologian and Professor of Hebrew who, with Newman and Keble, led the Oxford Movement *Oct 25*

Rinkart, Martin (1586–1649) German pastor at Eilenburg during the Thirty Years' War *Jun 14*

Rolle, Richard (?1300–49) English writer, hermit and mystic *Jan 26, 31; Jul 16; Oct 19; Dec 21*

Ruysbroeck, John (1293–1381) Flemish mystic *Nov 19*

Sayings of the Desert Fathers (Abraham) *Apr 27* (Agathon) *Apr 20* (John the Dwarf) *May 13* (Moses) *May 21* (Nilus) *Jun 16* (Orsisius) *Jul 12* (Syncletica) *Sep 5, Nov 18*

Simeon, Charles (1759–1836) Vicar of Holy Trinity, Cambridge, where his long evangelical ministry influenced generations of undergraduates *Nov 13*

Smith, Preserved (1880–1941) US historian *Jun 19*

Southwell, Robert (1561–95) English Jesuit priest and martyr *Jul 30*

Spurgeon, C. H. (1834–92) English Baptist preacher *Jul 20*

Symeon the New Theologian (c.949–1022) Byzantine monk and mystic *Nov 1*

Synesius of Cyrene (375–430) Bishop of Ptolemais, noted for his eloquence and philosophy *Aug 3*

Tate, Nahum (translator) *May 31*

Tauler, Johann (1300–61) German mystic and Dominican friar *Sep 18*

Taylor, Jeremy (1613–67) Anglican Bishop of Down and Connor *Sep 12*

Temple, William (1887–1944) Archbishop of Canterbury; theologian concerned with doctrine and social issues *Jun 28*

Teresa of Avila (1515–82) Spanish nun who initiated reform of the Carmelite order and wrote of her spiritual and mystical experiences *Jun 3; Aug 17; Sep 7; Oct 15; Nov 6–12; Dec 6*

Tersteegen, Gerhard (1697–1759) German Protestant devotional writer and spiritual director *Feb 5*

Theologia Germanica (late 14th century) *Jan 13; Dec 4, 22*

Thérèse de Lisieux (1873–97) French Carmelite nun who wrote an autobiographical account of her spiritual development *Jun 25*

Thomas Aquinas (1225–74) Theologian whose *Summa Theologiae* remains the foundation of Roman Catholic theology *Jan 28; Jul 8*

Traherne, Thomas (?1636–74) English clergyman and poet, noted for his sense of the divine in nature and his overwhelming sense of thanksgiving *Sep 14, 23*

Vaughan, Henry (1621–95) Welsh doctor and poet *Mar 30*

Watts, Isaac (1674–1748) English independent pastor and hymn-writer *Mar 27*

Wesley, Charles (1707–88) English clergyman and writer of many famous hymns; brother of John Wesley *May 16*

Wesley, John (1703–91) English clergyman, travelling preacher and founder of Methodism by his organisation of the new believers who had responded to his preaching *Jan 1; Feb 4; Apr 29; May 24; Jun 1; Aug 7*

Whitefield, George (1714–70) English clergyman who attracted huge crowds to his open-air preaching in both Britain and America *Aug 16*

Whittier, John Greenleaf (1807–92) US Quaker poet and anti-slavery campaigner *Feb 8*

Woolman, John (1720–72) US Quaker leader and anti-slavery campaigner *Jun 2*

INDEX OF THEMES